Applied Deep Learning with Keras

Solve complex real-life problems with the simplicity of Keras

Ritesh Bhagwat, Mahla Abdolahnejad, and Matthew Moocarme

Applied Deep Learning with Keras

Authors: Ritesh Bhagwat, Mahla Abdolahnejad, and Matthew Moocarme

Reviewer: Elder Santos

Managing Editor: Aditya Shah

Acquisitions Editor: Kunal Sawant

Production Editor: Shantanu Zagade

Editorial Board: David Barnes, Ewan Buckingham, Simon Cox, Manasa Kumar, Alex Mazonowicz, Douglas Paterson, Dominic Pereira, Shiny Poojary, Erol Staveley, Ankita Thakur, Mohita Vyas and Jonathan Wray

First Published: April 2019

Production Reference: 1220419

Published by Packt Publishing Ltd.

Livery Place, 35 Livery Street

Birmingham B3 2PB, UK

ISBN: 978-1-83855-507-8

Table of Contents

Preface   i

Introduction to Machine Learning with Keras   1

Introduction 2

Data Representation 3

    Tables of Data 4

    Loading Data 5

    Exercise 1: Loading a Dataset from the UCI Machine
    Learning Repository 7

Data Preprocessing 11

    Exercise 2: Cleaning the Data 12

    Appropriate Representation of the Data 23

    Exercise 3: Appropriate Representation of the Data 24

    Life Cycle of Model Creation 25

Machine Learning Libraries 25

scikit-learn 26

Keras 28

    Advantages of Keras 29

    Disadvantages of Keras 29

    More than Building Models 30

Model Training 31

    Classifiers and Regression Models 31

    Classification Tasks 32

    Regression Tasks 33

    Training and Test Datasets 34

    Model Evaluation Metrics 35

    Exercise 4: Creating a Simple Model 36

Model Tuning 40

    Baseline Models 40

    Exercise 5: Determining a Baseline Model 40

    Regularization 42

    Cross-Validation 43

    Activity 1: Adding Regularization to the Model 44

Summary 45

Machine Learning versus Deep Learning   47

Introduction 48

    Advantages of ANNs over Traditional Machine Learning Algorithms 50

    Advantages of Traditional Machine Learning Algorithms over ANNs 51

    Hierarchical Data Representation 51

Linear Transformations 52

    Scalars, Vectors, Matrices, and Tensors 53

    Tensor Addition 53

    Exercise 6: Perform Various Operations with Vectors, Matrices,
    and Tensors 54

    Reshaping 58

    Matrix Transposition 58

    Exercise 7: Matrix Reshaping and Transposition 59

    Matrix Multiplication 62

    Exercise 8: Matrix Multiplication 64

    Exercise 9: Tensor Multiplication 65

Introduction to Keras 68

    Layer Types 69

    Activation Functions 70

    Model Fitting 72

    Activity 2: Creating a Logistic Regression Model Using Keras 73

Summary 74

Deep Learning with Keras   77

Introduction 78

Building Your First Neural Network 78

    Logistic Regression to a Deep Neural Network 79

    Activation Functions 81

    Forward Propagation for Making Predictions 84

    Loss Function 85

    Backpropagation for Computing Derivatives of Loss Function 86

    Gradient Descent for Learning Parameters 87

    Exercise 10: Neural Network Implementation with Keras 90

    Activity 3: Building a Single-Layer Neural Network for Performing
    Binary Classification 94

Model Evaluation 96

    Evaluating a Trained Model with Keras 96

    Splitting Data into Training and Test Sets 97

    Underfitting and Overfitting 99

    Early Stopping 104

    Activity 4: Diabetes Diagnosis with Neural Networks 105

Summary 108

Evaluate Your Model with Cross-Validation using Keras Wrappers 111

Introduction 112

Cross-Validation 112

Drawbacks of Splitting a Dataset Only Once 113

K-Fold Cross-Validation 115

Leave-One-Out Cross-Validation 117

Comparing the K-Fold and LOO Methods 118

Cross-Validation for Deep Learning Models 119

Keras Wrapper with scikit-learn 119

Exercise 11: Building the Keras Wrapper with scikit-learn
for a Regression Problem 120

Cross-Validation with scikit-learn 122

Cross-Validation Iterators in scikit-learn 123

Exercise 12: Evaluate Deep Neural Networks with Cross-Validation 125

Activity 5: Model Evaluation Using Cross-Validation
for a Diabetes Diagnosis Classifier 127

Model Selection with Cross-validation 128

Cross-Validation for Model Evaluation versus Model Selection 129

Exercise 13: Write User-Defined Functions to Implement
Deep Learning Models with Cross-Validation 131

Activity 6: Model Selection Using Cross-Validation
for the Diabetes Diagnosis Classifier 137

Activity 7: Model Selection Using Cross-validation
on the Boston House Prices Dataset 139

Summary 141

Introduction 144

Regularization 144

    The Need for Regularization 145

    Reducing Overfitting with Regularization 146

L1 and L2 Regularization 147

    L1 and L2 Regularization Formulation 147

    L1 and L2 Regularization Implementation in Keras 149

    Activity 8: Weight Regularization on a Diabetes Diagnosis Classifier 150

Dropout Regularization 151

    Principles of Dropout Regularization 152

    Reducing Overfitting with Dropout 153

    Exercise 14: Dropout Implementation in Keras 154

    Activity 9: Dropout Regularization on Boston Housing Dataset 157

Other Regularization Methods 158

    Early Stopping 159

    Exercise 15: Implementing Early Stopping in Keras 161

    Data Augmentation 168

    Adding Noise 168

Hyperparameter Tuning with scikit-learn 169

    Grid Search with scikit-learn 170

    Randomized Search with scikit-learn 172

    Activity 10: Hyperparameter Tuning on the Diabetes Diagnosis Classifier 174

Summary 175

Model Evaluation   177

Introduction 178

Accuracy 178

    Exercise 16: Calculating Null Accuracy on a Dummy
Healthcare Dataset 179

    Advantages and Limitations of Accuracy 181

Imbalanced Datasets 182

    Working with Imbalanced Datasets 183

Confusion Matrix 183

    Metrics Computed from a Confusion Matrix 185

    Exercise 17: Computing Accuracy and Null Accuracy
with Healthcare Data 188

    Activity 11: Computing the Accuracy and Null Accuracy
of a Neural Network When We Change the Train/Test Split 199

    Activity 12: Derive and Compute Metrics Based
on a Confusion Matrix 200

    Exercise 18: Calculate the ROC and AUC Curves 201

Summary 205

Computer Vision with Convolutional Neural Networks   207

Introduction 208

Computer Vision 208

Convolutional Neural Networks 209

Architecture of a CNN 209

    Input Image 210

    Convolution Layer 210

    Pooling Layer 212

    Flattening 214

Image Augmentation 216

    Advantages of Image Augmentation 217

    Exercise 19: Build a CNN and Identify Images of Cats and Dogs 218

    Activity 13: Amending our Model with Multiple Layers and the
    Use of SoftMax 221

    Exercise 20: Amending our model by reverting to the Sigmoid
    activation function 222

    Exercise 21: Changing the Optimizer from Adam to SGD 224

    Exercise 22: Classifying a New Image 227

    Activity 14: Classify a New Image 229

Summary 230

Transfer Learning and Pre-Trained Models   233

Introduction 234

Pre-Trained Sets and Transfer Learning 234

    Feature Extraction 235

Fine-Tuning a Pre-Trained Network 238

    The ImageNet Dataset 238

    Some Pre-Trained Networks in Keras 238

    Exercise 23: Identify an Image Using the VGG16 Network 239

    Activity 15: Use the VGG16 Network to Train a Deep Learning
    Network to Identify Images 242

    Exercise 24: Classification of Images That Are Not Present
    in the ImageNet Database. 243

    Exercise 25: Fine-Tune the VGG16 Model 247

    Exercise 26: Image Classification with ResNet 252

    Activity 16: Image Classification with ResNet 255

Summary 256

Sequential Modeling with Recurrent Neural Networks   259

Introduction 260

Sequential Memory and Sequential Modeling 260

Recurrent Neural Networks (RNNs) 261

    The Vanishing Gradient Problem 266

Long Short-Term Memory (LSTM) 269

    Exercise 27: Predict the Trend of Apple's Stock Price
Using an LSTM with 50 Units (Neurons) 271

    Activity 17: Predict the Trend of Microsoft's Stock Price
Using an LSTM with 50 Units (Neurons) 277

    Exercise 28: Predicting the Trend of Apple's Stock Price
Using an LSTM with 100 units 278

    Activity 18: Predicting Microsoft's Stock Price
with Added Regularization 282

    Activity 19: Predicting the Trend of Microsoft's Stock Price Using
an LSTM with an Increasing Number of LSTM Neurons (100 Units) 283

Summary 284

Appendix   287

Index   387

Preface

About

This section briefly introduces the author, the coverage of this book, the technical skills you'll need to get started, and the hardware and software requirements required to complete all of the included activities and exercises.

About the Book

Applied Deep Learning with Keras takes you from a basic level of knowledge of machine learning and Python to an expert understanding of applying Keras to develop efficient deep learning solutions. To understand the difference between machine and deep learning, you will build a logistic regression model with scikit-learn and then with Keras. By building prediction models for several real-world scenarios, such as disease prediction and customer churn prediction, you will dive deep into Keras and its many models. You will also gain knowledge about how to evaluate, optimize, and improve your models to gain maximum information. You will learn how to use Keras wrappers with scikit-learn and implement cross-validation techniques on your findings, and apply L1, L2, and dropout regularization techniques to improve the accuracy of your model. To improve accuracy, you will learn how to apply the null accuracy, precision, sensitivity, specificity, and AUC-ROC score techniques to fine-tune your model. Then, you will explore convolutional and recurrent neural networks in detail.

By the end of this book, you will have all the skills you need to use Keras to your advantage and build superlative deep neural networks.

About the Authors

Ritesh Bhagwat has a master's degree in applied mathematics with a specialization in computer science. He has over 14 years of experience in data-driven technologies and has led and been a part of complex projects ranging from data warehousing and business intelligence to machine learning and artificial intelligence. He has worked with top-tier global consulting firms as well as large multinational financial institutions. Currently, he works as a data scientist. Besides work, he enjoys playing and watching cricket and loves to travel. He is also deeply interested in Bayesian statistics.

Mahla Abdolahnejad is a Ph.D. candidate in systems and computer engineering with Carleton University, Canada. She also holds a bachelor's degree and a master's degree in biomedical engineering, which first exposed her to the field of artificial intelligence and artificial neural networks, in particular. Her Ph.D. research is focused on deep unsupervised learning for computer vision applications. She is particularly interested in exploring the differences between a human's way of learning from the visual world and a machine's way of learning from the visual world, and how to push machine learning algorithms toward learning and thinking like humans.

Matthew Moocarme is a director and senior data scientist in Viacom's Advertising Science team. As a data scientist at Viacom, he designs data-driven solutions to help Viacom gain insights, streamline workflows, and solve complex problems using data science and machine learning.

Matthew lives in New York City and outside of work enjoys combining deep learning with music theory. He is a classically-trained physicist, holding a Ph.D. in Physics from The Graduate Center of CUNY and is an active Artificial Intelligence developer, researcher, practitioner, and educator.

Learning Objectives

In this book, you will be able to:

- Understand the difference between single-layer and multi-layer neural network models

- Use Keras to build simple logistic regression models, deep neural networks, recurrent neural networks, and convolutional neural networks

- Apply L1, L2, and dropout regularization to improve the accuracy of your model

- Implement cross-validate using Keras wrappers with scikit-learn

- Understand the limitations of model accuracy

Audience

If you have basic knowledge about data science and machine learning and want to upgrade your skills to learn about artificial neural networks and deep learning, you can accomplish a lot with this book. Prior experience of programming in Python and familiarity with statistics and logistic regression will help you get the most out of this book. Though not necessary, it will be an added bonus if you are familiar with the scikit-learn library.

Approach

Applied Deep Learning with Keras takes a practical approach to equip beginners with the most essential data analysis tools in the shortest possible time. The book contains multiple activities that use real-life business scenarios for you to practice and apply your new skills in a highly relevant context.

Hardware Requirements

For the optimal experience, we recommend the following hardware configuration:

- Any entry-level PC/Mac with Windows, Linux, or macOS is sufficient
- Processor: Intel Core i5 or equivalent
- Memory: 4 GB RAM
- Storage: 35 GB available space

Software Requirements

You'll also need the following software installed in advance:

- Operating system: Windows 7 SP1 64-bit, Windows 8.1 64-bit or Windows 10 64-bit, Ubuntu Linux, or the latest version of macOS
- Browser: Google Chrome/Mozilla Firefox (latest version)
- Notepad++/Sublime Text as IDE
- Python 3.4+ (latest is Python 3.7) installed (from https://python.org)
- Python libraries as needed (Jupyter, NumPy, pandas, Matplotlib, and others)

Conventions

Code words in the text, database table names, folder names, filenames, file extensions, pathnames, dummy URLs, user input, and Twitter handles are shown as follows: "We use the **skiprows** argument if there is a header that usually contains column names."

A block of code is set as follows:

```
import numpy as np
data = np.loadtxt(filename, delimiter=",", skiprows=1)
```

New terms and important words are shown in bold. Words that you see on the screen, for example, in menus or dialog boxes, appear in the text like this: "The printed output should look as follows, showing that **DataFrame** has **4521** rows and **17** columns."

Installation and Setup

Before you start this book, we'll install Python 3.6, pip, scikit-learn, and the other libraries used throughout this book. You will find the steps to install them here:

Installing Python

Install Python 3.6 by following the instructions at this link: https://realpython.com/installing-python/.

Installing the Jupyter Notebook

Install the Jupyter Notebook by following the instructions at this link: https://jupyter.org/install.

Installing pip

1. To install pip, go to this link and download the `get-pip.py` file: https://pip.pypa.io/en/stable/installing/.

2. Then, use the following command to install it:

   ```
   python get-pip.py
   ```

   You might need to use the `python3 get-pip.py` command, due to previous versions of Python on your computer that already use the Python command.

Installing libraries

Using the pip command, install the following libraries:

```
python -m pip install --user numpy scipy matplotlib jupyter pandas
```

Installing scikit-learn

Install scikit-learn by using the following command:

```
pip install -U scikit-learn
```

Installing Keras

Install Keras by following the instructions in this link: https://keras.io/#installation.

Installing the Code Bundle

Copy the code bundle for the class to the `C:/Code` folder.

Additional Resources

The code bundle for this book is also hosted on GitHub at https://github.com/TrainingByPackt/Applied-Deep-Learning-with-Keras.

We also have other code bundles from our rich catalog of books and videos available at https://github.com/PacktPublishing/. Check them out!

Introduction to Machine Learning with Keras

Learning Objectives

By the end of this chapter, you will be able to:

- Present data for use in machine learning models
- Explain how to preprocess data for a machine learning model
- Build a logistic regression model with scikit-learn
- Use regularization in machine learning models
- Evaluate model performance with model evaluation metrics

In this chapter, we will learn how to preprocess data for machine learning models. We will learn how to develop logistic regression models with scikit-learn. Lastly, we will evaluate model performance with model evaluation metrics.

Introduction

Machine learning is the science of utilizing machines to emulate human tasks and to have the machine improve their performance of that task over time. By feeding machines data in the form of observations of real-world events, they can develop patterns and relationships that will optimize an objective function, such as the accuracy of a binary classification task or the error in a regression task. In general, the usefulness of machine learning is in the ability to learn highly complex and non-linear relationships in large datasets and to replicate the results of that learning many times.

Take, for example, the classification of a dataset of pictures of either dogs or cats into classes of their respective type. For a human, this is trivial, and the accuracy would likely be very high. However, it may take around a second to categorize each picture, and scaling the task can only be achieved by increasing the number of humans, which may be infeasible. While it may be difficult, though certainly not impossible, for machines to reach the same level of accuracy as humans for this task, machines can classify many images per second, and scaling can be easily done by increasing the processing power of single machine, or making the algorithm more efficient.

Figure 1.1: A trivial classification task for humans, but quite difficult for machines

While the trivial task of classifying dogs and cats may be simple for us humans, the same principles that are used to create a machine learning model classify dogs and cats can be applied to other classification tasks that humans may struggle with. An example of this is identifying tumors in **Magnetic Resonance Images** (MRIs). For humans, this task requires a medical professional with years of experience, whereas a machine may only need a dataset of labeled images.

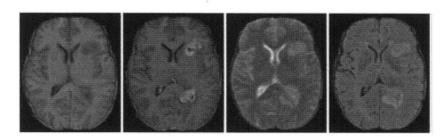

Figure 1.2: A non-trivial classification task for humans. Are you able to spot the tumors?

Data Representation

We build models so that we can learn something about the data we are training on and about the relationships between the features of the dataset. This learning can inform us

when we encounter new observations. However, we must realize that the observations we interact with in the real world and the format of data needed to train machine learning models are very different. Working with text data is a prime example of this. When we read text, we are able to understand each word and apply context given each word in relation to the surrounding words -- not a trivial task.However, machines are unable to interpret this contextual information. Unless it specifically encoded, they have no idea how to convert text into something that can be an input numerical. Therefore, we must represent the data appropriately, often by converting non-numerical data types, for example, converting text, dates, and categorical variables into numerical ones.

Tables of Data

Much of the data fed into machine learning problems is two-dimensional, and can be represented as rows or columns. Images are a good example of a dataset that may be three-or even four-dimensional. The shape of each image will be two-dimensional (a height and a width), the number of images together will add a third dimension, and a color channel (red, green, blue) will add a fourth.

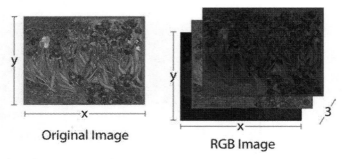

Original Image   RGB Image

Figure 1.3: A color image and its representation as red, green, and blue images

> **Note**
>
> We have used datasets from this repository: Dua, D. and Graff, C. (2019). UCI Machine Learning Repository [http://archive.ics.uci.edu/ml]. Irvine, CA: University of California, School of Information and Computer Science.

The following figure shows a few rows from a marketing dataset taken from the UCI repository. The dataset presents marketing campaign results of a Portuguese banking institution. The columns of the table show various details about each customer, while the final column, **y**, shows whether or not the customer subscribed to the product that was featured in the marketing campaign.

One objective of analyzing the dataset could be to try and use the information given to predict whether a given customer subscribed to the product (that is, to try and predict what is in column **y** for each row). We can then check whether we were correct by comparing our predictions to column **y**. The longer-term benefit of this is that we could then use our model to predict whether new customers will subscribe to the product, or whether existing customers will subscribe to another product after a different campaign.

	age	job	marital	education	default	balance	housing	loan	contact	day	month	duration	campaign	pdays	previous	poutcome	y
0	30	unemployed	married	primary	no	1787	no	no	cellular	19	oct	79	1	-1	0	unknown	no
1	33	services	married	secondary	no	4789	yes	yes	cellular	11	may	220	1	339	4	failure	no
2	35	management	single	tertiary	no	1350	yes	no	cellular	16	apr	185	1	330	1	failure	no
3	30	management	married	tertiary	no	1476	yes	yes	unknown	3	jun	199	4	-1	0	unknown	no
4	59	blue-collar	married	secondary	no	0	yes	no	unknown	5	may	226	1	-1	0	unknown	no
5	35	management	single	tertiary	no	747	no	no	cellular	23	feb	141	2	176	3	failure	no
6	36	self-employed	married	tertiary	no	307	yes	no	cellular	14	may	341	1	330	2	other	no
7	39	technician	married	secondary	no	147	yes	no	cellular	6	may	151	2	-1	0	unknown	no
8	41	entrepreneur	married	tertiary	no	221	yes	no	unknown	14	may	57	2	-1	0	unknown	no
9	43	services	married	primary	no	-88	yes	yes	cellular	17	apr	313	1	147	2	failure	no
10	39	services	married	secondary	no	9374	yes	no	unknown	20	may	273	1	-1	0	unknown	no
11	43	admin.	married	secondary	no	264	yes	no	cellular	17	apr	113	2	-1	0	unknown	no
12	36	technician	married	tertiary	no	1109	no	no	cellular	13	aug	328	2	-1	0	unknown	no
13	20	student	single	secondary	no	502	no	no	cellular	30	apr	261	1	-1	0	unknown	yes
14	31	blue-collar	married	secondary	no	360	yes	yes	cellular	29	jan	89	1	241	1	failure	no
15	40	management	married	tertiary	no	194	no	yes	cellular	29	aug	189	2	-1	0	unknown	no
16	56	technician	married	secondary	no	4073	no	no	cellular	27	aug	239	5	-1	0	unknown	no
17	37	admin.	single	tertiary	no	2317	yes	no	cellular	20	apr	114	1	152	2	failure	no
18	25	blue-collar	single	primary	no	-221	yes	no	unknown	23	may	250	1	-1	0	unknown	no
19	31	services	married	secondary	no	132	no	no	cellular	7	jul	148	1	152	1	other	no

Figure 1.4: An image showing the first 20 instances of the marketing dataset

Loading Data

Data can be in different forms and can be available in many places. Datasets for beginners are often given in a flat format, which means that they are two-dimensional, with rows and columns. Other common forms of data may include images, JSON objects, and text documents. Each type of data format has to be loaded in specific ways. For example, numerical data can be loaded into memory using the NumPy library, which is an efficient library for working with matrices in Python. However, we would not be able to load our marketing data .csv into memory using the NumPy library because the dataset contains string values. For our dataset, we will use the pandas library because of its ability to easily work with various data types, such as strings, integers, floats, and binary values. In fact, pandas is dependent on NumPy for operations on numerical data types. pandas is also able to read JSON, Excel documents, and databases using SQL queries, which makes the library common amongst practitioners for loading and manipulating data in Python.

Here is an example of how to load a CSV file using the NumPy library. We use the **skiprows** argument in case is there is a header, which usually contains column names:

```
import numpy as np

data = np.loadtxt(filename, delimiter=",", skiprows=1)
```

Here's an example of loading data using the pandas library:

```
import pandas as pd

data = pd.read_csv(filename, delimiter=",")
```

Here we are loading in a CSV file. The default delimiter is a comma, and so passing this as an argument is not necessary, but is useful to see. The pandas library can also handle non-numeric datatypes, which makes the library more flexible:

```
import pandas as pd

data = pd.read_json(filename)
```

The pandas library will flatten out the JSON and return a DataFrame.

The library can even connect to a database, and queries can be fed directly into the function, and the table returned will be loaded as a pandas DataFrame:

```
import pandas as pd

data = pd.read_sql(con, "SELECT * FROM table")
```

We have to pass a database connection to the function in order for this to work. There are a myriad of ways for this to be achieved, depending on the database flavor.

Other forms of data that are common in deep learning, such as images and text, can also be loaded in and will be discussed later in the book.

> **Note**
>
> You can find all the documentation for pandas at the following link: https://pandas.pydata.org/pandas-docs/stable/. The documentation for NumPy can be found at the following link: https://docs.scipy.org/doc/.

Exercise 1: Loading a Dataset from the UCI Machine Learning Repository

> **Note**
>
> For all exercises and activities in this chapter, you will need to have Python 3.6, Jupyter, and pandas installed on your system. They are developed in Jupyter notebooks. It is recommended to keep a separate notebook for different assignments. You can download all the notebooks from the GitHub repository. Here is the link: https://github.com/TrainingByPackt/Applied-Deep-Learning-with-Keras.

In this exercise, we will be loading the bank marketing dataset from the UCI Machine Learning Repository. The goal of this exercise will be to load in the CSV data, identify a target variable to predict, and feature variables with which to use to model the target variable. Finally, we will separate the feature and target columns and save them to CSV files to use in subsequent activities and exercises.

The dataset comes from a Portuguese banking institution and is related to direct marketing campaigns by the bank. Specifically, these marketing campaigns were composed of individual phone calls to clients, and the success of the phone call, that is, whether or not the client subscribed to a product. Each row represents an interaction with a client and records attributes of the client, campaign, and outcome. You can look at the bank-names.txt file provided in the **bank.zip** file, which describes various aspects of the dataset:

1. Open a Jupyter notebook from the start menu to implement this exercise.

2. Download the dataset from https://github.com/TrainingByPackt/Applied-Deep-Learning-with-Keras/tree/master/Lesson01/data.

3. To verify that the data looks as follows, we can look at the first 10 rows of the **.csv** file using the **head** function:

```
!head data/bank.csv
```

The output of the preceding code is as follows:

```
"age";"job";"marital";"education";"default";"balance";"housing";"loan";"contact";"day";"month";"duration";"campaig
n";"pdays";"previous";"poutcome";"y"
30;"unemployed";"married";"primary";"no";1787;"no";"no";"cellular";19;"oct";79;1;-1;0;"unknown";"no"
33;"services";"married";"secondary";"no";4789;"yes";"yes";"cellular";11;"may";220;1;339;4;"failure";"no"
35;"management";"single";"tertiary";"no";1350;"yes";"no";"cellular";16;"apr";185;1;330;1;"failure";"no"
30;"management";"married";"tertiary";"no";1476;"yes";"yes";"unknown";3;"jun";199;4;-1;0;"unknown";"no"
59;"blue-collar";"married";"secondary";"no";0;"yes";"no";"unknown";5;"may";226;1;-1;0;"unknown";"no"
35;"management";"single";"tertiary";"no";747;"no";"no";"cellular";23;"feb";141;2;176;3;"failure";"no"
36;"self-employed";"married";"tertiary";"no";307;"yes";"no";"cellular";14;"may";341;1;330;2;"other";"no"
39;"technician";"married";"secondary";"no";147;"yes";"no";"cellular";6;"may";151;2;-1;0;"unknown";"no"
41;"entrepreneur";"married";"tertiary";"no";221;"yes";"no";"unknown";14;"may";57;2;-1;0;"unknown";"no"
```

Figure 1.5: The first 10 rows of the dataset

4. Now let's load the data into memory using the pandas library with the **read_csv** function. First, import the pandas library:

```
import pandas as pd
bank_data = pd.read_csv('data/bank.csv', sep=';')
```

5. Finally, to verify that we have the data loaded into the memory correctly, we can print the first few rows. Then, print out the top 20 values of the variable:

```
bank_data.head(20)
```

The printed output should look like this:

	age	job	marital	education	default	balance	housing	loan	contact	day	month	duration	campaign	pdays	previous	poutcome	y
0	30	unemployed	married	primary	no	1787	no	no	cellular	19	oct	79	1	-1	0	unknown	no
1	33	services	married	secondary	no	4789	yes	yes	cellular	11	may	220	1	339	4	failure	no
2	35	management	single	tertiary	no	1350	yes	no	cellular	16	apr	185	1	330	1	failure	no
3	30	management	married	tertiary	no	1476	yes	yes	unknown	3	jun	199	4	-1	0	unknown	no
4	59	blue-collar	married	secondary	no	0	yes	no	unknown	5	may	226	1	-1	0	unknown	no
5	35	management	single	tertiary	no	747	no	no	cellular	23	feb	141	2	176	3	failure	no
6	36	self-employed	married	tertiary	no	307	yes	no	cellular	14	may	341	1	330	2	other	no
7	39	technician	married	secondary	no	147	yes	no	cellular	6	may	151	2	-1	0	unknown	no
8	41	entrepreneur	married	tertiary	no	221	yes	no	unknown	14	may	57	2	-1	0	unknown	no
9	43	services	married	primary	no	-88	yes	yes	cellular	17	apr	313	1	147	2	failure	no
10	39	services	married	secondary	no	9374	yes	no	unknown	20	may	273	1	-1	0	unknown	no
11	43	admin.	married	secondary	no	264	yes	no	cellular	17	apr	113	2	-1	0	unknown	no
12	36	technician	married	tertiary	no	1109	no	no	cellular	13	aug	328	2	-1	0	unknown	no
13	20	student	single	secondary	no	502	no	no	cellular	30	apr	261	1	-1	0	unknown	yes
14	31	blue-collar	married	secondary	no	360	yes	yes	cellular	29	jan	89	1	241	1	failure	no
15	40	management	married	tertiary	no	194	no	yes	cellular	29	aug	189	2	-1	0	unknown	no
16	56	technician	married	secondary	no	4073	no	no	cellular	27	aug	239	5	-1	0	unknown	no
17	37	admin.	single	tertiary	no	2317	yes	no	cellular	20	apr	114	1	152	2	failure	no
18	25	blue-collar	single	primary	no	-221	yes	no	unknown	23	may	250	1	-1	0	unknown	no
19	31	services	married	secondary	no	132	no	no	cellular	7	jul	148	1	152	1	other	no

Figure 1.6: The first 20 rows of the pandas DataFrame

6. We can also print the shape of the DataFrame:

```
bank_data.shape
```

The printed output should look as follows, showing that the DataFrame has 4,521 rows and 17 columns:

The following figure shows the output of the preceding code:

$$(4521, 17)$$

Figure 1.7: Output of the shape command on the DataFrame

We have successfully loaded the data into memory, and now we can manipulate and clean the data so that a model can be trained using this data. Remember that machine learning models require data to be represented as numerical data types in order to be trained. We can see from the first few rows of the dataset that some of the columns are string types, so we will have to convert them to numerical data types later in the chapter.

7. We can see that there is a given output variable for the dataset, known as **'y'**, which indicates whether or not the client has subscribed. This seems like an appropriate target to predict for, since it is conceivable that we may know all the variables about our clients, such as their age. For those variables that we don't know, substituting unknowns is acceptable. The **'y'** target may be useful to the bank to figure out as to which customers they want to focus their resources on. We can create feature and target datasets as follows, providing the **axis=1** argument:

```
feats = bank_data.drop('y', axis=1)
target = bank_data['y']
```

> **Note**
>
> The **axis=1** argument tells the function to drop columns rather than rows.

8. To verify that the shapes of the datasets are as expected, we can print out the number of rows and columns of each:

```
print(f'Features table has {feats.shape[0]} rows and {feats.shape[1]}
columns')
print(f'Target table has {target.shape[0]} rows')
```

The following figure shows the output of the preceding code:

```
Features table has 4521 rows and 16 columns
Target table has 4521 rows
```

Figure 1.8: Output of the shape commands on the feature and target DataFrames

We can see two important things here that we should always verify before continuing: first, the number of rows of the feature DataFrame and target DataFrame are the same. Here, we can see that both have 4,521 rows. Second, the number of columns of the feature DataFrame should be one fewer than the total DataFrame, and the target DataFrame has exactly one column.

On the second point, we have to verify that the target is not contained in the feature dataset, otherwise the model will quickly find that this is the only column needed to minimize the total error, all the way down to zero. It's also not incredibly useful to include the target in the feature set. The target column doesn't necessarily have to be one column, but for binary classification, as in our case, it will be. Remember that these machine learning models are trying to minimize some cost function, in which the target variable will be part of that cost function.

9. Finally, we will save our DataFrames to CSV so that we can use them later:

```
feats.to_csv('data/bank_data_feats.csv')
target.to_csv('data/bank_data_target.csv', header='y')
```

> **Note**
>
> The **header='y'** parameter is used to provide a column name. We will do this to reduce confusion later on.

In this topic, we have successfully demonstrated how to load data into Python using the pandas library. This will form the basis of loading data into memory for most tabular data. Images and large documents, other common forms of data for machine learning applications, have to be loaded in using other methods that are discussed later in the book.

Data Preprocessing

To fit models to the data, it must be represented in numerical format since the mathematics used to in all machine learning algorithms only work on matrices of numbers (you cannot perform linear algebra on an image). This will be one goal of this topic, to learn how to encode all features into numerical representations. For example, in binary text, values that contain one of two possible values may be represented as zeros or ones. An example is shown in the following figure. Since there are only two possible values, a value 0 is assumed to be a cat and the value 1 a dog We can also rename the column for interpretation..

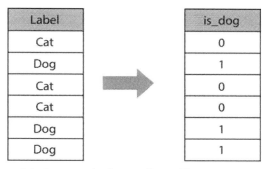

Figure 1.9: A numerical encoding of binary text values

Another goal will be to appropriately represent the data in numerical format – by appropriately, we mean that we want to encode relevant information numerically through the distribution of numbers. For example, one method to encode the months of the year would be to use the number of the month in the year. For example, January would be encoded as 1, since it is the first month, and December would be 12. Here's an example of how this would look in practice:

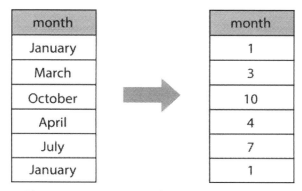

Figure 1.10: A numerical encoding of months

Not encoding information appropriately into numerical features can lead to machine learning models learning unintuitive representations, and relationships between the feature data and target variables that will prove useless for human interpretation.

An understanding of the machine learning algorithms you are looking to use will also help encode features into numerical representations appropriately. For example, algorithms for classification tasks such as **Artificial Neural Networks (ANNs)** and logistic regression are susceptible to large variations in the scale between the features that may hamper model-fitting ability. Take, for example, a regression problem attempting to fit house attributes, such as area in square feet and the number of bedrooms, to the house price. The bounds of the area may be anywhere from 0 to 5,000, whereas the number of bedrooms may only vary from 0 to 6, so there is a large difference between the scale of the variables. An effective way to combat the large variation in scale between the features is to normalize the data. Normalizing the data will scale the data appropriately so that it is all of a similar magnitude, so that any model coefficients or weights can be compared correctly. Algorithms such as decision trees are unaffected by data scaling, so this step can be omitted for models using tree-based algorithms.

In this topic, we demonstrate a number of different ways to encode information numerically. There is a myriad of alternative techniques that can be explored elsewhere. Here, we will show some simple and popular methods to tackle common data formats.

Exercise 2: Cleaning the Data

It is important that we clean the data appropriately so that it can be used for training models. This often includes converting non-numerical datatypes into numerical datatypes. This will be the focus of this exercise – to convert all columns in the feature dataset into numerical columns. To complete the exercise, perform the following steps:

1. First, we load the feature dataset into memory:

    ```
    %matplotlib inline
    import pandas as pd
    bank_data = pd.read_csv('data/bank_data_feats.csv', index_col=0)
    ```

    Note

    When pandas saves a DataFrame, it also includes the index column by default as the first column. So, when loading the data, we have to indicate which column number is the index column; otherwise, we will gain an extra column in our DataFrame.

2. Again, we can look at the first 20 rows to check out the data:

```
bank_data.head(20)
```

	age	job	marital	education	default	balance	housing	loan	contact	day	month	duration	campaign	pdays	previous	poutcome	y
0	30	unemployed	married	primary	no	1787	no	no	cellular	19	oct	79	1	-1	0	unknown	no
1	33	services	married	secondary	no	4789	yes	yes	cellular	11	may	220	1	339	4	failure	no
2	35	management	single	tertiary	no	1350	yes	no	cellular	16	apr	185	1	330	1	failure	no
3	30	management	married	tertiary	no	1476	yes	yes	unknown	3	jun	199	4	-1	0	unknown	no
4	59	blue-collar	married	secondary	no	0	yes	no	unknown	5	may	226	1	-1	0	unknown	no
5	35	management	single	tertiary	no	747	no	no	cellular	23	feb	141	2	176	3	failure	no
6	36	self-employed	married	tertiary	no	307	yes	no	cellular	14	may	341	1	330	2	other	no
7	39	technician	married	secondary	no	147	yes	no	cellular	6	may	151	2	-1	0	unknown	no
8	41	entrepreneur	married	tertiary	no	221	yes	no	unknown	14	may	57	2	-1	0	unknown	no
9	43	services	married	primary	no	-88	yes	yes	cellular	17	apr	313	1	147	2	failure	no
10	39	services	married	secondary	no	9374	yes	no	unknown	20	may	273	1	-1	0	unknown	no
11	43	admin.	married	secondary	no	264	yes	no	cellular	17	apr	113	2	-1	0	unknown	no
12	36	technician	married	tertiary	no	1109	no	no	cellular	13	aug	328	2	-1	0	unknown	no
13	20	student	single	secondary	no	502	no	no	cellular	30	apr	261	1	-1	0	unknown	yes
14	31	blue-collar	married	secondary	no	360	yes	yes	cellular	29	jan	89	1	241	1	failure	no
15	40	management	married	tertiary	no	194	no	yes	cellular	29	aug	189	2	-1	0	unknown	no
16	56	technician	married	secondary	no	4073	no	no	cellular	27	aug	239	5	-1	0	unknown	no
17	37	admin.	single	tertiary	no	2317	yes	no	cellular	20	apr	114	1	152	2	failure	no
18	25	blue-collar	single	primary	no	-221	yes	no	unknown	23	may	250	1	-1	0	unknown	no
19	31	services	married	secondary	no	132	no	no	cellular	7	jul	148	1	152	1	other	no

Figure 1.11: First 20 rows of the pandas feature DataFrame

We can see that there are a number of columns that need to be converted to numerical format. The numerical columns we may not need to touch the columns named **age**, **balance**, **day**, **duration**, **campaign**, **pdays**, and **previous**.

There are some binary columns, which have either one of two possible values. They are default, housing, and loan.

Finally, there are also categorical columns that are string types, but there are a limited number of choices (>2) that the column can take. They are **job**, **education**, **marital**, **contact**, **month**, and **poutcome**.

3. For the numerical columns, we can use the **describe** function, which can give us a quick indication of the bounds of the numerical columns:

```
bank_data.describe()
```

	age	balance	day	duration	campaign	pdays	previous
count	4521.000000	4521.000000	4521.000000	4521.000000	4521.000000	4521.000000	4521.000000
mean	41.170095	1422.657819	15.915284	263.961292	2.793630	39.766645	0.542579
std	10.576211	3009.638142	8.247667	259.856633	3.109807	100.121124	1.693562
min	19.000000	-3313.000000	1.000000	4.000000	1.000000	-1.000000	0.000000
25%	33.000000	69.000000	9.000000	104.000000	1.000000	-1.000000	0.000000
50%	39.000000	444.000000	16.000000	185.000000	2.000000	-1.000000	0.000000
75%	49.000000	1480.000000	21.000000	329.000000	3.000000	-1.000000	0.000000
max	87.000000	71188.000000	31.000000	3025.000000	50.000000	871.000000	25.000000

Figure 1.12: Output of the describe function in the feature DataFrame

4. We will convert the binary columns into numerical columns. For each column, we will follow the same procedure, examine the possible values, and convert one of the values to 1 and the other to 0. If appropriate, we will rename the column for interpretability.

For context, it is helpful to see the distribution of each value. We can do that using the **value_counts** function. We can try this out on the **default** column:

```
bank_data['default'].value_counts()
```

We can also look at these values as a bar graph by plotting the value counts:

```
bank_data['default'].value_counts().plot(kind='bar')
```

> **Note**
>
> The **kind='bar'** argument will plot the data as a bar graph. The default is a line graph. When plotting in the Jupyter Notebook, in order to make the plots within the notebook, the following command may need to be run: **%matplotlib inline**.

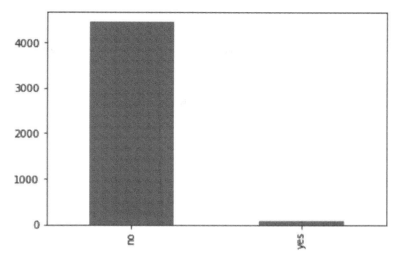

Figure 1.13: A plot of the distribution of values of the default column

5. We can see that this distribution is very skewed. Let's convert the column to numerical value by converting the **yes** values to 1, and the no values to 0. We can also change the name of the column from default to **is_default**. This makes it a bit more obvious what the column means:

```
bank_data['is_default'] = bank_data['default'].apply(lambda row: 1 if row
== 'yes' else 0)
```

Note

The **apply** function iterates through each element in the column and applies the function provided as the argument. A function has to be supplied as the argument. Here, a **lambda** function is supplied.

6. We can take a look at the original and converted columns side by side. We can take a sample of the last few rows to show examples of both values manipulated to numerical data types:

```
bank_data[['default','is_default']].tail()
```

> **Note**
>
> The **tail** function is identical to the **head** function, except the function returns the bottom **n** values of the DataFrame instead of the top **n**.

	default	is_default
4516	no	0
4517	yes	1
4518	no	0
4519	no	0
4520	no	0

Figure 1.14: The original and manipulated default column

We can see that **yes** is converted to **1** and **no** is converted to **0**.

1. Let's do the same for the other binary columns, **housing** and **loan**:

```
bank_data['is_loan'] = bank_data['loan'].apply(lambda row: 1 if row ==
'yes' else 0)
bank_data['is_housing'] = bank_data['housing'].apply(lambda row: 1 if row
== 'yes' else 0)
```

2. Next, we have to deal with categorical columns. We will approach the conversion of categorical columns to numerical values slightly differently, than with binary text columns but the concept will be the same. We will convert each categorical column into a set of dummy columns. With dummy columns, each categorical column will be converted to **n** columns, where **n** is the number unique values in the category. The columns will be zero or one depending on the value of categorical column.

   This is achieved with the **get_dummies** function. If we need any help understanding the function, we can use the **help** function, or any function:

```
help(pd.get_dummies)
```

```
Help on function get_dummies in module pandas.core.reshape.reshape:

get_dummies(data, prefix=None, prefix_sep='_', dummy_na=False, columns=None, sparse=False, drop_first=False)
    Convert categorical variable into dummy/indicator variables

    Parameters
    ----------
    data : array-like, Series, or DataFrame
    prefix : string, list of strings, or dict of strings, default None
        String to append DataFrame column names
        Pass a list with length equal to the number of columns
        when calling get_dummies on a DataFrame. Alternativly, `prefix`
        can be a dictionary mapping column names to prefixes.
    prefix_sep : string, default '_'
        If appending prefix, separator/delimiter to use. Or pass a
        list or dictionary as with `prefix.`
    dummy_na : bool, default False
        Add a column to indicate NaNs, if False NaNs are ignored.
    columns : list-like, default None
        Column names in the DataFrame to be encoded.
        If `columns` is None then all the columns with
        `object` or `category` dtype will be converted.
    sparse : bool, default False
        Whether the dummy columns should be sparse or not.  Returns
        SparseDataFrame if `data` is a Series or if all columns are included.
        Otherwise returns a DataFrame with some SparseBlocks.

        .. versionadded:: 0.16.1
    drop_first : bool, default False
        Whether to get k-1 dummies out of k categorical levels by removing the
        first level.
```

Figure 1.15: The output of the help command applied to the pd.get_dummies function

3. Let's demonstrate how to manipulate categorical columns with the `marital` column. Again, it is helpful to see the distribution of values, so let's look at the value counts and plot them:

```
bank_data['marital'].value_counts()
bank_data['marital'].value_counts().plot(kind='bar')
```

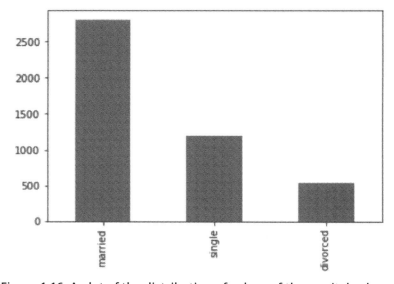

Figure 1.16: A plot of the distribution of values of the marital column

4. We can call the **get_dummies** function on the **marital** column and take a look at the first few rows alongside the original:

```
marital_dummies = pd.get_dummies(bank_data['marital'])
pd.concat([bank_data['marital'], marital_dummies], axis=1).head(n=10)
```

	marital	divorced	married	single
0	married	0	1	0
1	married	0	1	0
2	single	0	0	1
3	married	0	1	0
4	married	0	1	0
5	single	0	0	1
6	married	0	1	0
7	married	0	1	0
8	married	0	1	0
9	married	0	1	0

Figure 1.17: Dummy columns from the marital column

We can see that in each of the rows there can be one value of **1**, which is in the column corresponding the value in the **marital** column.

In fact, when using dummy columns there is some redundant information. Because we know there are three values, if two of the values in the dummy columns are zero for a particular row, then the remaining column must be equal to one. It is important to eliminate any redundancy and correlations in features as it becomes difficult to determine which feature is most important in minimizing the total error.

5. To remove the inter-dependency, let's drop the **divorced** column because it occurs with the lowest frequency. We can also change the name of the columns so that it is a little easier to read and include the original column:

```
marital_dummies.drop('divorced', axis=1, inplace=True)
marital_dummies.columns = [f'marital_{colname}' for colname in marital_
dummies.columns]
marital_dummies.head()
```

> **Note**
>
> In the **drop** function, the **inplace** argument will apply the function in place, so a new variable does not have to declared.

Looking at the first few rows, we can see what remains of our dummy columns for the original **marital** column.

	marital_married	marital_single
0	1	0
1	1	0
2	0	1
3	1	0
4	1	0

Figure 1.18: Final dummy columns from the marital column

6. Finally, we can add these dummy columns to the original feature data by concatenating the two DataFrames column-wise and dropping the original column:

```
bank_data = pd.concat([bank_data, marital_dummies], axis=1)
bank_data.drop('marital', axis=1, inplace=True)
```

7. We will repeat the exact same steps with the remaining categorical columns: **education**, **job**, **contact**, and **poutcome**. First, we will examine the distribution of column values, which is an optional step. Second, we will create dummy columns. Third, we will drop one of the columns to remove redundancy. Fourth, we will change the column names for interpretability. Fifth, we will concatenate the dummy columns into a feature dataset. Sixth, we will drop the original column if it remains in the dataset.

8. We could treat the **month** column like a categorical variable, although since there is some order to the values (January comes before February, and so on) they are known as ordinal values. We can encode this into the feature by converting the month name into the month number, for example, `January` becomes `1` as it is the first month in the year.

   This is one way to convert months into numerical features that may make sense in certain models. In fact, for a logistic regression model, this may not make sense since we are encoding some inherent weighting into the features. This feature will contribute 12 times as much for rows with December as the month compared to January, which there should be no reason to do. Regardless, in the spirit of showing multiple techniques to convert columns to numerical datatypes, we will continue.

   We can achieve this result by mapping the month names to month numbers by creating a Python dictionary of key-value pairs in which the keys will be the month names and the values will be the month numbers:

   ```
   month_map = {'jan':1, 'feb':2, 'mar':3, 'apr':4, 'may':5, 'jun':6,
    'jul':7, 'aug':8, 'sep':9, 'oct':10, 'nov':11, 'dec': 12}
   ```

   Then we can convert the column by utilizing the `map` function:

   ```
   bank_data['month'] = bank_data['month'].map(month_map)
   ```

   Since we have kept the column name the same, there is no need for us to concatenate back into the original feature dataset and drop the column.

9. Now we should have our entire dataset as numerical columns. Let's check the types of each column to verify:

```
bank_data.dtypes
```

```
age                     int64
balance                 int64
day                     int64
month                   int64
duration                int64
campaign                int64
pdays                   int64
previous                int64
is_default              int64
is_housing              int64
is_loan                 int64
marital_married         uint8
marital_single          uint8
job_admin.              uint8
job_blue-collar         uint8
job_entrepreneur        uint8
job_housemaid           uint8
job_management          uint8
job_retired             uint8
job_self-employed       uint8
job_services            uint8
job_student             uint8
job_technician          uint8
job_unemployed          uint8
education_primary       uint8
education_secondary     uint8
education_tertiary      uint8
contact_cellular        uint8
contact_telephone       uint8
poutcome_failure        uint8
poutcome_other          uint8
poutcome_success        uint8
dtype: object
```

Figure 1.19: The datatypes of the processed feature dataset

10. Now that we have verified the datatypes, we have a dataset we can use to train a model, so let's save this for later:

```
bank_data.to_csv('data/bank_data_feats_e2.csv')
```

11. Let's do the same for the target variable. First, load the data in, then convert the column to numerical datatype, and lastly, save the column as CSV:

```
target = pd.read_csv('data/bank_data_target.csv', index_col=0)
target.head(n=10)
```

	y
0	no
1	no
2	no
3	no
4	no
5	no
6	no
7	no
8	no
9	no
10	no

Figure 1.20: First 10 rows of the target dataset

We can see that this is a string datatype, and there are two unique values.

12. Let's convert this into a binary numerical column, much like we did the binary columns in the feature dataset:

```
target['y'] = target['y'].apply(lambda row: 1 if row=='yes' else 0)
target.head(n=10)
```

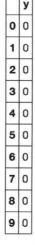

	y
0	0
1	0
2	0
3	0
4	0
5	0
6	0
7	0
8	0
9	0

Figure 1.21: First 10 rows of the target dataset when converted to integers

13. Finally, we save the target dataset to CSV:

```
target.to_csv('data/bank_data_target_e2.csv')
```

In this exercise, we learned how to clean the data appropriately so that it can be used to train models. We converted the non-numerical datatypes into numerical datatypes. That is, we converted all the columns in the feature dataset into numerical columns. Lastly, we saved the target dataset to a CSV file so that we can use them in the succeeding exercises or activities.

Appropriate Representation of the Data

In our bank marketing dataset, we have some columns that do not appropriately represent the data, which will have to be addressed if we want the models we build to learn useful relationships between the features and the target. One column that is an example of this is the **pdays** column. In the documentation, the column is described as follows:

pdays: number of days that passed by after the client was last contacted from a previous campaign (numeric, -1 means client was not previously contacted)

Here we can see that a value of **-1** means something quite different than a positive number. There are two pieces of information encoded in this one column that we may want to separate. They are as follows:

- Whether or not they were contacted

- If they were contacted, how long ago was that last contact made

When we create columns, they should ideally align with hypotheses we create of relationships between the features and the target.

One hypothesis may be that previously contacted customers are more likely to subscribe to the product. Given our column, we could test this hypothesis by converting the **pdays** column into a binary variable indicating whether they were previously contacted or not. This can be achieved by observing whether the value of **pdays** is **-1**. If so, we will associate that with a value of **0**; otherwise, they have been contacted, so the value will be **1**.

A second hypothesis is that the more recently the customer was contacted, the greater the likelihood that they will subscribe. There are many ways to encode this second hypothesis. I recommend encoding the first one, and if we see that this feature has predictive power, we can implement the second hypothesis.

Since building machine learning models is an iterative process, we can choose either or both hypotheses and evaluate whether their inclusion has increased the model's predictive performance.

Exercise 3: Appropriate Representation of the Data

In this exercise, we will encode the hypothesis that a customer will be more likely to subscribe to the product that they were previously targeted with. We will encode this hypothesis by transforming the **pdays** column. Wherever the value is **-1**, we will transform it to **0**, indicating the customer has never been previously contacted. Otherwise, the value will be **1**. To do so, we follow the following steps:

1. Open a Jupyter notebook.

2. Load the dataset into memory. We can use the same feature dataset as was the output from Exercise 2:

   ```
   import pandas as pd
   bank_data = pd.read_csv('data/bank_data_feats_e2.csv', index_col=0)
   ```

3. Use the **apply** function to manipulate the column and create a new column:

   ```
   bank_data['was_contacted'] = bank_data['pdays'].apply(lambda row: 0 if row == -1 else 1)
   ```

4. Drop the original column:

   ```
   bank_data.drop('pdays', axis=1, inplace=True)
   ```

5. Let's look at the column that was just changed:

   ```
   bank_data[['was_contacted']].head(n=10)
   ```

	was_contacted
0	0
1	1
2	1
3	0
4	0
5	1
6	1
7	0
8	0
9	1

Figure 1.22: The first 10 rows of the formatted column

6. Finally, let's save the dataset to a CSV file for later use:

```
bank_data.to_csv('data/bank_data_feats_e3.csv')
```

Great! Now we can test our hypothesis of whether previous contact will affect the target variable. This exercise has demonstrated how to appropriately represent data for use in machine learning algorithms. We have presented some techniques to convert data into numerical datatypes that cover many situations that may be encountered when working with tabular data.

Life Cycle of Model Creation

In this section, we will cover the life cycle of creating performant machine learning models from engineering features, to fitting models to training data, and evaluating our models using various metrics. Many of the steps to create models are highly transferable between all machine learning libraries – we'll start with scikit-learn, which has the advantage of being widely used, and as such there is a lot of documentation, tutorials, and learning to be found across the internet.

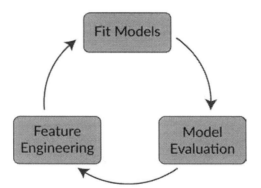

Figure 1.23: The life cycle of model creation

Machine Learning Libraries

While this book is an introduction to deep learning with Keras, as mentioned earlier, we will start by utilizing scikit-learn. This will help us establish the fundamentals of building a machine learning model using the Python programming language.

Similar to scikit-learn, Keras makes it easy to create models in the Python programming language through an easy-to-use API. However, the goal of Keras is for the creation and training of neural networks, rather than machine learning models in general. ANNs represent a large class of machine learning algorithms, and they are so called because their architecture resembles the neurons in the human brain. The Keras library has many general-purpose functions built in, such as optimizers, activation functions, and layer properties, so that users, like in scikit-learn, do not have to code these algorithms from scratch.

scikit-learn

scikit-learn was initially created in 2007 as a way to easily create machine learning models in the Python programming language by David Cournapeau. Since its inception, the library has grown immensely in popularity because of its ease of use, wide adoption within the machine learning community, and flexibility of use.

In the next section are a few of the advantages and disadvantages of using scikit-learn for machine learning purposes.

Advantages of scikit-learn are as follows:

- **Mature**: scikit-learn is well established within the community and used by members of the community of all skill levels. The package includes most of the common machine learning algorithms for classification, regression, and clustering tasks.

- **User-friendly**: scikit-learn features an easy-to-use API that enables beginners to efficiently prototype without having to have a deep understanding or code each specific mode.

- **Open source**: There is an active open source community working to improve the library, add documentation, and release regular updates, which ensures that the package is stable and up to date.

Disadvantage of scikit-learn is as follows:

- **Neural network support lacking**: Estimators with ANN algorithms are minimal.

> **Note**
>
> You can find all the documentation for the scikit-learn library here: https://scikit-learn.org/stable/documentation.html.

The estimators in scikit-learn can generally be classified into supervised learning and unsupervised learning techniques. Supervised learning occurs when a **target variable** is present. A target variable is a variable of the dataset for which you are trying to predict given the other variables. Supervised learning requires the target variable to be known and models are trained in order to correctly predict this variable. Binary classification using logistic regression is a good example of a supervised learning technique.

In unsupervised learning, there is no target variable given in the training data, but models aim to assign a target variable. An example of an unsupervised learning technique is k-means clustering. This algorithm partitions data into a given number of clusters based on proximity to neighboring data points. The target variable assigned may be either the cluster number or cluster center.

An example of utilizing a clustering example in practice may look as follows. Imagine that you are a jacket manufacturer and your goal is to develop dimensions for various jacket sizes. You cannot create a custom-fit jacket for each customer, so one option you have to determine the dimensions for jackets is to sample the population of customers for various parameters that may be correlated to fit, such as height and weight. Then, you can group the population into clusters using scikit-learn's k-means clustering algorithm with a cluster number that matches with the number of jacket sizes you wish to produce. The cluster-centers that are created from the clustering algorithm become the parameters on which the jacket sizes are based. This is visualized in the following figure:

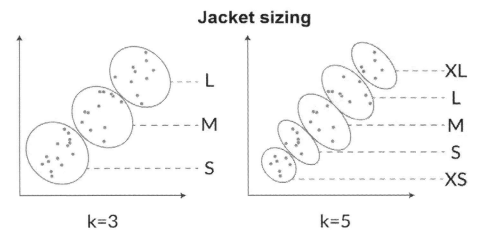

Figure 1.24: An unsupervised learning example of grouping customer parameters into clusters

There are even semi-supervised learning techniques in which unlabeled data is used in the training of machine learning models. This technique may be used if there is only a small amount of labeled data and a copious amount of unlabeled data. In practice, semi-supervised learning produces a significant improvement in model performance compared to unsupervised learning.

The scikit-learn library is ideal for beginners as the general concepts for building machine learning pipelines can be learned easily. Concepts such as data preprocessing, hyperparameter tuning, model evaluation, and many more are all included in the library. Even experienced users find the library easy to rapidly prototype models before using a more specialized machine learning library.

Indeed, the various machine learning techniques discussed such as supervised and unsupervised learning can be applied with Keras using neural networks with different architectures that will be discussed throughout the book.

Keras

Keras is designed to be a high-level neural network API that is built on top of frameworks such as TensorFlow, CNTK, or Theano. One of the great benefits of using Keras as an introduction to deep learning for beginners is that it is very user-friendly – advanced functions such as optimizers and layers are already built in to the library and do not have to be written from scratch. This is why Keras is popular not only amongst beginners, but also seasoned experts. Also, the library allows rapid prototyping of neural networks, supports a wide variety of network architectures, and can be run on both CPU and GPU.

> **Note**
>
> You can find the library and all documentation for Keras at the following link: https://Keras.io/.

Keras is used to create and train neural networks and does not offer much in terms of other machine learning algorithms, including supervised algorithms such as support vector machines and unsupervised algorithms such as k-means clustering. What Keras does offer, though, is a well-designed API to create and train neural networks, which takes away much of the effort required to apply linear algebra and multivariate calculus accurately.

The specific modules available from the Keras library, such as neural layers, cost functions, optimizers, initialization schemes, activation functions, and regularization schemes, will be explained thoroughly throughout the book. All these modules have relevant functions that can be used to optimize the performance for training neural networks for specific tasks.

Advantages of Keras

Here are a few of the main advantages and disadvantages of using Keras for machine learning purposes:

- **User-friendly**: Much like scikit-learn, Keras features an easy-to-use API that allows users to focus on model-building rather than the specifics of the algorithms.

- **Modular**: The API consists of fully configurable modules that can all be plugged together and work seamlessly.

- **Extensible**: It is relatively simple to add new modules to the library. This allows users to take advantage of the many robust modules within library while providing them the flexibility to create their own.

- **Open Source**: Keras is an open source library and is constantly improving and adding modules to its code base thanks to the work of many collaborators working in conjunction to build improvements and help create a robust library for all.

- **Works with Python**: Keras models are declared directly in Python rather than in separate configuration files, which allows Keras to take advantages of working with Python, such as ease of debugging and extensibility.

Disadvantages of Keras

- **Advanced customization**: While simple surface-level customization such as creating simple custom loss functions or neural layers is facile, it can be difficult to change how the underlying architecture works.

- **Lack of examples**: Beginners often rely on examples to kick-start their learning. Advanced examples can be lacking in Keras documentation that can prevent beginners from advancing in their learning.

Keras offers those familiar with the Python programming language and machine learning the ability to create neural network architectures easily. Since neural networks are quite complicated, we will use scikit-learn to introduce many machine learning concepts before applying them out in the Keras library.

More than Building Models

While machine learning libraries such as scikit-learn and Keras were created to help build and train predictive models, their practicality extends much further. One common use case of building models is that they can be utilized to perform predictions on new data. Once a model is trained, new observations can be fed into the model to generate predictions. Models may even be used as intermediate steps. For example, neural network models can be used as feature extractors, classifying objects in an image that can then be fed into a subsequent model, as illustrated in the following figure:

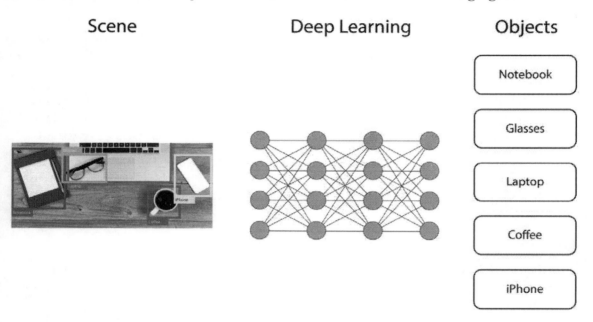

Figure 1.25: Classifying objects using deep learning

Another common use case for models is that they can be used to summarize datasets by learning representations of the data. Such models are known as auto-encoders, a type of neural network architecture that can be used to learn such representations of a given dataset. The dataset can thus be represented in a reduced dimension with minimal loss of information.

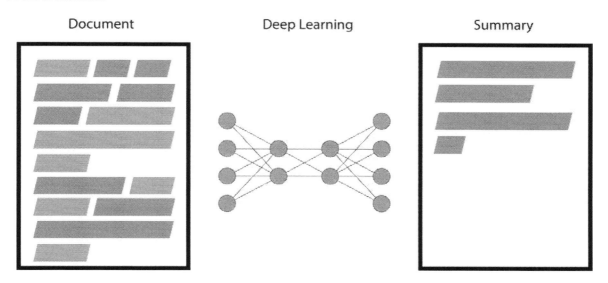

Figure 1.26: An example of using deep learning for text summarization

Model Training

In this topic, we will begin fitting our model to the datasets that we have created. In this chapter, we will review the minimum steps required to create a machine learning model that can be applied to building models with any machine learning library, including scikit-learn and Keras.

Classifiers and Regression Models

This book is concerned with applications of deep learning. The vast majority of deep learning tasks are supervised learning, in which there is a given target, and we want to fit a model so that we can understand the relationship between the features and the target.

An example of supervised learning is identifying whether a picture contains a dog or a cat. We want to determine the relationship between the input (a matrix of pixel values) and the target variable, that is, whether the image is of a dog or a cat.

Image	Label

Figure 1.27: A simple supervised learning task to classify images into dogs and cats

Ofcourse, we may need many more images in our training dataset to robustly classify new images, but models that are trained on such a dataset are able to identify the various relationships that differentiate cats and dogs, which can then be used to predict labels for new data.

Supervised learning models are generally used for either classification or regression tasks.

Classification Tasks

The goal of classification tasks is to fit models from data with discrete categories that can be used to label unlabeled data. For example, these types of models can be used to classify images into dogs or cats. But it doesn't stop at binary classification; multi-label classification is also possible.

Most classification tasks output a probability for each unique class. The prediction is determined as the class with the highest probability, as can be seen in the following figure:

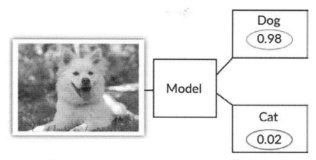

Figure 1.28: An illustration of a classification model labeling an image

Some of the most common classification algorithms are the following:

- **Logistic regression**: This algorithm similar to linear regression, in which feature coefficients are learned and predictions are made by taking the sum of the product of the feature coefficients and features.

- **Decision trees**: This algorithm follows a tree-like structure. Decisions are made at each node and branches represent possible options at the node, terminating in the predicted result.

- **ANNs**: ANNs replicate the structure and performance of a biological neural network to perform pattern recognition tasks. An ANN consists of interconnected neurons, laid out with a set architecture, that pass information to each other until a result is achieved.

Regression Tasks

While the aim of classification tasks is to label datasets with discrete variables, the aim of regression tasks is to provide input data with continuous variables, and output a numerical value. For example, if you have a dataset of stock market prices, a classification task may predict whether to buy, sell, or hold, whereas a regression task will predict what the stock market price will be.

A simple, yet very popular, algorithm for regression tasks is linear regression. It consists of only one independent feature (x), whose relation with its dependent feature (y) is linear. Due to its simplicity, it is often overlooked, even though it performs very well for simple data problems.

Some of the most common classification algorithms are the following:

- **Linear regression**: This algorithm learns feature coefficients and predictions are made by taking the sum of the product of the feature coefficients and features.

- **Support Vector Machines**: This algorithm uses kernels to map input data into a multi-dimensional feature space to understand relationships between features and the target.

- **ANNs**: ANNs replicate the structure and performance of a biological neural network to perform pattern recognition tasks. An ANN consists of interconnected neurons, laid out with a set architecture, that pass information to each other until a result is achieved.

Training and Test Datasets

Whenever we create machine learning models, we separate the data into training and test datasets. The training data is the set of data used to train the model. Typically, it is a large proportion, around 80%, of the total dataset. The test dataset is a sample of the dataset that is held out from the beginning and is used to provide an unbiased evaluation of the model. The test dataset should as accurately as possible represent real-world data. Any model evaluation metrics that are reported should be applied on the test dataset unless it's explicitly stated that the metrics have been evaluated on the training dataset. The reason for this is that models will typically perform better on the data they are trained on. Furthermore, models can overfit the training dataset, meaning that they perform well on the training dataset but perform poorly on the test dataset. A model is said to be overfitted to the data if the model performance is very good when evaluated on the training dataset, but performs poorly on the test dataset. Conversely, a model can be underfitted to the data. In this case, the model will fail to learn relationships between the features and the target, which will lead to poor performance when evaluated on both the training and test datasets. We aim for a balance of the two, not relying so heavily on the training dataset that we overfit, but allowing the model to learn the relationships between features and target so that the model generalizes well to new data. This concept is illustrated in the following figure:

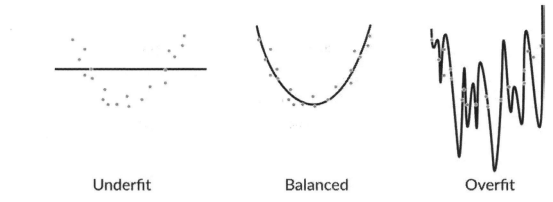

Figure 1.29: A example of under- and overfitting a dataset

There are many ways to split the dataset via sampling methods. One method to split a dataset into training is to simply randomly sample the data until you have the desired number of data points. This is often the default method in functions such as the scikit-learn `train_test_spilt` function. Another method is to stratify the sampling. In stratified sampling, each subpopulation is sampled independently. Each subpopulation is determined by the target variable. This can be advantageous in examples such as binary classification where the target variable is highly skewed toward one value or another, and random sampling may not provide data points of both values in the training and test datasets. There are also validation datasets, which we will address later in the chapter.

Model Evaluation Metrics

It is important to be able to evaluate our models effectively, not just in terms of the model's performance but also in the context of the problem we are trying to solve. For example, let's say we built a classification task to predict whether to buy, sell, or hold stock based on historical stock market prices. If our model only predicted to buy every time, this would not be a useful result because we may not have infinite resources to buy stocks. It may be better to be less accurate yet also include some sell predictions.

Common evaluation metrics for classification tasks are accuracy, precision, recall, and f1 score. Accuracy is defined as the number of correct predictions divided by the total number of predictions. Accuracy is very interpretable and relatable, and good for when there are balanced classes. When the classes are highly skewed, the accuracy can be misleading, however.

$$\text{Accuracy} = \frac{\text{Number of correct predictions}}{\text{Total number of predictions}}$$

Figure 1.30: Formula to calculate accuracy

Precision is another useful metric. It's defined as the number of true positive results divided by the total number of positive results (true and false) predicted by the model.

$$\text{Precision} = \frac{\text{True Positives}}{\text{True Positives} + \text{False Positives}}$$

Figure 1.31: Formula to calculate precision

Recall is defined as the number of correct positive results divided by all positive results from the ground truth.

$$\text{Recall} = \frac{\text{True Positives}}{\text{True Positives} + \text{False Negatives}}$$

Figure 1.32: Formula to calculate recall

Both precision and recall are scored between zero and one, but scoring well on one may mean scoring poorly on the other. For example, a model may have high precision but low recall, which indicates that the model is very accurate but misses a large number of positive instances. It is useful to have a metric that combines recall and precision. Enter the f1 score, which determines how precise and robust your model is.

$$\text{F1 Score} = 2 \times \frac{1}{\frac{1}{\text{Precision}} + \frac{1}{\text{Recall}}}$$

Figure 1.33: Formula to calculate f1 score

When evaluating models, it is helpful to look at a range of different evaluation metrics. They will help determine the most appropriate model and evaluate where the model is misclassifying predictions.

Exercise 4: Creating a Simple Model

In this exercise, we will create a simple logistic regression model from the scikit-learn package. We will then create some model evaluation metrics and test the predictions against those model evaluation metrics.

We should always approach training any machine learning model training as an iterative approach, beginning first with a simple model, and using model evaluation metrics to evaluate the performance of the models. In this model, our goal is to classify the customers in the bank dataset into training and test datasets:

1. Load in the data:

    ```
    import pandas as pd
    feats = pd.read_csv('data/bank_data_feats_e3.csv', index_col=0)
    target = pd.read_csv('data/bank_data_target_e2.csv', index_col=0)
    ```

2. We first begin by creating a test and train dataset. We will train the data using the training dataset and evaluate the performance of the model on the test dataset.

   We will use **test_size = 0.2**, which means that 20% of the data will be reserved for testing, and we will set a number for the **random_state** parameter:

```
from sklearn.model_selection import train_test_split
test_size = 0.2
random_state = 42
X_train, X_test, y_train, y_test = train_test_split(feats, target, test_
size=test_size, random_state=random_state)
```

3. We can print out the shape of each DataFrame to verify that the dimensions are correct:

```
print(f'Shape of X_train: {X_train.shape}')
print(f'Shape of y_train: {y_train.shape}')
print(f'Shape of X_test: {X_test.shape}')
print(f'Shape of y_test: {y_test.shape}')
```

The following figure shows the output of the preceding code:

```
Shape of X_train: (3616, 32)
Shape of y_train: (3616, 1)
Shape of X_test: (905, 32)
Shape of y_test: (905, 1)
```

Figure 1.34: Shape of the test and training feature and target DataFrames

These dimensions look correct; each of the target datasets have a single column, the training feature and target DataFrames have the same number of rows, the same applies to the test feature and target DataFrames, and the test DataFrames are 20% of the total dataset.

4. Next, we have to instantiate our model:

```
from sklearn.linear_model import LogisticRegression
model = LogisticRegression(random_state=42)
```

While there are many arguments we can add to scikit-learn's logistic regression model, such as the type and value of regularization parameter, the type of solver, and the maximum number of iterations for the model to have, we will only pass **random_state**.

5. We then fit the model to the training data:

```
model.fit(X_train, y_train['y'])
```

6. To test the performance of the model, we compare the predictions of the model with the true values:

```
y_pred = model.predict(X_test)
```

There are many types of model evaluation metrics that we can use. Let's start with the accuracy, which is defined as the proportion of predicted values that equal the true values:

```
from sklearn import metrics
accuracy = metrics.accuracy_score(y_pred=y_pred, y_true=y_test)
print(f'Accuracy of the model is {accuracy*100:.4f}%')
```

The following figure shows the output of the preceding code:

```
Accuracy of the model is 89.9448%
```

Figure 1.35: Accuracy of the model

7. Other common evaluation metrics for classification models are the precision, recall, and f1 score. Scikit-learn has a function that can calculate all three, so we can use that:

```
precision, recall, fscore, _ = metrics.precision_recall_fscore_support(y_
pred=y_pred, y_true=y_test, average='binary')
print(f'Precision: {precision:.4f}\nRecall: {recall:.4f}\nfscore:
{fscore:.4f}')
```

Note

The underscore is used in Python for many reasons. It can be used to recall the value of the last expression in the interpreter, but in this case, we're using it to ignore specific values that are output by the function.

The following figure shows the output of the preceding code:

```
Precision: 0.5814
Recall: 0.2551
fscore: 0.3546
```

Figure 1.36: The other common evaluation metrics of the model

Since these metrics are scored between 0 and 1, the recall and fscore are not as impressive as the accuracy, though looking at all of these metrics together can help us to find where our models are doing well and where they could be improved by examining in which observations the model gets predictions incorrect.

8. We can also look at the coefficients that the model outputs to observe which features have a greater impact on the overall result of the prediction:

```
coef_list = [f'{feature}: {coef}' for coef, feature in sorted(zip(model.
coef_[0], X_train.columns.values.tolist())))]
for item in coef_list:
    print(item)
```

The following figure shows the output of the preceding code:

```
job_entrepreneur: -0.9322678224144281
poutcome_failure: -0.7360703558361755
is_loan: -0.6882901627079451
job_blue-collar: -0.5956734567765051
job_unemployed: -0.5897709614775752
is_housing: -0.5855613749463311
is_married: -0.45533425225057506
job_technician: -0.4434429614039016
job_services: -0.41934097407934096
job_self-employed: -0.2776596010239553
is_single: -0.2744267718174345
education_primary: -0.24801126222989317
job_housemaid: -0.17467680632343618
job_management: -0.15326446615040326
education_secondary: -0.14223659400871758
job_admin.: -0.12121238888910131
campaign: -0.08326986863874576
poutcome_other: -0.04754007400341722
month: -0.02740659107463574
age: -0.0031618607032899973
day: -0.0007529413012959553
balance: 2.031345304027948e-06
duration: 0.00405371895577842
previous: 0.01911757379686975
education_tertiary: 0.12860374054901927
job_student: 0.17240984850358923
is_default: 0.4342166153789329
job_retired: 0.4747213803112326
was_contacted: 0.7673862962443289
contact_telephone: 0.9095323487299974
contact_cellular: 0.9292906229946546
poutcome_success: 1.5509967260839006
```

Figure 1.37: The sorted important features of the model with their respective coefficients

This activity has taught us how to create and train a predictive model to predict a target variable given feature variables. We split the feature and target dataset into training and test datasets. Then, we trained our model on the training dataset and evaluated our model on the test dataset. Finally, we observed the trained coefficients for this model.

Model Tuning

In this topic, we will delve further into evaluating model performance and examine techniques of generalizing models to new data using regularization. Providing the context of a model's performance is extremely important. Our aim is to determine whether our model is performing well compared to trivial or obvious approaches. We do this by creating a baseline model against which machine learning models we train are compared. It is important to stress that all model evaluation metrics are evaluated and reported via the test dataset, since that will give us an understanding of how the model will perform on new data.

Baseline Models

A **baseline** model should be a simple and well-understood procedure, and the performance of this model should be the lowest acceptable performance for any model we build. For classification models, a useful and easy baseline model is to calculate the mode outcome value. For example, in our example, if there are 60% false values, our baseline model would be to predict false for every value, which would give us an accuracy of 60%.

Exercise 5: Determining a Baseline Model

In this exercise, we will put model performance into context. The accuracy we attained from our model seemed good, but we need something to compare it to. Since machine learning model performance is relative, it is important to develop a robust baseline with which to compare models. We are again using the bank dataset, and our target variable is whether or not each customer subscribed to a product. Follow these steps to perform the exercise:

1. Import all the necessary dependencies and load in the target dataset:

```
import pandas as pd
target = pd.read_csv('data/bank_data_target_e2.csv', index_col=0)
```

2. Next, we have to calculate the relative proportion of each value of the target variables:

```
target['y'].value_counts()/target.shape[0]*100
```

The following figure shows the output of the preceding code:

```
0      88.476001
1      11.523999
Name: y, dtype: float64
```

Figure 1.38: Relative proportion of each value

3. We can see in the dataset that 0 is represented 88.476% of the time – these are the customers that didn't subscribe to any product, and this is our baseline accuracy. Now for the other model evaluation metrics:

```
from sklearn import metrics
y_baseline = pd.Series(data=[0]*target.shape[0])
precision, recall, fscore, _ = metrics.precision_recall_fscore_support(y_
pred=y_baseline, y_true=target['y'], average='macro')
```

Here, we've set the baseline model to predict 0 and have repeated the value to be the same as the number of rows in the test dataset.

> **Note**
>
> The average parameter in the **precision_recall_fscore_support** function has to be set to **macro** because when it is set to **binary**, as it was before, the function is looking for true values, and our baseline model consists of only false values.

4. Print the final output for precision, recall, and fscore:

```
print(f'Precision: {precision:.4f}\nRecall:{recall:.4f}\nfscore:
{fscore:.4f}')
```

The following figure shows the output of the preceding code:

```
Precision: 0.4424
Recall: 0.5000
fscore: 0.4694
```

Figure 1.39: Final output values for precision, recall, and fscore

Now we have a baseline model that we can compare to our previous model, as well as any subsequent models. Now we can tell that while the accuracy of our previous model seemed high, it did not score much better than this baseline model.

Regularization

We learned earlier in the chapter about overfitting and what it looks like. The hallmark of overfitting is when a model is trained to the training data and performs extremely well, yet performs terribly on test data. One reason for this could be that the model may be relying too heavily on certain features that lead to good performance in the training dataset but do not generalize well to new observations of data or the test dataset. One technique of avoiding this is called **regularization**. Regularization constrains the values of the coefficients toward zero, which discourages a complex model. There are many different types of regularization techniques. For example, in **linear** and **logistic** regression, ridge and lasso regularization are most common. In **tree-based** models, limiting the maximum depth of the trees acts as regularization.

There are two different types of regularization, namely **L1** and **L2**. This term is either the L2 norm (the sum of the squared values) of the weights, or the L1 norm (the sum of the absolute values) of the weights. Since the **l1** regularization parameter acts as a feature selector, it is able to reduce the coefficient of features to zero. We can use the output of this model to observe which features do not contribute much to the performance and remove them entirely if desired. The **l2** regularization parameter will not reduce the coefficient of features to zero, so we will observe that they all have non-zero values.

The following code shows how to instantiate the models using these regularization techniques:

```
model_l1 = LogisticRegressionCV(Cs=Cs, penalty='l1', cv=10,
solver='liblinear', random_state=42)

model_l2 = LogisticRegressionCV(Cs=Cs, penalty='l2', cv=10, random_state=42)
```

The following code shows how to fit the models:

```
model_l1.fit(X_train, y_train['y'])

model_l2.fit(X_train, y_train['y'])
```

The same concepts in **lasso** and **ridge** regularization can be applied to ANNs. However, the penalization occurs on the weight matrices rather than the coefficients. **Dropout** is another form of regularization that's used to prevent overfitting in ANNs. Dropout randomly selects nodes at each iteration and removes them, along with their connections:

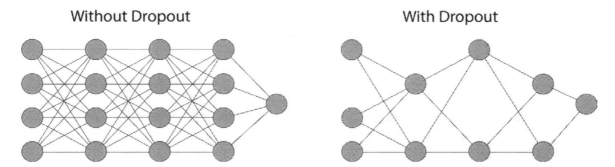

Figure 1.40: Dropout regularization in ANNs

Cross-Validation

Cross-validation is often used in conjunction with regularization to help tune hyperparameters. Take, for example, the `penalization` parameter in **ridge** and **lasso regression**, or the proportion of nodes to drop out at each iteration using the **dropout** technique with ANNs. How will you determine which parameter to use? One way is to run models for each value of the regularization parameter and evaluate on the test set; however, using the test set often can introduce bias into the model.

One popular example of cross-validation is called **k-fold cross-validation**. This technique gives us the ability to test our model on unseen data, while retaining a test set that we will use to test at the end. Using this method, the data is divided into k subsets. In each of the k iterations, k-1 of the subsets are used as training data and the remaining subset is used as a validation set. This is repeated k times until all k subsets have been used as validation sets. By using this technique, there is a significant reduction in bias, since most of the data is used for fitting. There is also a reduction in variation since most of the data is also used for validation. Typically, there are between 5 and 10 folds, and the technique can even be stratified, which is useful when there is a large imbalance of classes.

The following example shows 5-fold cross-validation with 20% held out as a test set. The remaining 80% is separated into 5 folds. 4 of those folds comprise the training data, and the remaining fold is the validation data. This repeated a total of 5 times until every fold has been used once as for validation.

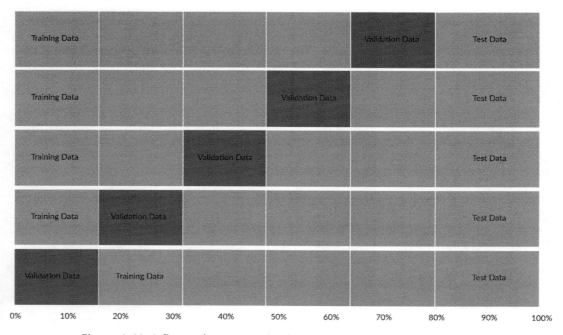

Figure 1.41: A figure demonstrating how 5-fold cross-validation works

Activity 1: Adding Regularization to the Model

In this activity, we will utilize the same logistic regression model from the scikit-learn package. This time, however, we will add regularization to the model and search for the optimum regularization parameter, a process often called hyperparameter tuning. After training the models, we will test the predictions and compare the model evaluation metrics to those produced by the baseline model and the model without regularization.

The steps we will take are as follows:

1. Load in the feature and target datasets of the bank dataset from `'data/bank_data_feats_e3.csv'` and `'data/bank_data_target_e2.csv'`.

2. Create training and testing datasets for each of the feature and target datasets. The training datasets will be used to train on, and the models will be evaluated using the test datasets.

3. Instantiate a model instance of the `LogisticRegressionCV` class of scikit-learn's `linear_model` package.

4. Fit the model to the training data.

5. Make predictions of the test dataset using the trained model.

6. Evaluate the models by comparing how they scored against the true values using the evaluation metrics.

> **Note**
>
> The solution for this activity can be found on page 288.

Summary

In this chapter, we have covered how to prepare data and construct machine learning models. We have achieved this utilizing Python and libraries such as pandas and scikit-learn. We have also used the algorithms in scikit-learn to build our machine learning models.

In this chapter, we learned how to load data into Python, and how to manipulate data so that a machine learning model can be trained on the data. This involved converting all columns to numerical data types. We also learned to create a basic logistic regression classification model using scikit-learn algorithms. We divided the dataset into training and test datasets and fit the model to the training dataset. We evaluated the performance of the model on the test dataset using the model evaluation metrics: accuracy, precision, recall, and f1 score.

Finally, we iterated on this basic model by creating two models with different types of regularization to the model. We utilized cross-validation to determine the optimal parameter to use for the regularization parameter.

In the next chapter, we will use the same concept learned in this chapter; however, we will create the model using the Keras library. We will use the same dataset, and attempt to predict the same target value, for the same classification task. We will cover how to use regularization, cross-validation, and model evaluation metrics when fitting our neural network to the data.

Machine Learning versus Deep Learning

Learning Objectives

By the end of this chapter, you will be able to:

- Explain deep learning and how it is different from machine learning
- Apply linear transformations with Python
- Build a logistic regression model with Keras

In this chapter, we will learn how deep learning is different from machine learning. We will apply linear transformations and lastly build regression models.

Introduction

In the previous chapter, we discussed some applications of machine learning and even built models with the scikit-learn Python package. In this chapter, we will continue learning how to build machine learning models and extend our knowledge to build an **Artificial Neural Network (ANN)** with the Keras package. (Remember that ANNs represent a large class of machine learning algorithms that are so called because their architecture resembles the neurons in the human brain.)

Keras is a machine learning library designed specifically for building neural networks. While scikit-learn functionality spans a broader area of machine learning algorithms, the functionality of scikit-learn for neural networks is minimal.

ANNs can be used for the same machine learning tasks as other algorithms that we have encountered, such as logistic regression for classification tasks, linear regression for regression problems, and k-means for clustering. Whenever we begin any machine learning problem, to determine what kind of task it is (regression, classification, or clustering), we need to ask the following questions:

- *What outcomes matter the most to me or my business?* For example, if you are predicting the value of stock market indices, you could predict whether the price is higher or lower than the previous time point, which would be a classification task, or you could predict the value itself, which would be a regression problem. Each may lead to a different subsequent action or trading strategy. Figure 2.1 shows a candlestick chart; a classification task would predict a positive or negative change (whether the bar color is green or red), whereas a regression task aims to predict the value.

- *Do I have the appropriately labeled data to train a model?* For a supervised learning task, we must have at least some labeled data in order to train a model. ANNs can often need a lot of data to develop accurate models so that the factor for consideration when deciding which algorithm is appropriate for a given task.

The following figure shows an trend of the stock price using candlestick chart:

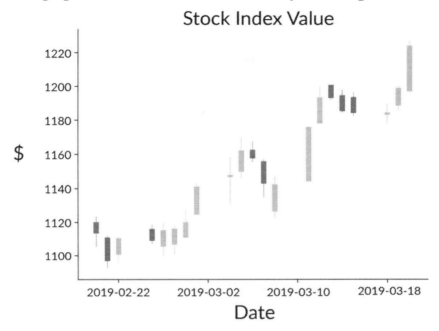

Figure 2.1: A candlestick chart indicating the movement of a stock index over the book of a month

ANNs are a type of machine learning algorithm that can be used to solve a task. They excel in certain respects and have drawbacks in others, and these pros and cons should be considered before choosing this type of algorithm. Deep learning networks are distinguished from single-layer ANNs by their depth – the total number of hidden layers within the network.

So, deep learning is really just a specific subgroup of machine learning that relies on ANNs with multiple layers.

Advantages of ANNs over Traditional Machine Learning Algorithms

- **Best performance**: For any supervised learning task, the best models have been ANNs that are trained on a lot of data. For example, in classification tasks such as classifying images from ImageNet, ANNs can attain greater accuracy than humans.

- **Scales effectively with data**: Traditional machine learning models plateau in performance, whereas ANNs architecture are able to learn higher-level representations. This enables ANNs to perform better when provided large amounts of data, and is especially the case for ANNs with deep architecture.

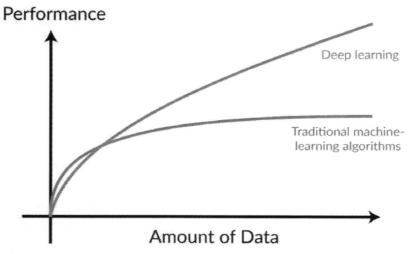

Figure 2.2: Performance scaling with the amount of data for both deep learning algorithms and traditional machine learning algorithms

- **No need for feature engineering**: ANNs are able to identify which features are important in modeling, so they are able to model directly from raw data. In traditional machine learning algorithms, the features must be engineered in an iterative process that can be manual and time-consuming.

- **Adaptable and transferable**: Weights and features learned from ANNs can be applied to similar tasks. In computer vision tasks, pre-trained classification models can be used as the starting point to build models for other classification tasks. For example, VGG-16 is a 16-layer deep learning model used for ImageNet to classify 1,000 random objects. The weights learned in the model can be transferred to classify other objects given new training data in significantly less time.

Advantages of Traditional Machine Learning Algorithms over ANNs

- **When the training data available is small**: In order to attain high performance, ANNs require a lot of data, and the deeper the network, the more data is required. This is because ANNs need to learn the optimal values for a large number of parameters. For example, VGG-16 is a pre-trained model used for the ImageNet challenge that has over 138 million parameters. This ANN was provided over 14 million hand-labeled images to train and learn all the parameters.

- **Cost effective**: Both financially and computationally, deep networks can take a lot of computing power and time to train. This demands a lot of resources that may not be available to all. Moreover, these models are time-consuming to tune effectively and require a domain expert who's familiar with the inner workings of the model to achieve optimal performance.

- **Easy to interpret**: Many traditional machine learning models are easy to interpret, so identifying which feature had most predictive power in the model is straightforward. This can be incredibly useful when working with non-technical team members who wish to understand and interpret the results of the model. ANNs are more of a black box, in that understanding the structure of the network or values of the various weights do not provide insight into how the results are generated. As such, interpretation of the results requires more effort.

Hierarchical Data Representation

One reason that ANNs are able to perform so well is that the large number of layers enable the network to learn representations of the data at many different levels. This is illustrated in Figure 2.3, in which the representation of an ANN used to identify faces is shown. At lower levels of the model, simple features are learned, such as edges and gradients. As the model progresses, combinations of lower-level features activate to form face parts, and at later layers of the model, generic faces are learned. This is known as **feature hierarchy** and illustrates the power that this layered representation has for model building and interpretation.

Many examples of input to real-world applications of deep neural networks involve images, video, and natural language text. The feature hierarchy that is learned by deep neural networks enables them to discover latent structures within unlabeled, unstructured data, such as images, video, and natural language text, which makes them useful for processing real-world data, which is most often raw and unprocessed.

The following figure shows an example of learned representation of a deep learning model:

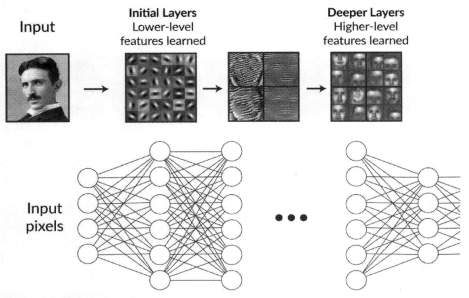

Figure 2.3: Learned representation at various parts of a deep learning model

As deep neural networks become more accessible, their applications are being exploited by various companies. The following are some examples of some companies that use ANNs:

- **Yelp**: Yelp use deep neural networks to process, classify, and label their images more efficiently. Since photos are one important aspect of Yelp reviews, the company has placed an emphasis on classifying and categorizing them. This is achieved more efficiently with deep neural networks.

- **Clarifai**: This cloud-based company is able to classify images and videos using deep neural network-based models.

- **Enlitic**: This company uses deep neural networks to analyze medical image data such as X-rays or MRIs. The use of such networks in this application increases diagnostic accuracy and decreases diagnostic time and cost.

Linear Transformations

In this topic, we will introduce linear transformations. Linear transformations are the backbone of modeling with ANNs. In fact, all the processes of ANN modeling can be thought of as a series of linear transformations. The working components of linear transformations are scalars, vectors, matrices, and tensors. Operations such as additions, transpositions, and multiplications are performed on these components.

Scalars, Vectors, Matrices, and Tensors

Scalars, vectors, matrices, and tensors are the actual components of any deep learning model. While they may be simple in principle, having a fundamental understanding of how to utilize all types, as well as the operations that can be performed on them. It is key to the mathematics of ANNs. Scalars, vectors, and matrices are examples of the general entity known as a tensor, so the term tensors may be used throughout this chapter but may refer to any component. Scalars, vectors, and matrices refer to tensors with a specific number of dimensions. The rank of a tensor is an attribute that determines the number dimensions the tensor spans. The definitions of each are listed here:

- **Scalar**: They are single numbers and are an example of 0-order tensors.

- **Vector**: Vectors are 1-dimensional arrays of single numbers and are an example of first-order tensors.

- **Matrix**: Matrices are rectangular arrays that span over two dimensions that consist of single numbers. They are an example of second-order tensors.

- **Tensor**: Tensors are the general entity that encapsulates scalars, vectors, and matrices. In general, the name is reserved for tensors of order 3 or more.

In figure 2.4 are some examples of a scalar, vector, matrix, and a 3-dimensional tensor:

Figure 2.4: A visual representation of scalars, vectors, matrices, and tensors

Tensor Addition

Tensors can be added together to create new tensors. We will use the example of matrices in this chapter, but the concept extends to tensors with any rank. Matrices may be added to scalars, vectors, and other matrices under certain conditions.

Two matrices may be added (or subtracted) together if they have the same shape. For such matrix-matrix addition, the resultant matrix is determined by element-wise addition of the input matrices. The resultant matrix will therefore have the same shape as the two input matrices. We can define the matrix $C = [c_{ij}]$ as the matrix sum $C = A + B$ where $c_{ij} = a_{ij} + b_{ij}$ each element in C is the sum of the same element in A and B. Matrix addition is commutative, which means that the order of A and B does not matter − $A + B = B + A$. Matrix addition is also associative, which means that the same result is achieved even when the order of additions is different or even if the operation is applied more than once. $A + (B + C) = (A + B) + C$.

The same matrix addition principles apply for scalars, vectors, and tensors. An example is shown in figure 2.5:

$$A + B = \begin{bmatrix} 1 & 4 & 1 \\ 9 & 2 & 5 \\ 7 & 3 & 1 \end{bmatrix} + \begin{bmatrix} 5 & 2 & 4 \\ 7 & 4 & 2 \\ 2 & 3 & 8 \end{bmatrix} = \begin{bmatrix} 6 & 6 & 5 \\ 16 & 6 & 7 \\ 9 & 6 & 9 \end{bmatrix} = C$$

Figure 2.5: An example of matrix-matrix addition

Scalars can also be added to matrices. Here, each element of the matrix is added to the scalar individually, as is shown in figure 2.6:

$$A + 4 = \begin{bmatrix} 1 & 4 & 1 \\ 9 & 2 & 5 \\ 7 & 3 & 1 \end{bmatrix} + 4 = \begin{bmatrix} 5 & 8 & 5 \\ 13 & 6 & 9 \\ 11 & 7 & 5 \end{bmatrix} = B$$

Figure 2.6: An example of matrix-scalar addition

It is possible to add vectors to matrices if the number of columns between the two match each other. This is known as **broadcasting**.

Exercise 6: Perform Various Operations with Vectors, Matrices, and Tensors

> **Note**
>
> For the exercises and activities within this chapter, you will need to have Python 3.6, Jupyter, and NumPy installed on your system. All exercises and activities will be primarily developed in the Jupyter Notebook. It is recommended to keep a separate notebook for different assignments, unless advised not to. Here is the link to download them from GitHub repository: https://github.com/TrainingByPackt/ Applied-Deep-Learning-with-Keras/tree/master/Lesson02.

In this exercise, we are going to demonstrate how to create and work with vectors, matrices, and tensors within Python. We will assume familiarity with scalars. This can all be achieved with the NumPy library using the **array** and **matrix** functions. Tensors of any rank can be created with NumPy **array** function. Follow the steps to perform this exercise:

1. Open the Jupyter Notebook to implement this exercise. Import all the necessary dependencies. We can create a 1-dimensional array, or a vector, as follows:

```
import numpy as np
vec1 = np.array([1, 2, 3, 4, 5, 6, 7, 8, 9, 10])
vec1
```

The following figure shows the output of the preceding code:

array([1,   2,   3,   4,   5,   6,   7,   8,   9, 10])

Figure 2.7: Output of the created vector

2. We can also create 2-dimensional array, or matrix, with the **array** function:

```
mat1 = np.array([[1, 2, 3], [4, 5, 6], [7, 8, 9], [10, 11, 12]])
mat1
```

The following figure shows the output of the preceding code:

**array([[1,   2,   3],
        [4,   5,   6],
        [7,   8,   9],
        [10, 11, 12]])**

Figure 2.8: Screenshot of the output of the created matrix

3. We also use the **matrix** function to create matrices, which will show a similar output:

```
mat2 = np.matrix([[1, 2, 3], [4, 5, 6], [7, 8, 9], [10, 11, 12]])
```

4. We can create a 3-dimensional array, or tensor, using the **array** function:

```
ten1 = np.array([[[1, 2, 3], [4, 5, 6]], [[7, 8, 9], [10, 11, 12]]])
ten1
```

The following figure shows the output of the preceding code:

```
array([[[ 1,  2,  3],
        [ 4,  5,  6]],

       [[ 7,  8,  9],
        [10, 11, 12]]])
```

Figure 2.9: Output of the created tensor

5. Determining the shape of a given vector, matrix, or tensor is important since certain operations, such as addition and multiplication, can only be applied to components of certain shapes. The shape of an n-dimensional array can be determined using the **shape** method. Following is the code for determining the shape of **vec1**:

    ```
    vec1.shape
    ```

    The following figure shows the output of the preceding code:

    ```
    (10,)
    ```

    Figure 2.10: Output of the shape of the vector

    Following is the code for determining the shape of **mat1**:

    ```
    mat1.shape
    ```

    The following figure shows the output of the preceding code:

    ```
    (4, 3)
    ```

    Figure 2.11: Output of the shape of the matrix

    Following is the code for determining the shape of **ten1**:

    ```
    ten1.shape
    ```

    The following figure shows the output of the preceding code:

    ```
    (2, 2, 3)
    ```

    Figure 2.12: Output of the shape of the tensor

6. Matrices can be added or subtracted if the shapes of the matrices are the same. These are the input values for matrix 1:

    ```
    mat1 = np.matrix([[1, 2, 3], [4, 5, 6], [7, 8, 9], [10, 11, 12]])
    mat1
    ```

The following figure shows the output of the preceding code:

```
matrix([[ 1,  2,  3],
        [ 4,  5,  6],
        [ 7,  8,  9],
        [10, 11, 12]])
```

Figure 2.13: Values in matrix 1

These are the input values for matrix 2:

```
mat2 = np.matrix([[2, 1, 4], [4, 1, 7], [4, 2, 9], [5, 21, 1]])
mat2
```

The following figure shows the output of the preceding code:

```
matrix([[ 2,  1,  4],
        [ 4,  1,  7],
        [ 4,  2,  9],
        [ 5, 21,  1]])
```

Figure 2.14: Values in matrix 2

7. Here, we will add matrix 1 and matrix 2:

```
mat3 = mat1 + mat2
mat3
```

The following figure shows the output of the preceding code:

```
matrix([[ 3,  3,  7],
        [ 8,  6, 13],
        [11, 10, 18],
        [15, 32, 13]])
```

Figure 2.15: Addition of matrix 1 and matrix 2

8. Scalars can be added to arrays as follows:

```
mat1 + 4
```

The following figure shows the output of the preceding code:

```
matrix([[ 5,  6,  7],
        [ 8,  9, 10],
        [11, 12, 13],
        [14, 15, 16]])
```

Figure 2.16: Matrix addition with a scalar

In this exercise, we learned how to perform various operations with vectors, matrices, and tensors. We also learned how to determine the shape of the matrix.

Reshaping

A tensor of any size can be reshaped as long as the number of total elements remains the same. For example, a (4x3) matrix can be reshaped into a (6x2) matrix since they both have a total of 12 elements. The rank, or number of dimensions, can also be changed in the reshaping process. For example, a (4x3) matrix can be reshaped into a (3x2x2) tensor. Here, the rank has changed from 2 to 3. The (4x3) matrix can also be reshaped into a (12x1) vector, in which the rank has changed from 2 to 1. Figure 2.17 illustrates tensor reshaping– on the left is a tensor with shape (4x1x3), which can be reshaped to a tensor of shape (4x3). Here, the number of elements (12) has remained constant, though the shape and rank of the tensor have changed.

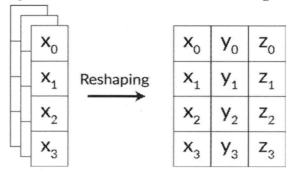

Figure 2.17: Visual representation of reshaping a (4x1x3) tensor to a (4x3) tensor

Matrix Transposition

The transpose of a matrix is an operator that flips the matrix over its diagonal. When this occurs, the rows become the columns and vice versa. The transpose operation is usually denoted as a T superscript upon the matrix. Tensors of any rank can also be transposed.

$$n\begin{bmatrix} & m & \end{bmatrix}^{T} = m\begin{bmatrix} & n & \end{bmatrix}$$

Figure 2.18: A visual representation of matrix transposition

The following figure shows the matrix transposition properties of matrices A and B:

$$(A^T)^T = A$$

$$(A+B)^T = A^T + B^T$$

$$(AB)^T = B^T A^T$$

$$(A_1 A_2 ... A_k)^T = A_k^T ... A_2^T A_1^T$$

$$(A^{-1})^T = (A^T)^{-1}$$

Figure 2.19: Matrix transposition properties where A and B are matrices

A square matrix, a matrix with equivalent number of rows and columns, is said to be symmetrical if the transpose of a matrix is equivalent to the original matrix.

Exercise 7: Matrix Reshaping and Transposition

In this exercise, we are going to demonstrate how to reshape and transpose matrices. This will become important since some operations can only be applied to components if certain tensor dimensions match. For example, tensor multiplication can only be applied if the inner dimensions of the two tensors match. Reshaping or transposition of tensors is one way to modify the dimensions of the tensor to ensure that certain operations can be applied.

1. Open a Jupyter notebook from the start menu to implement this exercise. We can create a 2-dimensional array, with 4 rows and 3 columns, as follows:

```
import numpy as np
mat1 = np.array([[1, 2, 3], [4, 5, 6], [7, 8, 9], [10, 11, 12]])
mat1
```

We can check the shape by looking at the shape of the matrix to confirm the shape:

```
mat1.shape
```

2. We can reshape the array to have 3 rows and 4 columns instead, as follows:

```
mat2 = np.reshape(mat1, [3,4])
mat2
```

The following figure shows the output of the preceding code:

```
array([[ 1,  2,  3,  4],
       [ 5,  6,  7,  8],
       [ 9, 10, 11, 12]])
```

Figure 2.20: Matrix reshaping

3. We can confirm this by printing the shape:

```
mat2.shape
```

The following figure shows the output of the preceding code:

$$(3, 4)$$

Figure 2.21: Shape of the reshaped matrix

4. We can also reshape to 3-dimensional arrays as follows:

```
mat3 = np.reshape(mat1, [3,2,2])
mat3
```

The following figure shows the output of the preceding code:

```
array([[[ 1,  2],
        [ 3,  4]],

       [[ 5,  6],
        [ 7,  8]],

       [[ 9, 10],
        [11, 12]]])
```

Figure 2.22: Reshaped matrix to a 3-dimensional tensor

The number of dimensions can be confirmed by printing the shape of the array:

```
mat3.shape
```

5. We can also reshape to a 1-dimensional array as follows:

```
mat4 = np.reshape(mat1, [12])
mat4
```

The following figure shows the output of the preceding code:

```
array([ 1,  2,  3,  4,  5,  6,  7,  8,  9, 10, 11, 12])
```

Figure 2.23: Reshaped matrix to a 1-dimensional tensor

The number of dimensions can be confirmed by printing the shape of the array:

```
mat4.shape
```

The following figure shows the output of the preceding code:

$$(12,)$$

Figure 2.24: Shape of the reshaped matrix

6. Taking the transpose of an array will flip it across its diagonal. For a 1-dimensional array, a row-vector will be converted to a column vector and vice versa. For a 2-dimensional array, or matrix, each row becomes a column and vice versa. The transpose of an array can be called using the **T** method:

```
mat = np.matrix([[1, 2, 3], [4, 5, 6], [7, 8, 9], [10, 11, 12]])
mat.T
```

The following figure shows the output of the preceding code:

mat= matrix([[1, 2, 3],
          [4, 5, 6],
          [7, 8, 9],
          [10, 11, 12]])

mat^T= matrix([[1, 4, 7, 10],
          [2, 5, 8, 11],
          [3, 6, 9, 12]])

Figure 2.25: Visual demonstration of the transpose function

7. We can check the shape of the matrix and its transpose to verify that the dimensions have changed.

```
mat.shape
```

The following figure shows the output of the preceding code:

$$(4, 3)$$

Figure 2.26: Shape of a matrix

Here is the code for checking the shape of the transposed matrix:

```
mat.T.shape
```

The following figure shows the output of the preceding code:

$$(3, 4)$$

Figure 2.27: Shape of the matrix transposition

8. To reinforce the notion that reshaping and transposing are different, we can see which elements of each array match:

```
np.reshape(mat1, [3,4]) == mat1.T
```

The following figure shows the output of the preceding code:

```
array([[ True, False, False, False],
       [False, False, False, False],
       [False, False, False,  True]], dtype=bool)
```

Figure 2.28: The Boolean matrix showing element-wise equivalence

We can see that only the first and last elements match.

In this topic, we have introduced some of the basic components of linear algebra, including scalars, vectors, matrices, and tensors. We also covered some basic manipulation of linear algebra components, such as addition, transposition, and reshaping.

Matrix Multiplication

Matrix multiplication is fundamental to neural network operation. While the rules for addition are simple and intuitive, the rules for multiplication for matrices and tensors are more complex. Matrix multiplication involves more than simple element-wise multiplication of the elements. Rather, a more complicated procedure is implemented that involves the entire row of one matrix and an entire column of the other. We will explain how multiplication works for 2-dimensional tensors, or matrices; however, tensors of higher orders can also be multiplied.

Given a matrix, $A = [a_{ij}]_{m \times n}$ and another matrix, $B = [b_{ij}]_{n \times p}$, the product of the two matrices is $C = AB = [c_{ij}]_{m \times p}$, and each element, c_{ij}, is defined element-wise as $c_{ij} = \sum_{k=1}^{n} a_{ik} b_{kj}$. We note that the shape of the resultant matrix is the same as the outer dimensions of the matrix product, or the number of rows of the first matrix and the number of columns of the second matrix. In order for the multiplication to work, the inner dimensions of the matrix product must match, or the number of columns of the first matrix and the number of columns of the second matrix. The concept of inner and outer dimensions of matrix multiplication is shown in the following figure:

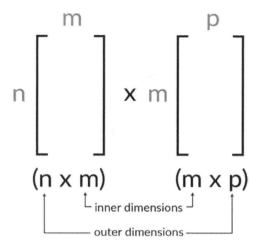

Figure 2.29: A visual representation of inner and outer dimensions in matrix multiplication

Unlike matrix addition, matrix multiplication is not commutative, which means that the order of the matrices in the product matters.

$$AB \neq BA$$

Figure 2.30: Matrix multiplication is non-commutative

For example, let's say we have the following two matrices:

$$A = \begin{bmatrix} 2 & 5 & 1 \\ 7 & 3 & 6 \end{bmatrix}, B = \begin{bmatrix} 1 & 8 \\ 9 & 4 \\ 3 & 5 \end{bmatrix}$$

Figure 2.31: Two matrices, A and B

One way to construct the product is to have matrix **A** first, multiplied by **B**:

$$AB = \begin{bmatrix} 2 \times 1 + 5 \times 9 + 1 \times 3 & 2 \times 8 + 5 \times 4 + 1 \times 5 \\ 7 \times 1 + 3 \times 9 + 6 \times 3 & 7 \times 8 + 3 \times 4 + 6 \times 5 \end{bmatrix} = \begin{bmatrix} 50 & 41 \\ 52 & 98 \end{bmatrix}$$

Figure 2.32: Visual representation of matrix A multiplied by B, A·B

This results in a 2x2 matrix. Another way to construct the product is to have **B** first, multiplied by **A**:

$$BA = \begin{bmatrix} 1 \times 2 + 8 \times 7 & 1 \times 5 + 8 \times 3 & 1 \times 1 + 8 \times 6 \\ 9 \times 2 + 4 \times 7 & 9 \times 5 + 4 \times 3 & 9 \times 1 + 4 \times 6 \\ 3 \times 2 + 5 \times 7 & 3 \times 5 + 5 \times 3 & 3 \times 1 + 5 \times 6 \end{bmatrix} = \begin{bmatrix} 58 & 29 & 49 \\ 46 & 57 & 33 \\ 41 & 30 & 33 \end{bmatrix}$$

Figure 2.33: Visual representation of matrix B multiplied by A, B·A

Here we can see that matrix formed from the product **BA** is a 3x3 matrix and is very different from matrix formed from the product **AB**.

Scalar-matrix multiplication is much more straightforward and is simply the product of every element in the matrix multiplied by the scalar so that $\lambda A = [\lambda a_{ij}]_{m \times n}$, where λ is a scalar and **A** is a matrix.

Exercise 8: Matrix Multiplication

In this exercise, we are going to demonstrate how to multiply matrices together:

1. Open a Jupyter Notebook from the start menu to implement this exercise.

   To demonstrate the fundamentals of matrix multiplication, we will begin with two matrices of the same shape:

   ```
   import numpy as np
   mat1 = np.array([[1, 2, 3], [4, 5, 6], [7, 8, 9], [10, 11, 12]])
   mat2 = np.array([[2, 1, 4], [4, 1, 7], [4, 2, 9], [5, 21, 1]])
   ```

2. Since both matrices have the same shape and they are not square, they cannot be multiplied as is, since the inner dimensions of the product must match. One way we could resolve this is to take the transpose of one of the matrices, then we would be able to perform the multiplication.

   We could take the transpose of the second matrix, which would mean that a (4x3) matrix is getting multiplied by a (3x4) matrix. The result would be a (4x4) matrix. Multiplication is performed using the **dot** method:

   ```
   mat1.dot(mat2.T)
   ```

   The following figure shows the output of the preceding code:

   ```
   array([[ 16,  27,  35,  50],
          [ 37,  63,  80, 131],
          [ 58,  99, 125, 212],
          [ 79, 135, 170, 293]])
   ```

   Figure 2.34: Matrix multiplication

3. We can also take the transpose of the first matrix, which would mean that a (3x4) matrix is getting multiplied by a (4x3) matrix. The result would be a (3x3) matrix:

   ```
   mat1.T.dot(mat2)
   ```

The following figure shows the output of the preceding code:

```
array([[ 96, 229, 105],
       [111, 254, 126],
       [126, 279, 147]])
```

Figure 2.35: Matrix multiplication by transposing first

4. We can also reshape one of the arrays to make sure the inner dimension of the matrix multiplication matches. For example, we can reshape the first array to make it a (3x4) matrix instead of transposing. We note that the result is not the same as with transposing:

```
np.reshape(mat1, [3,4]).dot(mat2)
```

The following figure shows the output of the preceding code:

```
array([[ 42,  93,  49],
       [102, 193, 133],
       [162, 293, 217]])
```

Figure 2.36: The matrix multiplication with matrix reshaping

In the previous exercise, we have learned how to multiply two matrices together. The same concept can be applied to tensors of all ranks, not just second-order tensors. Tensors of different ranks can even be multiplied together if their inner dimensions match. The next exercise demonstrates how to multiply 3-dimensional tensors together.

Exercise 9: Tensor Multiplication

In this exercise, we are going to apply our knowledge of matrix multiplication to higher-order tensors:

1. Open a Jupyter notebook from the start menu to implement this exercise. We will begin by creating a 3-dimensional tensor using the NumPy library and the **array** function. Import all the necessary dependencies:

```
import numpy as np
mat1 = np.array([[[1, 2, 3], [4, 5, 6]], [[1, 2, 3], [4, 5, 6]]])
mat1
```

The following figure shows the output of the preceding code:

```
array([[[1, 2, 3],
        [4, 5, 6]],

       [[1, 2, 3],
        [4, 5, 6]]])
```

Figure 2.37: A screenshot of the output of the 3-dimensional tensor created

2. The shape can be confirmed using the **shape** method:

```
mat1.shape
```

This tensor has the shape (2x2x3).

3. Now we create a new 3-dimensional tensor that we will be able to multiply the tensor by. We can take the transpose of the original matrix:

```
mat2 = mat1.T
mat2
```

The following figure shows the output of the preceding code:

```
array([[[1, 1],
        [4, 4]],

       [[2, 2],
        [5, 5]],

       [[3, 3],
        [6, 6]]])
```

Figure 2.38: The transpose of the 3-dimensional tensor

4. The shape can be confirmed using the **shape** method:

```
mat1.shape
```

This tensor has the shape (3x2x2).

5. Now we can take the **dot** product of the two matrices as follows:

```
mat3 = mat2.dot(mat1)
mat3
```

The following figure shows the output of the preceding code:

```
array([[[[ 5,  7,  9],
         [ 5,  7,  9]],

        [[20, 28, 36],
         [20, 28, 36]]],


       [[[10, 14, 18],
         [10, 14, 18]],

        [[25, 35, 45],
         [25, 35, 45]]],


       [[[15, 21, 27],
         [15, 21, 27]],

        [[30, 42, 54],
         [30, 42, 54]]]])
```

Figure 2.39: Output of the product of the two 3-dimensional tensors

6. We can look at the shape of this resultant tensor:

```
mat3.shape
```

The following figure shows the output of the preceding code:

$$(3, 2, 2, 3)$$

Figure 2.40: Output of the shape of the product of tensors

Now we have a 4-dimensional tensor.

In this topic, we have learned how to perform matrix multiplication using the NumPy library in Python. While we do not have to perform the matrix multiplication directly when we create ANNs with Keras, it is nevertheless useful to understand the underlying mathematics.

Introduction to Keras

Building ANNs involves creating layers of nodes. Each node can be thought of as a tensor of weights that are learned in the training process. Once the ANN is fitted to the data, a prediction is made by multiplying the input data by the weight matrices layer by layer, applying any other linear transformation when needed, such as activation functions, until the final output layer is reached. The size of each weight tensor is determined by the size of the shape of input nodes and the shape of the output nodes. For example, in a single-layer ANN, the size of our single hidden layer can be thought of as follows:

$$n\begin{bmatrix} & m & \\ & & \\ & & \\ & & \end{bmatrix} \times ?\begin{bmatrix} & ? & \\ & & \\ & & \\ & & \end{bmatrix} = n\begin{bmatrix} 1 \\ \\ \\ \end{bmatrix}$$

Figure 2.41: Solving the dimensions of the hidden layer of a single-layer ANN

If the input matrix of features has n rows, or observations, and m columns, or features, and we want our predicted target to have n rows (one for each observation) and 1 column (the predicted value), we can determine the size of our hidden layer by what is needed to make the matrix multiplication valid. Here is the representation of a single-layered ANN:

$$A_{n \times m} B_{? \times ?} = C_{n \times 1}$$

Figure 2.42: Representation of single-layer ANN

Here, we can determine that the weight matrix will be of size (mx1), since this will give us the desired output according to what the inner and outer dimensions should be in order for the matrix multiplication to be valid.

If we have more than one hidden layer in an ANN, then we have much more freedom with the size of these weight matrices. In fact, the possibilities are endless, depending on how many layers there are, and how many nodes we want in each layer. In practice, however, certain architecture designs work better than others, as we will be learning throughout the book.

In general, Keras abstracts much of the linear algebra out of building neural networks so that users can focus on designing the architecture. For most networks, only the input size, output size, and the number of nodes in each hidden layer are needed as minimum requirements to create networks in Keras.

The simplest model structure in Keras is the **Sequential** model, which can be imported from **keras.models**. The model of the **Sequential** class describes an ANN that consists of a linear stack of layers. A **Sequential** model can be instantiated as follows:

```
from keras.models import Sequential
model = Sequential()
```

Layers can be added to this model instance to create the structure of the model.

Layer Types

The notion of layers is part of the Keras core API. A layer can be thought of as a composition of nodes, and at each node a set of computations happen. In Keras, all the nodes of a layer can be initialized by simply initializing the layer itself. The depiction of the individual operation of a generalized layer node is shown in figure 2.42. At each node, the input data is multiplied by a set of weights, using matrix multiplication, as we learned earlier in the chapter. The sum of the product between the weights and the input is the generally applied, which may or may not include a bias. Further functions may be applied to the output of this matrix multiplication, such as activation functions:

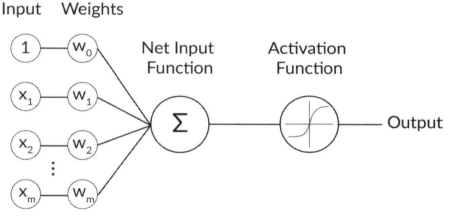

Figure 2.43: A depiction of a layer node

Some common layer types in Keras are as follows:

- **Dense**: This is a fully-connected layer in which all nodes of the layer are directly connected to all inputs and all outputs.

- **Convolutional**: This layer type creates a convolutional kernel that is convolved with the input layer to produce a tensor of outputs. The convolution can occur in one or multiple dimensions.

- **Pooling**: This type of layer is used to reduce the dimensionality of an input layer. Common types of pooling include max-pooling, in which the maximum value of a given window is passed through to the output, or average-pooling, in which the average value of a window passed through.

- **Recurrent**: Recurrent layers learn patterns from sequences, so each output is dependent on the results from the previous step. Recurrent layers are appropriate when modeling sequential data such as natural language or time-series data.

There are other layer types in Keras; however, these are the most common types when learning how to build models using Keras.

We demonstrate how to add layers to a model by instantiating a model of the `Sequential` class and add a `Dense` layer to the model. Successive layers can be added to the model in the order in which we wish the computation to be performed, and can be imported from `keras.layers`. The number of units, or nodes, needs to be specified. This value will also determine the shape of the result from the layer. A `Dense` layer can be added to a `Sequential` model in the following way:

```
from keras.layers import Dense
from keras.models import Sequential
input_shape = 20
units = 1
model.add(Dense(units, input_dim=input_shape))
```

> **Note**
>
> After the first layer, the input dimension does not need to be specified, since it is determined from the previous layer.

Activation Functions

An activation function is generally applied to the output of a node to limit or bound its value. The value from each node is unbounded and may have any value from negative to positive infinity. These can be troublesome within neural networks in which values of weights and losses calculated can head towards infinity and produce unusable results. Activation functions can help in this regard by bounding the value, often these activation functions push the value to two limits. Activation functions are also useful for deciding whether the node should be "fired" or not. Common activation functions are as follows:

- **Step** function: The value is nonzero if it is above a certain threshold, otherwise it is zero.

- **Linear** function: $A(x) = cx$, which is a scalar multiplication of the input value.

- **Sigmoid** function: $A(x) = \frac{1}{1+e^{-x}}$, like a smoothed-out step function with smooth gradients. This activation function is useful for classification since the values are bound from zero to one.

- **Tanh** function: $A(x) = \tanh(x) = \frac{2}{1+e^{-2x}} - 1$, which is a scaled version of the sigmoid with steeper gradients around x=0.

- **ReLU** function: $A(x) = x, \ x > 0$, otherwise 0.

Now that we have some of the main components we can begin to see how we might create useful neural networks out of these components. In fact, we can create a logistic regression model with all the concepts we have learned in this chapter. A logistic regression model operates by taking the sum of the product of an input and a set of learned weights, followed by the output being passed through a logistic function. This can be achieved with a single layer neural network with a sigmoid activation function.

Activation functions can be added to models in the same manner that layers are added to models. The activation function will be applied to the output of the previous step in the model. A **tanh** activation function can be added to a **Sequential** model as follows:

```
from keras.layers import Dense, Activation
from keras.models import Sequential
input_shape = 20
units = 1
model.add(Dense(units, input_dim=input_shape))
model.add(Activation('tanh'))
```

> **Note**
>
> Activation functions can also be added to a model by including them as an argument when defining the layers.

Model Fitting

Once a model's architecture has been created, the model must be compiled. The compilation process configures all the learning parameters, including which optimizer to use, the loss function to minimize, as well as optional metrics, such as accuracy, to calculate at various stages of model training. Models are compiled using the `compile` method as follows:

```
model.compile(optimizer='adam', loss='binary_crossentropy',
metrics=['accuracy'])
```

After the model has been compiled, it is ready to be fit to the training data. This is achieved with an instantiated model using the `fit` method. Useful arguments to the `fit` method are as follows:

- **X**: The array of training feature data to fit the data to.
- **y**: The array of training target data.
- **epochs**: The number of epochs to run the model for. An epoch is an iteration over the entire training dataset.
- **batch_size**: The number of training data samples to use per gradient update.
- **validation_split**: The proportion of the training data to be used for validation that is evaluated after each epoch.

The `fit` method can be used on a model in the following way:

```
history = model.fit(x=X_train, y=y_train['y'], epochs=10, batch_size=32,
validation_split=0.2)
```

It is beneficial to save the output of calling the `fit` method of the model since it contains information on the model's performance throughout training, including the loss, which is evaluated after each epoch. If a validation split is defined, the loss is evaluated after each epoch on the validation split. Likewise, if any metrics are defined in training they are also calculated after each epoch. It is useful to plot such loss and evaluation metrics to determine model performance as a function of epoch. The model's loss as a function of the epoch can be visualized as follows:

```
import matplotlib.pyplot as plt

%matplotlib inline


plt.plot(history.history['loss'])

plt.show()
```

Keras models can be evaluated by utilizing the **evaluate** method of the model instance. This method returns the loss and any metrics that were passed to the model for training. The method can be called as follows when evaluating an out-of-sample test dataset:

```
test_loss = model.evaluate(X_test, y_test['y'])
```

These model-fitting steps represent the basic steps in order to build, train, and evaluate models using the Keras package. From here, there are an infinite number of ways to build and evaluate a model depending on the task you wish to accomplish.

Activity 2: Creating a Logistic Regression Model Using Keras

In this activity, we are going to create a basic model using the Keras library. We will perform the same classification task as we did in *Chapter 1, Introduction to Machine Learning with Keras*. We will use the same bank dataset and attempt to predict the same variable.

In the previous chapter, we used a logistic regression model to predict whether a client would subscribe to a given product given various attributes of each client, such as their age and occupation. In this activity, we will introduce the Keras library, though we'll continue to utilize the libraries we introduced previously, such as **pandas** for easy loading in of data, and **sklearn** for any data preprocessing and model evaluation metrics.

The steps to complete the activity are as follows:

1. Load in the feature and target datasets from the previous chapter.

2. Split the training and target data into training and test datasets. The model will be fit to the training dataset and the test dataset will be used to evaluate the model.

3. Instantiate a model of the **Sequential** class from the **keras.models** library.

4. Add a single layer of the **Dense** class from the **keras.layers** package to the model instance. The number of nodes should be equal to the number of features in the feature dataset.

5. Add a sigmoid activation function to the model.

6. Compile the model instance, specifying the optimizer to use, the loss metric to evaluate, and any other metrics to evaluate after each epoch.

7. Fit the model to the training data, specifying the number of epochs to run for and validation split to use.

8. Plot loss and other evaluation metrics with respect to the epoch, evaluated on the training and validation datasets.

9. Evaluate the loss and other evaluation metrics on the test dataset.

> **Note**
>
> The solution for this activity can be found on page 294.

In this topic, we looked at some of the fundamental concepts of creating ANNs in Keras, including various layer types and activation functions. We have used these components to create a simple logistic regression model using a package that gives us similar results to the logistic regression model used in *Chapter 1, Introduction to Machine Learning with Keras*.

Summary

In this chapter, we have covered the various types of linear algebra components and operations that pertain to machine learning. The components include scalars, vectors, matrices, and tensors. The operations that were applied to these tensors included addition, transposition, and multiplication, all of which are fundamental for understanding the underlying mathematics of ANNs.

We also learned some basics of the Keras package, including the mathematics that occurs at each node. We also replicated the model from the first chapter, in which we built a logistic regression model to predict the same target from the bank data; however, we used the Keras library to create the model using an ANN instead of the scikit-learn logistic regression model. We achieved a similar level of accuracy using ANNs.

The next chapters in this book will use the same concepts learned in this chapter; however, we will continue building ANNs with the Keras package. We will extend our ANNs to more than a single layer, creating models that have multiple hidden layers. We will put the "deep" into "deep learning". We will also tackle the issues of under- and overfitting as they relate to training models with ANNs.

3

Deep Learning with Keras

Learning Objectives

By the end of this chapter, you will be able to:

- Define Keras as a sequential model

- Develop single-layer and multi-layer Keras models

- Evaluate a trained model

- Explain overfitting and underfitting

- Perform early stopping as a technique to reduce overfitting

In this chapter, we will learn how to develop single-layer and multi-layer models. We will learn how to evaluate trained models and determine whether they are overfitting or not.

Introduction

In this chapter, you will learn how to implement your first **neural network** using Keras. This chapter covers the basics of deep learning and will provide you with the foundation necessary to build highly complex neural network architectures. We start by extending the **logistic regression** model to a simple single-layer neural network and then proceed to more complicated neural networks with multiple hidden layers. In this process, you will learn about the underlying basic concepts of neural networks, including forward propagation for making predictions, computing loss, backpropagation for computing derivative of loss with respect to model parameters, and finally gradient descent for learning optimal parameters for the model. You will also learn about the various choices available to build and train a neural network in terms of **activation functions**, **loss functions**, and **optimizers**.

Furthermore, you will learn how to evaluate your model while understanding issues such as overfitting and underfitting, looking at how they can impact the performance of your model and how to detect them. You will learn about the drawbacks of evaluating a model on the same dataset used for training, and the alternative approach of holding back a part of the available dataset for evaluation purposes. Subsequently, you will learn how comparing the model error rate on each of these two subsets of the dataset can be used to detect problems such as high bias and high variance in the model. Lastly, you will learn about a technique called **early stopping** to reduce overfitting, which is again based on comparing the model's error rate on the two subsets of the dataset.

Building Your First Neural Network

In this section, you will first learn about the representations and concepts of deep learning such as forward propagation, backpropagation, and gradient descent. We will not delve deeply into these concepts, as it isn't required for this book. However, the coverage will essentially help anyone who wants to apply deep learning to a problem.

We then will move on to implementing neural networks using Keras. Also, we will stick to the simplest case, which is a neural network with a single hidden layer. You will learn how to define a model in Keras, choose the **hyperparameters**, and then train your model. At the end of this section, you will have the opportunity to practice what you have learned by implementing a neural network in Keras to perform classification on a dataset and observe how neural networks outperform simpler models such as logistic regression.

Logistic Regression to a Deep Neural Network

You learned in the previous chapter about the logistic regression model and how to implement it as a sequential model using Keras. Technically speaking, logistic regression involves a very simple neural network with only one hidden layer and only one node in its hidden layer.

An overview of the logistic regression model with two-dimensional input is shown in Figure 3.1. What you see in this figure is called one **node** or **unit** in the deep learning world. As you may have noticed from the figure, there are some differences between logistic regression terminology and deep learning terminology. In logistic regression, we call the parameters of the model **coefficients** and **intercepts**. In deep learning models, the parameters are referred to as **weights** (w) and **biases** (b):

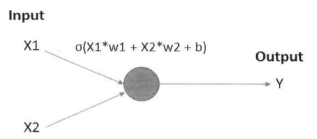

Figure 3.1: Overview of logistic regression model with two-dimensional Input

At each node/unit, the inputs are multiplied by some weights and then a bias term is added to the sum of these weighted inputs. Next, a nonlinear function (for example, a sigmoid function in the case of a logistic regression model) is applied to the sum of the weighted inputs and the bias term to compute the final output of the node. In deep learning, the nonlinear function is called the **activation function** and the output of the node is called the **activation** of that node.

It is possible to build a single-layer neural network by stacking logistic regression nodes/units on top of each other in a layer, as shown in Figure 3.2. It is also possible to build multi-layer neural networks by stacking multiple layers of processing nodes after each other, as shown in Figure 3.3:

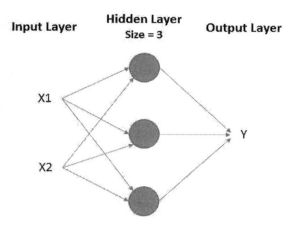

Figure 3.2: Overview of a single-layer neural network with two-dimensional input and a hidden layer of size 3

The following figure shows a two-layer neural network with two-dimensional input:

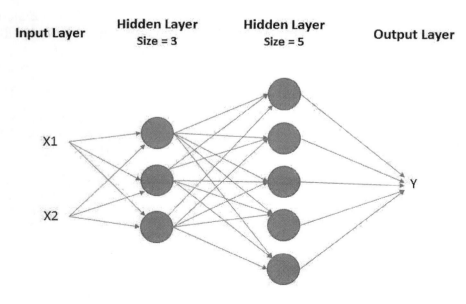

Figure 3.3: Overview of a two-layer neural network with two-dimensional input

Figure 3.2 and Figure 3.3 show the most common way of representing a neural network. Every neural network consists of an **input layer**, an **output layer**, and one or many **hidden layers**. If there is only one hidden layer, the network is called a **shallow neural network**. On the other hand, neural networks with many hidden layers are called **deep neural networks** and the process of training them is called **deep learning**.

> **Note**
>
> You may see in some resources that a network, such as the one shown in Figure 3.3, is referred to as a four-layer network. This is because the input and output layers are counted along with the hidden layers. However, the more common convention is to count only the hidden layers and therefore, the network mentioned previously will be referred to as a two-layer network.

In a deep learning setting, the number of nodes in the input layer is equal to the number of features/dimensions of the input data, and the number of nodes in the output layer is equal to the number of dimensions of the output data. However, you need to select the number of nodes in the hidden layers, or the size of the hidden layers. If you choose a larger size layer, the model becomes more flexible and will be able to model more complex functions. This increase in flexibility comes at the cost of the need for more training data and more computations to train the model. The parameters that are required to be selected by the developer are called **hyperparameters**. The number of nodes in a hidden layer is an example of a hyperparameter.

Activation Functions

In addition to the size of the layer, you need to choose an activation function for each hidden layer that you add to the model, and also do the same for the output layer. We learned about the sigmoid activation function in the logistic regression model. However, there are more options for activation functions that you can choose from when building a neural network in Keras depending on the problem that you are working on. Some commonly used activation functions for deep learning are **sigmoid**/**logistic**, **tanh** (**hyperbolic tangent**), and **Rectified Linear Unit** (**ReLU**).

The following figure shows a sigmoid activation function:

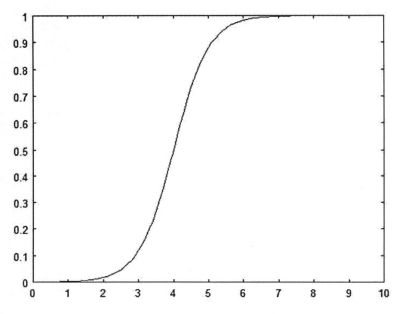

Figure 3.4: Sigmoid activation function

The following figure shows a tanh activation function:

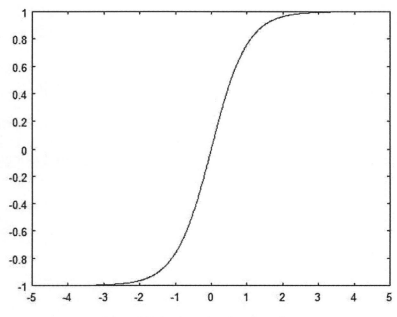

Figure 3.5: tanh activation function

The following figure shows a ReLU activation function:

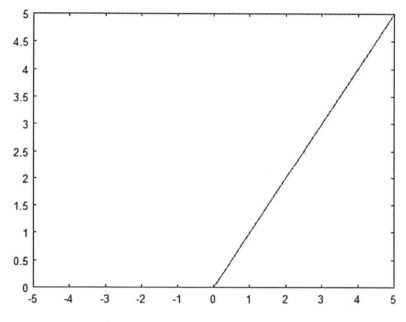

Figure 3.6: ReLU activation function

As you can see in Figure 3.4 and Figure 3.5, the output of a sigmoid function is always between 0 and 1, and the output of tanh is always between -1 and 1. This makes tanh a better choice for hidden layers since it keeps the average of the outputs in each layer close to zero. In fact, sigmoid is only a good choice for the activation function of the output layer when building a binary classifier, as its output can be interpreted as the probability of a given input belonging to one class.

Therefore, tanh and ReLU are the most common choices of activation function for hidden layers. It turns out that the learning process is faster when using the ReLU activation function because it has a fixed slope/derivative for input greater than 0, and a slope of 0 everywhere else.

> **Note**
>
> You can read more about all the available choices for activation functions in Keras here: https://keras.io/activations/.

Forward Propagation for Making Predictions

Neural networks make a prediction about the output by performing **forward propagation**. Forward propagation entails the computations that are performed on the input in every layer of a neural network until the output layer is reached. It is best to understand forward propagation through an example.

Let's go through forward propagation equations one by one for a two-layer neural network as shown in Figure 3.7, where the input data is two-dimensional and the output data is a one-dimensional binary class label. The activation functions for layer 1 and layer 2 will be tanh, and the activation function in the output layer is sigmoid.

The weights and biases for each layer are shown as matrices and vectors with proper indexes. For each layer, the number of rows in the weights matrix is equal to the number of nodes in the previous layer, and the number of columns is equal to the number of nodes in that layer. The bias, however, is always a vector with the size equal to the number of nodes in that layer. The total number of parameters in a deep learning model is equal to the total number of elements in all the weights matrices and the biases vectors:

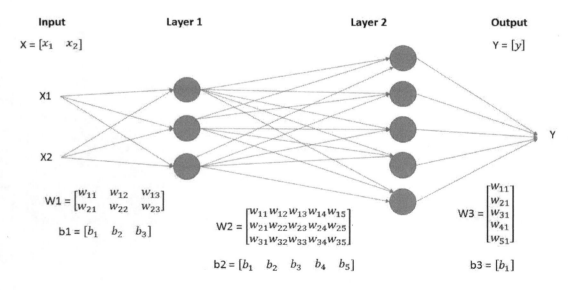

Figure 3.7: A two-layer neural network

Steps to perform forward propagation:

1. X is the network input and therefore, it is the input for the first hidden layer:

    $z1 = X*W1 + b1$

2. The layer 1 output is computed by applying an activation function to $z1$:

    $a1 = tanh(z1)$

3. $a1$ is the output of layer 1 and it is called the **activation** of layer 1. The output of layer 1 is, in fact, the **input** for layer 2. Therefore, the following is true:

    $z2 = a1 * W2 + b2$

4. The layer 2 output/activation is computed by applying an activation function to $z2$:

    $a2 = tanh(z2)$

5. The output of layer 2 is, in fact, the input for the next layer (the network output layer here). Therefore, the following is true:

    $z3 = a2 * W3 + b3$

6. The network output is computed by applying the sigmoid activation function to $z3$:

    $Y = sigmoid(z3)$

The total number of parameters in this model is equal to the sum of the number of elements in W1, W2, W3, b1, b2, and b3. Therefore, the number of parameters is equal to 6 + 15 + 5 + 3 + 5 + 1 = 35. These are the parameters that need to be trained in the process of deep learning.

Loss Function

When learning the optimal parameters (weights and biases) of a model, we need to define a function to measure error. This function is called the **loss function** and it provides us with a measure of how different network-predicted outputs are from the real outputs in the dataset.

The loss function can be defined in several different ways, depending on the problem and the goal. For example, in the case of a classification problem, one common way to define loss is to compute the proportion of misclassified inputs in the dataset and use that as the probability of the model making an error. On the other hand, in the case of a regression problem, the loss function is usually defined by computing the distance between the predicted outputs and their corresponding real outputs and then averaging over all examples in the dataset.

Brief descriptions of some commonly used loss functions available in Keras are provided here:

- **mean_squared_error** is a loss function for regression problems that calculates *(real output – predicted output)*^2 for each example in the dataset and then returns their average.

- **mean_absolute_error** is a loss function for regression problems that calculates *abs(real output – predicted output)* for each example in the dataset and then returns their average.

- **mean_absolute_percentage_error** is a loss function for regression problems that calculates *abs[(real output – predicted output) / real output]* for each example in the dataset and then returns their average multiplied by 100%.

- **binary_crossentropy** is a loss function for two-class/binary classification problems. In general, cross-entropy loss is for calculating the loss for models where the output is a probability number between 0 and 1.

- **categorical_crossentropy** is a loss function for multi-class (more than two classes) classification problems.

> **Note**
>
> You can read more about all the available choices for loss functions in Keras here: https://keras.io/losses/.

During the training, we keep changing the model parameters until the minimum difference between model-predicted outputs and the real outputs is reached. This is called an **optimization process**, and we will learn more about how it works in later sections.

Backpropagation for Computing Derivatives of Loss Function

Backpropagation is the process of performing the chain rule of calculus from the output layer to the input layer of a neural network, in order to compute the derivatives of the loss function with respect to the model parameters in each layer. The derivative of a function is simply the slope of that function. We are interested in the slope of the loss function because it provides us with the direction in which model parameters need to change in order for the loss value to be minimized.

The chain rule of calculus states that if, for example, z is a function of y, and y is a function of x, then the derivative of z with respect to x can be reached by multiplying the derivative of z with respect to y by the derivative of y with respect to x. This can be written as follows:

dz/dx = dz/dy * dy/dx

In deep neural networks, the loss function is a function of predicted outputs. We can show this through the equation given here:

loss = L(y_predicted)

On the other hand, according to forward propagation equations, the predicted output by the model is a function of the model parameters, that is, the weights and biases in each layer. Therefore, according to the chain rule of calculus, the derivative of the loss with respect to the model parameters can be computed by multiplying the derivative of the loss with respect to the predicted output by the derivative of the predicted output with respect to the model parameters.

Gradient Descent for Learning Parameters

In this section, we will learn how a deep learning model learns its optimal parameters. In other words, we are going to learn about how model parameters keep updating until the values for which the error rate or loss is minimized are found. This process is called **learning parameters**, and it is done through the use of an optimization algorithm. One very common optimization algorithm used for learning parameters in machine learning is **gradient descent**. Let's see how gradient descent works.

If we plot the average of loss over all examples in the dataset for all possible values of the model parameters, it is usually a convex shape such as the one shown in Figure 3.8. In gradient descent, our goal is to find the minimum point (Pt) on the plot. The algorithm starts by initializing the model parameters with some random values (P1). Then it computes the loss and the derivatives of the loss with respect to the parameters at that point. It was mentioned before that derivative of a function is, in fact, the slope of the function. Therefore, by computing the slope at an initial point, we have the direction in which we need to update the parameters.

The hyperparameter called **learning rate** (**alpha**) determines how big a step the algorithm will take from the initial point. After selecting the proper alpha value, the algorithm updates the parameters from their initial values to the new values shown as point P2 in Figure 3.8. You can see from the figure that P2 is a bit closer to the target point, and if we keep moving in that direction, we will eventually get to the target point, Pt. Therefore, the algorithm computes the slope of the function again at P2 and takes another step. The process is repeated until the slope is equal to zero and therefore no direction for further movement is provided:

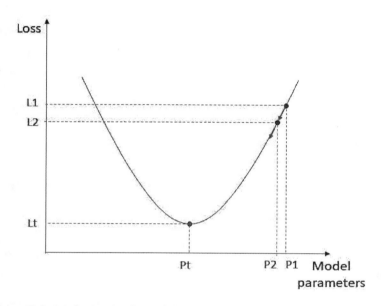

Figure 3.8: A schematic view of the gradient descent algorithm finding
the set of parameters that minimize loss

The pseudo-code for the gradient descent algorithm is provided here:

```
Initialize all the weights (w) and biases (b) arbitrarily
Repeat Until converge {
Compute loss given w and b
    Compute derivatives of loss with respect to w (dw), and with respect to
b (db) using backpropagation
    Update w to w - alpha * dw
    Update b to b - alpha * db
}
```

To summarize, the following steps are repeated in training a deep neural network (after initializing the parameters to some random values):

1. Use forward propagation and current parameters to predict the outputs for the entire dataset.

2. Use the predicted outputs to compute the loss over all the examples.

3. Use backpropagation to compute the derivatives of the loss with respect to the weights and biases at each layer.

4. Update the weights and biases using the derivative values and the learning rate.

What we discussed here was the standard gradient descent algorithm, which computes the loss and the derivatives using the entire dataset in order to update the parameters. There is another version of gradient descent called **stochastic gradient descent** (**SGD**), which computes the loss and the derivatives each time using a subset or a batch of data examples only; therefore, its learning process is faster.

> **Note**
>
> Another common choice is an optimization algorithm called Adam. Adam usually outperforms SGD for training deep learning models. As we learned, SGD uses a single hyperparameter called a learning rate to update the parameters. However, Adam improves this process by using a learning rate, a weighted average of gradients, and a weighted average of squared gradients to update the parameters at each iteration.

Usually, when building a neural network, you need to choose two hyperparameters, called the **batch size** and the number of **epochs**, for your optimization process. The `batch_size` argument determines the number of data examples to be included at each iteration of the optimization algorithm. `batch_size=None` is equivalent to the standard version of gradient descent, which uses the entire dataset in each iteration. The `epochs` argument determines how many times the optimization algorithm passes through the entire training dataset before it stops.

For example, imagine we have a dataset of size **n=400** and we chose **batch_size=5** and **epochs=20**. In this case, the optimizer will have 400/5 = 80 iterations in one pass through the entire dataset. Since it is supposed to go through the entire dataset 20 times, it will have 80 * 20 iterations in total.

> **Note**
>
> When building a model in Keras, you need to choose the type of optimizer to be used in training your model. There are some other options other than SGD and Adam available in Keras. You can read more about all the possible options for optimizers in Keras here: https://keras.io/optimizers/.

> **Note**
>
> All activities will be developed in a Jupyter notebook. Please download the GitHub repository with all the prepared templates from https://bit.ly/2WsoFin.

Exercise 10: Neural Network Implementation with Keras

In this exercise, you will learn about the step-by-step process of implementing a neural network using Keras. First, execute the following code block to generate a simulated dataset of 200 data points of two classes, where each data example has 10 feature values:

```
# create some simulated classification data
import numpy
from sklearn.datasets import make_classification
X, y = make_classification(n_samples=200, n_features=10, n_classes=2)

# Print the sizes of the dataset
print("Number of Examples in the Dataset = ", X.shape[0])
print("Number of Features for each example = ", X.shape[1])
print("Possible Output Classes = ", numpy.unique(y))
```

Expected Output:

```
Number of Examples in the Dataset =  200
Number of Features for each example =  10
Possible Output Classes =  [0 1]
```

Figure 3.9: A simulated dataset of 200 data points of 2 classes

Since each data example in this dataset can only belong to one of the two classes, this is a binary classification problem. Binary classification problems are very important and very common in real-life scenarios. For example, let's assume that the examples in this dataset are the information for 200 customers of a particular bank. The goal is to build a model using this dataset that allows the bank to predict whether a customer is going to leave the bank soon or not. Each customer is identified by an ID number ranging between 1 and 200. The 10 features for the customers can include predictors such as age, credit score, current balance, and so on. The output class **0** means that the customer will stay with the bank, and the output class **1** means that the customer will leave the bank soon.

Now let's go through the steps for building and training a Keras model to perform the classification:

1. Define your model as a Keras sequential model.

    Sequential models are, in fact, stacks of layers. After defining the model, we can add to it as many layers as desired:

    ```
    from keras.models import Sequential
    model = Sequential()
    ```

2. Add one hidden layer of size **10** with activation function of type **tanh** to your model (remember that the input dimension is equal to 10).

    There are different types of layers available in Keras. For now, we will use only the simplest type of layer, called the **Dense** layer. A Dense layer is equivalent to the **fully connected layers** that we have seen in all the examples so far:

    ```
    from keras.layers import Dense, Activation
    model.add(Dense(10, activation='tanh', input_dim=10))
    ```

3. Add another hidden layer, this time of size **5** and with an activation function of type **tanh**, to your model:

   Please note that the input dimension argument is only provided for the first layer, since the input dimension for the next layers is known:

   ```
   model.add(Dense(5, activation='tanh'))
   ```

4. Add the output layer with the sigmoid activation function.

   Please note that the number of units in the output layer is equal to the output dimension:

   ```
   model.add(Dense(1, activation='sigmoid'))
   ```

5. Choose the loss function to be binary cross-entropy and the optimizer to be SGD for training the model, using the **compile()** method:

   ```
   model.compile(optimizer='sgd', loss='binary_crossentropy')
   ```

6. Train your model for 100 epochs and set a batch size equal to 5 using the **fit()** method. Remember that you need to pass the input data, **X**, and its corresponding outputs, **y**, to the **fit()** method to train the model.

   Also, keep in mind that training a network may take a long time depending on the size of dataset, the size of network, the number of epochs, and the number of CPUs or GPUs available:

   ```
   model.fit(X, y, epochs=100, batch_size=5, verbose=0)
   ```

   The **verbose** argument can take any of these three values: **0**, **1**, or **2**. By choosing **verbose=0**, no information will be printed during training. **verbose=1** will print a full progress bar at every iteration, and **verbose=2** will print only the epoch number.

7. Use your trained model to predict the output class for the first 10 input data examples (**X[0:10,:]**):

   ```
   y_predicted = model.predict(X[0:10,:])
   ```

   You can print the predicted classes using the code block given here:

   ```
    # print the predicted classes
   print("Predicted probability for each of the examples belonging to class
   1: "),
   print(y_predicted)
   print("Predicted class label for each of the examples: "),
   print(numpy.round(y_predicted))
   ```

Expected Output:

```
Predicted probability for each of the examples belonging to class 1:
[[0.11604196]
 [0.94832146]
 [0.0205036 ]
 [0.0457067 ]
 [0.72578007]
 [0.05553623]
 [0.03615896]
 [0.3093823 ]
 [0.08713455]
 [0.98204064]]
Predicted class label for each of the examples:
[[0.]
 [1.]
 [0.]
 [0.]
 [1.]
 [0.]
 [0.]
 [0.]
 [0.]
 [1.]]
```

Figure 3.10: Predicted classes for the first 10 examples in the simulated dataset

Here, we used the trained model to predict the output for the first 10 customers in the dataset and, as you can see, the model predicted that the customers with ID numbers equal to 2, 5, and 10 have a high chance of leaving the bank.

Please note that you can extend the steps by adding more hidden layers to your network. In fact, you can add as many layers as you want to your model before proceeding to adding the output layer. However, the input dimension argument is only provided for the first layer, since the input dimension for the next layers is known. Now that you have learned how to implement a neural network in Keras, you are ready to practice with them further by implementing a neural network to perform classification in the following activity.

Activity 3: Building a Single-Layer Neural Network for Performing Binary Classification

In this activity, we will use a Keras sequential model to build a binary classifier. The dataset used for this includes 400 two-dimensional points, each belonging to one of two possible classes. It is a simulated dataset created using the `sklearn.datasets.make_circles` method. The reason to use a simulated dataset in this activity is for you to observe the visualization of different models' performance. It will help you gain a better sense of how going from one processing unit to a layer of processing units changes the flexibility and performance of the model.

Let's assume that this dataset contains two features, for example, the age and salary, of 400 individuals who have been contacted by an internet provider company (the age and salary features are normalized to have values between –1 and 1). The output is the likelihood of a purchase; *purchase=1* indicates that the individual will purchase the internet package, and *purchase=0* indicates that the individual will not purchase the internet package. The company would like to focus its marketing resources on individuals who have a higher chance of purchasing. Therefore, the goal is to build a model that can predict whether an individual will purchase some specific internet package or not based on their age and salary. In this activity, you will first build a logistic regression model, then a single-layer neural network with three units, and finally a single-layer neural network with six units to perform the classification:

1. Import the required packages:

    ```
    # import required packages from Keras
    from keras.models import Sequential
    from keras.layers import Dense, Activation
    import numpy
    # import required packages for plotting
    import matplotlib.pyplot as plt
    import matplotlib
    %matplotlib inline
    # import the simulated dataset and the function for plotting decision
    boundary
    from utils import load_dataset, plot_decision_boundary
    ```

2. Set up a seed for a random number generators, so that the results will be reproducible:

    ```
    # define a seed for random number generator so the result will be
    reproducible
    seed = 1
    ```

3. Load the dataset using `X, Y = load_dataset()`. Print the X and Y sizes and the number of examples in the training dataset using `X.shape`, `Y.shape`, and `X.shape[0]`.

4. Plot the dataset using this:

```
plt.scatter(X[:,0], X[:,1], s=40, c=Y, cmap=plt.cm.Spectral)
```

5. Implement a logistic regression model as a sequential model in Keras. Remember that the activation function for binary classification needs to be sigmoid.

6. Train the model with `optimizer='sgd'`, `loss='binary_crossentropy'`, `batch_size = 5`, and `epochs = 100`. Observe the loss values in each iteration by using `verbose=1`. Plot the decision boundary of the trained model using this:

```
plot_decision_boundary(lambda x: model.predict(x), X, Y)
```

7. Implement a single-layer neural network with three nodes in the hidden layer and the ReLU activation function for 200 epochs. It is important to remember that the activation function for the output layer still needs to be sigmoid, since it is a binary classification problem. Choosing ReLU or having no activation function for the output layer will not produce outputs that can be interpreted as class labels. Train the model with `verbose=1` and observe the loss in every iteration. After model is trained, plot the decision boundary.

8. Repeat step 7 for the hidden layer of size 6 and 400 epochs and compare the final loss value and the decision boundary plot with the models of steps 5 and 7.

9. Repeat steps 7 and 8 using the `tanh` activation function for the hidden layer and compare the results with the models with `relu` activation. Which activation function do you think is a better choice for this problem?

In this activity, you observed how stacking multiple processing units in a layer can create a much more powerful model than a single processing unit. This is the basic reason why neural networks are such powerful models. You also observed that increasing the number of units in the layer increases the flexibility of the model, meaning a non-linear separating decision boundary can be estimated more precisely. However, a model with more processing units takes longer to learn the patterns and requires more epochs to be trained. As such, neural networks are computationally expensive models. You also observed that using the tanh activation function results in a slower training process in comparison to using the ReLU activation function.

> **Note**
>
> The solution for this activity can be found on page 299.

Model Evaluation

In this section, we will move on to multi-layer or deep neural networks while learning about techniques for assessing the performance of a model. As you may have already realized, there are many hyperparameter choices to be made when building a deep neural network. Some very important challenges of applied deep learning are how to find the right values for the number of hidden layers, the number of units in each hidden layer, the type of activation function to use for each layer, the type of optimizer and loss function for training the network, among others. Model evaluation is required for making these decisions. By performing model evaluation, you can say whether a specific deep architecture or a specific set of hyperparameters is working poorly or well on a particular dataset, and therefore decide whether to change them or not.

Furthermore, you will learn about overfitting and underfitting in this section. These are two very important issues that can arise when building and training deep neural networks. Understanding the concepts of overfitting and underfitting and being able to know whether they are happening in practice is essential in order to find the right deep neural network for a particular problem and improve its performance as much as possible.

Evaluating a Trained Model with Keras

In *Activity 3*, we plotted the decision boundary of the model by predicting the output for every possible value of input. Such visualization of model performance was possible because we were dealing with two-dimensional input data. The number of features or measurements in the input space is almost always way more than two, and so visualization by 2D plotting is not an option. One way to figure out how well a model is doing on a particular dataset is by computing the overall loss when predicting outputs for many examples. This can be done by using the **evaluate()** method in Keras. The method receives a set of inputs (**X**) and their corresponding outputs (**y**) and calculates and returns the overall loss of the model on the inputs, **X**.

For example, let's consider a case of building a neural network with two hidden layers of sizes 8 and 4, respectively, for performing binary or two-class classification. The available data points and their corresponding class labels are stored in **X, y** arrays. We can build and train the mentioned model as follows:

```
model = Sequential()
model.add(Dense(8, activation='tanh', input_dim=2))
model.add(Dense(4, activation='tanh'))
model.add(Dense(1, activation='sigmoid'))
model.compile(optimizer='sgd', loss='binary_crossentropy')
model.fit(X, y, epochs=epochs, batch_size=batch_size)
```

Now, instead of using **model.predict()** to predict the output for a given set of inputs, we can evaluate the overall performance of the model by calculating the loss on the whole dataset by writing the following:

```
model.evaluate(X, y, batch_size=None, verbose=0)
```

If you include other metrics, such as accuracy, when defining the **compile()** method for the model, the **evaluate()** method will return those metrics along with the loss when it is called. For example, if we add metrics to the **complie()** arguments, as shown in the following code, then calling the **evaluate()** method will return the overall loss and the overall accuracy of the trained model on the whole dataset:

```
model.compile(optimizer='sgd', loss='binary_crossentropy',
metrics=['accuracy'])

model.evaluate(X, y, batch_size=None, verbose=0)
```

> **Note**
>
> You can check out all the possible options for the **metrics** argument in Keras here: https://keras.io/metrics/

Splitting Data into Training and Test Sets

In general, evaluating a model on the same dataset that has been used for training the model is a methodological mistake. Since the model has been trained to reduce the errors on this dataset, performing evaluation on it will result in a biased estimation of the model performance. In other words, the error rate on the dataset that has been used for training is always an underestimation of the error rate on new unseen examples. On the other hand, when building a machine learning model, the goal is not to achieve a good performance on the training data only. The more important goal is to achieve good performance on future examples that the model has not seen during training. That is why we are very interested in evaluating the performance of a model using a dataset that has not been used for training the model.

One way to achieve this is to split the available dataset into two sets: a training set and a test set. The training set is used to train the model and the test set is used for performance evaluation. More precisely, the role of the training set is to provide enough examples for the model that it will learn the relations and patterns in the data, while the role of the test set is to provide us with an unbiased estimation of the model performance on new unseen examples. The common practice in machine learning is to perform 70%-30% or 80%-20% splitting for training-test sets. This is usually the case for relatively small datasets. When dealing with a dataset with millions of examples and the goal is to train a very large deep neural network, the training-test splitting can be done using 98%-2% or 99%-1% ratios:

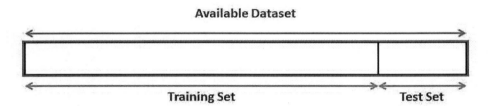

Figure 3.11: Illustration of splitting a dataset into training and test sets

You can easily perform splitting on your dataset using scikit-learn's **train_test_split()**. For example, the code here will perform a 70%-30% training-test split on the dataset:

```
from sklearn.model_selection import train_test_split

X_train, X_test, y_train, y_test = train_test_split(X, y, test_size=0.3,
random_state=None)
```

The **test_size** argument represents the proportion of the dataset to be kept in the test set and therefore, it should be between 0 and 1. By assigning **int** to the **random_state** argument, you can choose the seed to be used to generate the random split between the training and test sets.

After splitting the data into training and test sets, we can change the code from the previous section by providing only the training set as an argument to **fit()**:

```
model = Sequential()
model.add(Dense(8, activation='tanh', input_dim=2))
model.add(Dense(4, activation='tanh'))
model.add(Dense(1, activation='sigmoid'))
model.compile(optimizer='sgd', loss='binary_crossentropy')
model.fit(X_train, y_train, epochs=epochs, batch_size=batch_size)
```

Now we can compute the model error rate on the training set and the test set separately:

```
model.evaluate(X_train, y_train, batch_size=None, verbose=0)

model.evaluate(X_test, y_test, batch_size=None, verbose=0)
```

Another way of doing the splitting is by including the `validation_split` argument for the `fit()` method in Keras. For example, by only changing the `model.fit(X, y)` line in the code from the previous section to `model.fit(X, y, validation_split=0.3)`, the model will keep the last 30% of the data examples in a separate test set. It will train the model only on the other 70% of the samples, and it will evaluate the model on the training set and the test set at the end of each epoch. In doing so, it would be possible to observe the changes in the training error rate as well as the test error rate as the training progresses.

Underfitting and Overfitting

In this section, you will learn about two very important issues you may face when building a machine learning model to fit to a dataset. The issues are called **overfitting** and **underfitting**, and are similar to the concepts of **bias** and **variance** for a model. In general, if a model is not flexible enough to learn the relations and patterns in a dataset, there will be a high training error. We can call such a model a model with high bias. On the other hand, if a model is too flexible for a given dataset, it will learn the noise in the training data as well as the relations and patterns in the data. Such a system will cause a large increase in the test error in comparison to the training error. We discussed before that it is always the case that the test error is slightly higher than the training error. However, having a large gap between the test error and the training error is an indicator of a system with high variance. In data analysis, neither of these situations (high bias and high variance) are desirable. In fact, the aim is to find the model with the lowest possible amount of bias and variance at the same time.

For example, let's consider a set of two-dimensional data points of two different classes, as shown in Figure 3.12. The goal is to find a model to separate these two classes. Clearly, the separating line between the two classes in not linear. Therefore, if we choose a simple model such as logistic regression (a neural network with one hidden layer of size one) to perform the classification on this dataset, we will get a linear separating line/decision boundary between two classes that is not able to capture the true pattern in the dataset:

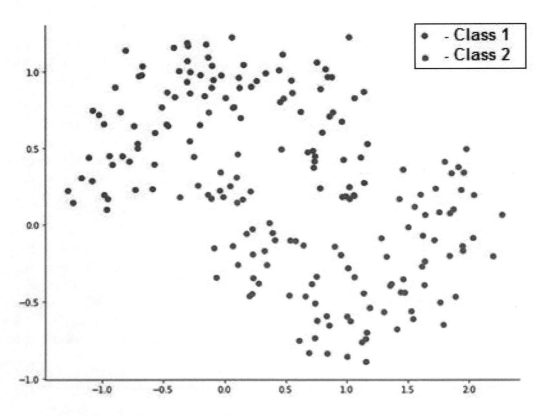

Figure 3.12: Two-dimensional data points of two different classes

Figure 3.13 illustrates the decision boundary achieved by such a model. By evaluating this model, it will be observed that the training error rate is high and the test error rate is slightly higher than the training error. Having a high training error rate is indicative of a model with high bias and having a slight difference between the training error and test error is representative of a low-variance model. This is a clear case of underfitting; the model fails to fit the true separating line between the two classes:

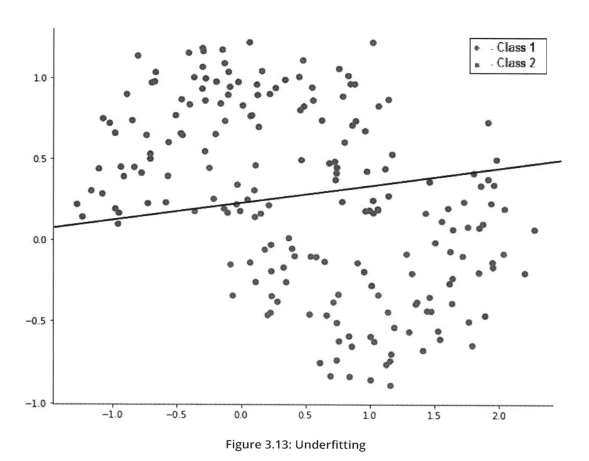

Figure 3.13: Underfitting

If we increase the flexibility of the neural network by adding more layers to it and increasing the number of units in each layer, we can train a better model and succeed in capturing the non-linearity in the decision boundary. Such a model is shown in Figure 3.14. This is a model with a low training error rate and low test error rate (again, the test error rate is slightly higher than the training error rate). Having a low training error rate and a slight difference between the test error rate and training error rate is indicative of a model with low bias and low variance. A model with low bias and low variance represents the right amount of fitting for a given dataset:

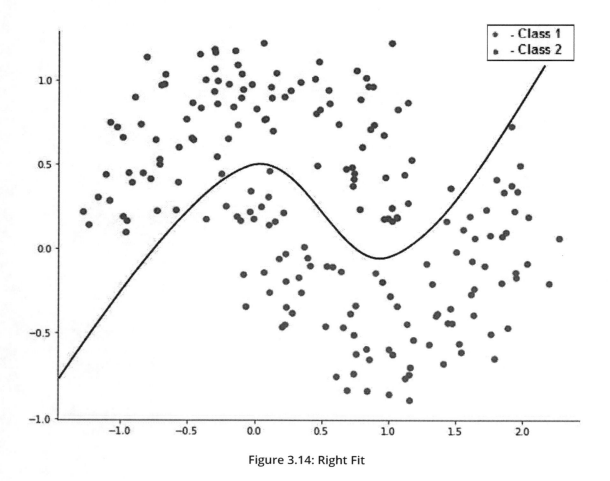

Figure 3.14: Right Fit

But what will happen if we increase the flexibility of the neural network even more? By adding too much flexibility to the model, it will learn not only the patterns and relations in the training data but also the noise in them. In other words, the model will fit to each individual training example as opposed to fitting only to the overall trends and relations in them. Figure 3.15 shows such a system. Evaluating this model will show a very low training error rate and a high test error rate (with a large difference between the training error rate and test error rate). This is a model with low bias and high variance, and this situation is called overfitting:

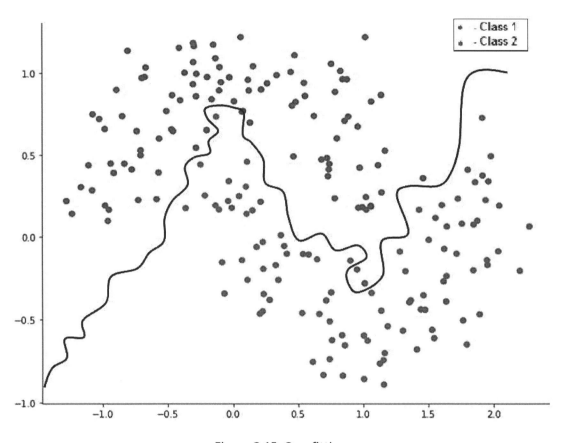

Figure 3.15: Overfitting

Evaluating the model on both the training set and the test set and comparing their error rates provide valuable information on whether the current model is right for a given dataset or not. Also, in cases where the current model is not fitting the dataset right, it is possible to determine whether it is overfitting or underfitting to the data and change the model accordingly to find the right model. For example, if the model is underfitting, you can make the network larger. On the other hand, if the model is overfitting, you can reduce the overfitting by making the network smaller or providing more training data to it.

Early Stopping

Sometimes the flexibility of a model is quite right for the dataset but overfitting or underfitting is still happening. This is because we are training the model for either too many iterations or too few iterations. When using an iterative optimizer such as gradient descent, the optimizer tries to fit to the training data better and better in every iteration. Therefore, if we keep updating the parameters after the patterns in the data are learned, it will start fitting to the individual data examples. By observing the training and test error rates in every iteration, it is possible to determine when the network is starting to overfit to the training data and stop the training process before this happens. Regions associated with underfitting and overfitting are labeled on the following plot. The right number of iterations for training the model can be determined from the region at which the test error rate has its lowest value. We labeled this region as the right fit on the plot and it can be seen that in this region, both the training error rate and test error rate are low:

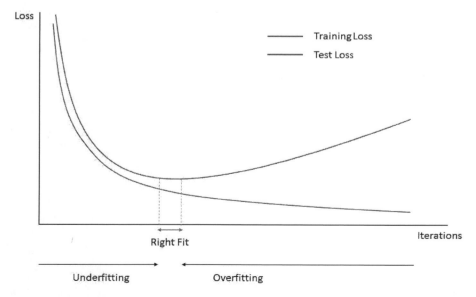

Figure 3.16: Plot of training error rate and test error rate during the training of a model

You can easily store the values for training loss and test loss in every epoch during training with Keras. To do this, you need to provide the test set as the `validation_data` argument when defining the `fit()` method for the model and store it in a `history` dictionary:

```
history = model.fit(X_train, y_train, validation_data=(X_test, y_test))
```

You can later plot the values stored in `history` to find the right number of iterations for training your model:

```
import matplotlib.pyplot as plt
import matplotlib


# plot training loss
plt.plot(history.history['loss'])
# plot test loss
plt.plot(history.history['val_loss'])
```

In general, since deep neural networks are highly flexible models, the chance of overfitting happening is very high. There is a whole group of techniques called **regularization** techniques developed for reducing overfitting in machine learning models in general and deep neural networks in particular. You will learn more about these techniques in *Chapter 5, Improving Model Accuracy* of this book.

Activity 4: Diabetes Diagnosis with Neural Networks

In this activity, you are going to use a real dataset to predict whether a patient has diabetes or not, based on measurements such as age, BMI, and insulin level in their blood. The dataset consists of information for 768 patients and for each patient, 8 different measurements are available, as well as a class label, which can only take two values: 1, indicating diabetic, and 0, indicating non-diabetic. Therefore, this is a binary/two-class classification problem with an input dimension equal to 8.

You will learn how to implement different deep neural network architectures for performing this classification and plot the trends in training error rates and test error rates and determine how many epochs the final classifier needs to be trained for:

> **Note**
>
> The source of the dataset is https://www.kaggle.com/uciml/pima-indians-diabetes-database. You can also download the dataset from the GitHub repository. Here is the link for this: https://bit.ly/2HHTkF7.

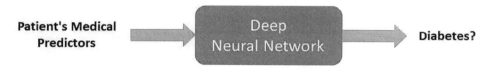

Figure 3.17: Schematic view of the binary classifier for diabetes diagnosis

1. Import all the necessary dependencies. Load the dataset from the **data** subfolder of **Lesson03** folder from GitHub:

    ```
    data=numpy.loadtxt("./data/pima-indians-diabetes.csv", delimiter=",")
    ```

2. Store the training data in **X** using **X = data[:,0:8]** and the class labels in **y** using **y = data[:,8]**. Print the number of examples in the dataset, the number of features available, and the possible values for the class labels.

3. Split the dataset into the training set and test set with a 7:3 ratio, and print the number of examples in each set after splitting.

4. Implement a shallow neural network with one hidden layer of size 8 and a **'relu'** activation function to perform the classification. Use the following values for the hyperparameters:

    ```
    optimizer = 'adam', loss = 'binary_crossentropy', metrics = ['accuracy'],
    batch_size = 5, epochs = 300
    ```

    Store the values for training error rate and test error rate during the training.

5. Plot the training error rate and test error rate for every epoch of training. Use the plot to determine at which epoch the network is starting to overfit to the dataset. Also, print the values of the best accuracy reached on the training set and on the test set.

6. Repeat steps 4 and 5 for a deep neural network with two hidden layers (the first layer of size 16, and the second layer of size 8) and a `'relu'` activation function for both layers to perform the classification. Also, set **epochs** = **350**, since it is a larger network.

7. Repeat the previous step for a deep neural network with three hidden layers (the first layer of size 16, the second layer of size 8, and the third layer of size 4) and a `'relu'` activation function for all three layers to perform the classification. Also, set **epochs** = **400**, since it is a larger network.

Please note that all the three models were able to get a better accuracy on the training set, and the training error rate kept decreasing when trained for a great number of epochs. However, the test error rate decreased during training to a certain value and after that, it started increasing, which is indicative of overfitting to the training data. The maximum test accuracy corresponds to the point on the plots where the test loss is at its lowest and is truly representative of how well the model will perform on independent examples later.

It can be seen from the results that the model with two hidden layers is able to reach a lower test error rate, in comparison to the other models. We may conclude that this model is the best match for this particular problem. However, its test error shows lots of fluctuation, which can make this conclusion unreliable (you will learn how to better evaluate a model in the next chapter). Also, since the models with two and three hidden layers are more flexible, they show a higher amount of overfitting (that is, a larger gap between the training error rate and test error rate at the end of training). On the other hand, the model with one hidden layer shows a lower amount of overfitting (that is, a smaller gap between the training error rate and test error rate). Lastly, it can be concluded from the plots that we should stop the training around the region where the test error rate starts increasing, to prevent the model from overfitting to the data points.

Note

The solution for this activity can be found on page 308.

Summary

In this chapter, you learned about the basics of deep learning, including the common representations and terminology and essential underlying concepts. You learned how forward propagation in neural networks works and how it is used for predicting outputs. You learned about the loss function as a measure of model performance and learned how backpropagation is used to compute the derivatives of loss function with respect to model parameters. Finally, you learned about gradient descent, which uses the gradients computed by backpropagation to gradually update the model parameters. In addition to basic theory and concepts, you also learned how to implement and train shallow and deep neural networks with Keras and how to use a trained network to make predictions about the output of a given input. You also learned how to evaluate the overall performance of the network over all data examples, and the reasons why evaluating a model on training examples can be misleading. You learned about splitting a dataset into a training set and a test set as an alternative approach to improve the network evaluation. You also learned about the very important issues of overfitting and underfitting that can happen when training a model. You learned what each of these issues mean and how you can use the training error rate and test error rate to detect overfitting and underfitting in a network. Lastly, you learned about a technique called early stopping in order to reduce overfitting in a network. You also had a chance to practice what you learned through completing multiple exercises and activities.

In the next chapter, we will learn about the Keras wrapper with scikit-learn and how to use it to further improve model evaluation by using resampling methods such as cross-validation, and you will see how to find the best set of hyperparameters for a deep neural network.

Evaluate Your Model with Cross-Validation using Keras Wrappers

Learning Objectives

By the end of this chapter, you will be able to:

- Build a Keras wrapper with scikit-learn
- Apply cross-validation to evaluate deep learning models
- Create user-defined functions to implement deep learning models along with cross-validation

In this chapter, we will learn how to build a Keras wrapper with scikit-learn. We will perform cross-validation to evaluate deep learning models and also develop user-defined functions in order to perform cross-validation on multiple models.

Introduction

In this chapter, you will learn about **cross-validation**, a **resampling technique** that leads to a very accurate and robust estimation of a model's performance in comparison to the model evaluation approaches discussed in the previous chapters. This chapter starts with an in-depth discussion about why we need to use cross-validation for model evaluation, the underlying basics of cross-validation, its variations, and a comparison between them. Next, we will move on to implementing cross-validation on Keras deep learning models. We will also focus on how to use Keras wrappers with scikit-learn to allow Keras models to be treated as estimators in a scikit-learn workflow. You will then learn how to implement cross-validation in scikit-learn, and finally bring it all together and perform cross-validation using scikit-learn on Keras deep learning models. Lastly, you will learn about using cross-validation to perform more than just model evaluation. You will learn how a cross-validation estimation of model performance can be used to compare different models and select the one that results in the best performance on a particular dataset. You will also learn to use cross-validation to improve the performance of a given model by finding the best set of hyperparameters for it. We will implement the concepts learned in this chapter in three activities, each involving a real-life dataset.

Cross-Validation

Resampling techniques are an important group of techniques in statistical data analysis. They involve repeatedly drawing samples from a dataset to create the training set and the test set. At each repetition, they fit and evaluate the model using the samples drawn from the dataset   for the training set and the test set at that repetition. Using these techniques can provide us with information about the model that is otherwise not obtainable by fitting and evaluating the model only once using one training set and one test set. Since resampling methods involve fitting a model to the training data several times, they are computationally expensive. Therefore, when it comes to deep learning, we only implement them in the cases where the dataset and the network are relatively small and the available computational power allows us to do so.

In this section, you will learn about a very important resampling method called **cross-validation**. Cross-validation is one of the most important and the most commonly used resampling methods. It computes the best estimation of model performance on new, unseen examples given a limited dataset. We will also explore the basics of cross-validation, its two different variations, and a comparison between them.

Drawbacks of Splitting a Dataset Only Once

In the previous chapter, we mentioned that evaluating a model on the same dataset that has been used to train the model is a methodological mistake. Since the model has been trained to reduce the error on this particular set of examples, its performance on it is highly biased. That is why the error rate on training data is always an underestimation of the error rate on new examples. We have learned that one way to solve this problem is to randomly hold out a subset of the data as a test set for evaluation, and fit the model on the rest of the data, which is called the training set. An illustration of this approach is shown in Figure 4.1:

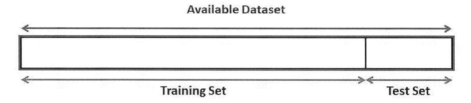

Available Dataset

Training Set   **Test Set**

Figure 4.1: Overview of training set/test set split

As we mentioned, the assignment of data to either the training set or the test set is completely random. It means that if we repeat the process, different data will be assigned to the test set and training set each time. The test error rate reported by this approach can vary a lot, depending on which examples are in the test set and which examples are in the training set.

Example

Let's look at an example. We built a single layer neural network for the diabetes dataset that you saw previously in *Activity 4, Diabetes Diagnosis with Neural Networks of Chapter 3, Deep Learning with Keras.* We used the training set/test set approach to compute the test error associated with this model. Instead of splitting and training only once, we repeated this process five times. The test error rates for each of these five experiments are shown in the plot in Figure 4.2. As you can see, the test error rate is quite different in each experiment. This variation in the models' evaluation results indicates that the simple strategy of splitting the dataset into a training set and a test set only once may not lead to a robust and accurate estimation of the model's performance.

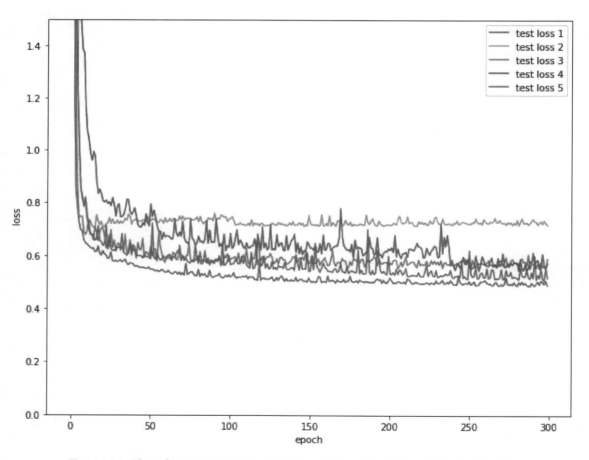

Figure 4.2: Plot of test error rates with five different training set/test set splits
on the diabetes dataset

To summarize, the training set/test set approach that we learned in the previous chapter has the obvious advantage of being simple, easy to implement, and computationally inexpensive. However, it has drawbacks, which are as follows:

- The first drawback is that its estimation of the model's error rate strongly depends on exactly which data is assigned to the test set and which data is assigned to the training set.

- The second drawback is that in this approach, we are only training the model on a subset of the data. Machine learning models tend to perform worse when they are trained using a small amount of data.

Since the performance of a model can be improved by training it on the entire dataset, we are always looking for ways to include all the available data points in training. Additionally, we are interested in finding a robust estimation of the model's performance by including all the available data points in the evaluation as well. These objectives can be accomplished by the use of cross-validation technique. These are the two methods of cross-validation:

- K-fold cross-validation
- Leave-one-out cross-validation

K-Fold Cross-Validation

In **k-fold cross-validation**, instead of dividing the dataset into two subsets, we divide the dataset into k approximately equal-sized subsets, or folds. In the first iteration of the method, the first fold is considered as a test set. The model is trained on the remaining k-1 folds, and then it is evaluated on the first fold (the first fold is used to estimate the test error rate). This process is repeated k times, and a different fold is used as the test set in each iteration, while the remaining folds are used as the training set. Eventually, the method results in k different test error rates. The final k-fold cross-validation estimate of the model's error rate is computed by averaging these k test error rates.

The following figure illustrates the dataset splitting process in the k-fold cross-validation method:

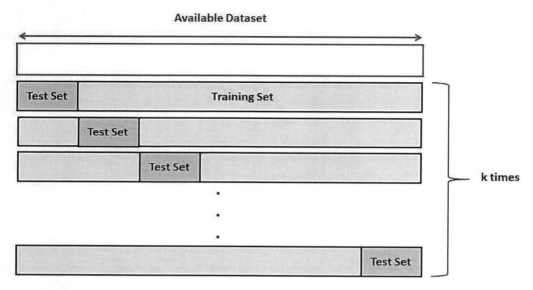

Figure 4.3: Overview of dataset splitting in the k-fold cross-validation method

In practice, we usually perform k-fold cross-validation with $k=5$ or $k=10$, and these are the recommended values if you are struggling to select a value for your dataset. Deciding on the number of folds to use is dependent on the number of examples in the dataset and the available computational power. If $k=5$, the model will be trained and evaluated 5 times, while if $k=10$, this process will be repeated 10 times. The higher the number of folds, the longer it will take to perform k-fold cross-validation.

In k-fold cross-validation, the assignment of examples to each fold is completely random. However, by looking at Figure 4.3, you can see that, in the end, every single piece of data is used for both training and evaluation. That is why, if you repeat k-fold cross-validation many times on the same dataset and the same model, the final reported test error rates will be *almost identical*. Therefore, k-fold cross-validation does not suffer from high variance in its results, in contrast to the training set/test set approach.

Leave-One-Out Cross-Validation

Leave-One-Out (LOO) is a variation of cross-validation technique in which, instead of dividing the dataset into two comparable-sized subsets for the training set and test set, only one single piece of data example is used for evaluation. If there are n data examples in the entire dataset, at each iteration of LOO cross-validation, the model is trained on $n-1$ examples and the single remaining example is used to compute the test error rate. Using only one example for estimating test error rate leads to an unbiased but high variance estimation of model performance; it is unbiased because this one example has not been used in training the model, and it has high variance because it is computed based on only one data example, and it will vary depending on which exact data example is used. However, this process is repeated n times and, at each iteration, a different data example is used for evaluation. In the end, the method will result in n different test error rates, and the final LOO cross-validation test error estimation is computed by averaging these n error rates. An illustration of the dataset splitting process in the LOO cross-validation method is shown in the following figure:

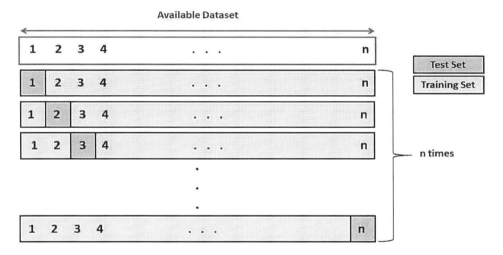

Figure 4.4: Overview of dataset splitting in the LOO cross-validation method

In each iteration of LOO cross-validation, *almost* all the examples in the dataset are used to train the model. On the other hand, in the training set/test set approach, a relatively large subset of data is used for evaluation and not used in training. Therefore, the LOO estimation of model performance is much closer to the performance of a model that is trained on the entire dataset, and this is the main advantage of LOO cross-validation over the training set/test set approach.

Additionally, since in each iteration of LOO cross-validation only one unique data example is used for evaluation, and every single data example is used for training as well, there is no randomness associated with this method. Therefore, if you repeat LOO cross-validation many times on the same dataset and the same model, the final reported test error rates will be *exactly the same each time.*

The drawback of LOO cross-validation is that it is computationally expensive. The reason for this is that the model needs to be trained n times, and in cases where n is large and/or the network is large, it will take a long time to complete.

Comparing the K-Fold and LOO Methods

By comparing Figure 4.3 and Figure 4.4, it is obvious that LOO cross-validation is, in fact, a special case of k-fold cross-validation, where **k=n**. However, as was mentioned before, choosing **k=n** is computationally very expensive in comparison to choosing **k=5** or **k=10**. Therefore, the first advantage of k-fold cross-validation over LOO cross-validation is that it is computationally less expensive. The following figure compares the k-fold and LOO methods with respect to bias and variance:

	Bias	Variance
Simple Train-Test Split Approach	Highest	Lowest
K-fold Cross Validation with smaller k	Higher	Lower
K-fold Cross Validation with larger k	Lower	Higher
LOO Cross Validation k=n	Lowest	Highest

Figure 4.5: Comparing the train-test split, k-fold cross-validation, and LOO cross validation methods

The following figure compares training set/test set approach, k-fold cross-validation, and LOO cross-validation in terms of bias and variance:

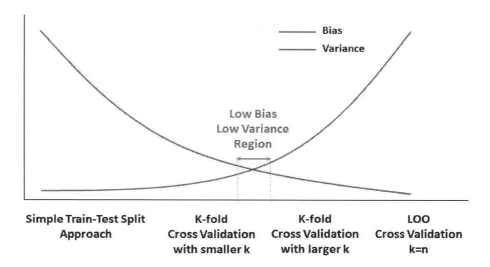

Figure 4.6: Comparing the training set/test set approach, k-fold cross-validation, and LOO cross-validation in terms of bias and variance

Generally, in machine learning and data analysis, the most desirable model is the one with the lowest bias and the lowest variance. As we can see in Figure 4.6, the region labeled in the middle of the graph, where both bias and variance are low, is of interest. It turns out that this region is equivalent to k-fold cross-validation with k value between 5 and 10.

Cross-Validation for Deep Learning Models

In this section, you will learn about using the Keras wrapper with scikit-learn, a very helpful tool that allows us to use Keras models as part of a scikit-learn workflow. As a result, scikit-learn methods and functions, such as the one for performing cross-validation, can be easily applied to Keras models. You will learn, step-by-step, how to implement what you learned about cross-validation in the previous section using scikit-learn. Furthermore, you will learn to use cross-validation in order to evaluate Keras deep learning models using the Keras wrapper with scikit-learn. Lastly, you will practice what you learned on a problem involving a real dataset.

Keras Wrapper with scikit-learn

When it comes to general machine learning and data analysis, the scikit-learn library is much richer and easier to use than Keras. That is why being able to use scikit-learn methods on Keras models will be of great value.

Fortunately, Keras comes with a helpful wrapper, **keras.wrappers.scikit_learn**, that allows us to build a scikit-learn interface for deep learning models that can be used as classification or regression estimators in scikit-learn. There are two types of wrapper: one for classification estimators and one for the regression estimators. Following is the code to define these scikit-learn interfaces:

```
keras.wrappers.scikit_learn.KerasClassifier(build_fn=None, **sk_params)
# wrappers for classification estimators
```

```
keras.wrappers.scikit_learn.KerasRegressor(build_fn=None, **sk_params)
# wrappers for regression estimators
```

The **build_fn** argument needs to be a callable function within whose body a Keras sequential model is defined, compiled, and returned.

The **sk_params** argument can take both parameters for building the model (such as activation functions for layers) and parameters for fitting the model (such as the number of epochs and batch size).

> **Note**
>
> All activities will be developed in a Jupyter Notebook. Please download the GitHub repository with all the prepared templates from https://github.com/ TrainingByPackt/Applied-Deep-Learning-with-Keras/tree/master/Lesson04.

Exercise 11: Building the Keras Wrapper with scikit-learn for a Regression Problem

In this exercise, you will learn the step-by-step process of building the wrapper for a Keras deep learning model to be used in scikit-learn workflow. First, execute the following code block to generate a simulated dataset of 500 data points of a regression problem, where each data example has 2 feature values:

```
# create some simulated regression data

import numpy

from sklearn.datasets import make_regression

X, y = make_regression(n_samples=500, n_features=2, n_informative=2,
noise=5, random_state=0)


# Print the sizes of the dataset

print("Number of Examples in the Dataset = ", X.shape[0])
```

```
print("Number of Features for each example = ", X.shape[1])
# print output range
print("Output Range = [%f, %f]" %(min(y), max(y)))
```

This is the expected output:

```
Number of Examples in the Dataset =  500
Number of Features for each example =  2
Output Range = [-288.225754, 271.270135]
```

Figure 4.7: The properties of the simulated dataset with 500 data points

Since the output in this dataset takes a numerical value, this is a regression problem. You may come across different regression problems in many real-life scenarios. For example, let's assume that this dataset contains the changes in a company's stock price over 500 days. The two features included in the dataset are, for example, the changes in the stock price for the two previous trading days, and the output is the change in the stock price today. The goal is to build a model to predict how much the stock price for this company will change on a specific day, based on the changes in the two previous trading days. Now, let's go through the steps:

1. Define a function that builds and returns a Keras model for this regression problem. The Keras model that you define must have two hidden layers with ReLU activation functions, the first layer of size 16 and the second layer of size 8. Also use the Mean Squared Error (MSE) loss function and the Adam optimizer to compile the model:

```
from keras.models import Sequential
from keras.layers import Dense, Activation
# Create the function that returns the keras model
def build_model():
    # build the Keras model
    model = Sequential()
    model.add(Dense(16, input_dim=2, activation='relu'))
    model.add(Dense(8, activation='relu'))
    model.add(Dense(1))
    # Compile the model
    model.compile(loss='mean_squared_error', optimizer='adam')
    # return the model
    return model
```

2. Now use the Keras wrapper with scikit-learn to create the scikit-learn interface for your model. Remember that you need to provide the **epochs**, **batch_size**, and **verbose** arguments here:

```
# build the scikit-Learn interface for the keras model
from keras.wrappers.scikit_learn import KerasRegressor
YourModel = KerasRegressor(build_fn= build_model, epochs=300, batch_
size=10, verbose=1)
```

3. Now, **YourModel** is ready to be used as a regression estimator in scikit-learn.

In this exercise, we learned how to build a Keras wrapper with scikit-learn for a regression problem by using a simulated dataset. We will continue implementing cross-validation using this dataset in the next exercises of this chapter.

Cross-Validation with scikit-learn

We learned in the previous chapter that you can perform training set/test set splitting easily in scikit-learn. Assume that your original dataset is stored in **X**, **y** arrays. You can split them randomly into a training set and a test set using the following commands:

```
from sklearn.model_selection import train_test_split
```

```
X_train, X_test, y_train, y_test = train_test_split(X, y, test_size=0.3,
random_state=0)
```

The **test_size** argument can be assigned to any number between 0 and 1 depending on how large you would like the test set to be. By providing an **int** number for a **random_state** argument, you will be able to select the seed for random number generator.

To perform cross-validation in scikit-learn, the easiest way is to use the **cross_val_score** function. In order to do this, you need to define your estimator first (in our case, the estimator will be a Keras model). Then you will be able to perform cross-validation on your estimator/model using the following commands:

```
from sklearn.model_selection import cross_val_score
```

```
scores = cross_val_score(YourModel, X, y, cv=5)
```

Notice that we provide the Keras model and the original dataset as arguments to the **cross_val_score** function, along with the number of folds (the **cv** argument). Here, we used **cv=5**, and therefore, the **cross_val_score** function will randomly split the dataset into five folds and perform training and fitting on the model five times using five different training and test sets. It will compute the default metric for model evaluation (or the metrics given to the Keras model when defining it) at each iteration/fold and store them in scores. We can print the final cross-validation score as follows:

```
print(scores.mean())
```

It was mentioned earlier that the score returned by the **cross_val_score** function is the default metric for our model, or the metric that we determined for it when defining our model. However, it is possible to change the cross-validation metric by providing the desired metric as a **scoring** argument when calling the **cross_val_score** function.

> **Note**
>
> You can read more about how to provide the desired metric in the **scoring** argument of the **cross_val_score** function here:
>
> https://scikit-learn.org/stable/modules/model_evaluation.html#scoring-parameter

By providing an integer number for the **cv** argument of the **cross_val_score** function, we are in fact telling the function to perform k-fold cross-validation on the dataset. However, there are several other iterators available in scikit-learn that we can assign to **cv** to perform other variations of cross-validation on the dataset. For example, the following code block will perform LOO cross-validation on the dataset:

```
from sklearn.model_selection import LeaveOneOut

loo = LeaveOneOut()

scores = cross_val_score(YourModel, X, y, cv=loo)
```

Cross-Validation Iterators in scikit-learn

A list of the most commonly-used cross-validation iterators available in scikit-learn is provided here, along with a brief description of each of them:

- **KFold(n_splits=?)**

  This divides the dataset into k folds or groups. The **n_splits** argument is required to determine how many folds to use. If **n_splits=n**, it will be equivalent to LOO cross-validation.

- **RepeatedKFold(n_splits=?, n_repeats=?, random_state=random_state)**

  This will repeat k-fold cross-validation **n_repeats** times.

- **LeaveOneOut()**

  This will perform splitting the dataset for LOO cross-validation.

- **ShuffleSplit(n_splits=?, test_size=?, random_state= random_state)**

  This will generate an **n_splits** number of random and independent training set/test set dataset splits. It is possible to store the seed for random number generator using the **random_state** argument; if you do this, the dataset splits will be reproducible.

In addition to the regular iterators such as the ones mentioned here, there are **stratified** versions as well. Stratified sampling is useful when the number of examples in different classes of a dataset is unbalanced. For example, imagine we want to design a classifier to diagnose whether a patient has a particular disease or not, where almost 80% of the examples in the dataset are in the **negative** class. Stratified sampling makes sure that the relative class frequencies are preserved in each training set/test set split. It is recommended to use the stratified versions of iterators for such cases.

Usually, before using a training set in order to train and evaluate a model, we perform preprocessing on it to scale the examples to have mean equal 0 and standard deviation equal 1. In training set - test set approach, we need to scale the training set and store the transformation. The code block below will do this:

```
from sklearn.preprocessing import StandardScaler
scaler = StandardScaler()
X_train = scaler.fit_transform(X_train)
X_test = scaler.transform(X_test)
```

Here's an example of performing **stratified k-fold cross-validation** with **k=5** on our **X, y** dataset:

```
from sklearn.model_selection import StratifiedKFold
skf = StratifiedKFold(n_splits=5)
scores = cross_val_score(YourModel, X, y, cv=skf)
```

> **Note**
>
> You can read more about cross-validation iterators in scikit-learn here:
>
> https://scikit-learn.org/stable/modules/cross_validation.html#cross-validation-iterators

Exercise 12: Evaluate Deep Neural Networks with Cross-Validation

In this exercise, we will bring together all the concepts and methods that we learned in this topic about cross-validation. We will go through all the steps one more time, from defining a Keras deep learning model to transferring it to scikit-learn workflow, and performing cross-validation in order to evaluate its performance. In a sense, this exercise is a recap of the topic and what is covered here will be extremely helpful for implementing Activity 5:

1. The first step always is to load the dataset that you would like to build the model for. Execute the following code block to generate a simulated dataset of 500 data points of a regression problem, where each data point has 2 feature values. Similar to Exercise 11, let's assume that this dataset contains the changes in a company's stock price over 500 days. The two features included in the dataset are the changes of the stock price over the two previous trading days, and the output is the change of the stock price today. The goal is to build a model to predict how much the stock price of this company will change on a specific day, based on the changes on the two previous trading days:

    ```python
    # create some simulated regression data
    import numpy
    from sklearn.datasets import make_regression
    X, y = make_regression(n_samples=500, n_features=2, n_informative=2,
    noise=5, random_state=0)

    # Print the sizes of the dataset
    print("Number of Examples in the Dataset = ", X.shape[0])
    print("Number of Features for each example = ", X.shape[1])
    # print output range
    print("Output Range = [%f, %f]" %(min(y), max(y)))
    ```

2. Define the function that returns the Keras model with two hidden layers with ReLU activation functions, the first layer of size 16 and the second layer of size 8, and using the Mean Squared Error (MSE) loss function and the Adam optimizer:

    ```python
    from keras.models import Sequential
    from keras.layers import Dense, Activation
    # Create the function that returns the keras model
    def build_model():
        # build the Keras model
        model = Sequential()
        model.add(Dense(16, input_dim=2, activation='relu'))
        model.add(Dense(8, activation='relu'))
        model.add(Dense(1))
    ```

```
# Compile the model
model.compile(loss='mean_squared_error', optimizer='adam')
# return the model
return model
```

3. Use the wrapper to build the scikit-learn interface for the Keras model defined in the function in step 2:

```
# build the scikit-Learn interface for the keras model
from keras.wrappers.scikit_learn import KerasRegressor
YourModel = KerasRegressor(build_fn= build_model, epochs=300, batch_
size=10, verbose=1)
```

4. Define the iterator to use for cross-validation. Let's perform 5-fold cross-validation:

```
# define the iterator to perform 5-fold cross-validation
from sklearn.model_selection import KFold
kf = KFold(n_splits=5)
```

5. Call the **cross_val_score** function to perform the cross-validation. This step will take a while to complete, depending on the computational power available:

```
# perform cross-validation on X, y
from sklearn.model_selection import cross_val_score
results = cross_val_score(YourModel, X, y, cv=kf)
```

6. Once cross-validation is completed, print the final cross-validation estimation of model performance (the default metric for performance will be the test loss):

```
# print the result
print("Final Cross-validation Loss =", abs(results.mean()))
```

Here's an example output:

```
Final Cross Validation Loss = 25.39843524932861
```

Figure 4.8: Final cross-validation estimation of the model's performance

The cross-validation loss states that the Keras model trained on this dataset is able to predict how much the stock price of this company will change today, based on the changes on the past two trading days, with a 25.4% error rate (or 74.6% accuracy). We will try to examine this model further in the next exercise.

These were all the steps required in order to evaluate a Keras deep learning model using cross-validation in scikit-learn.

Activity 5: Model Evaluation Using Cross-Validation for a Diabetes Diagnosis Classifier

We learned about the diabetes dataset in *Activity 4, Diabetes Diagnosis with Neural Networks* of *Chapter 3, Deep Learning with Keras*. The dataset consists of information for 768 patients and for each patient, 8 different measurements are available, as well as a class label that can only take 2 values: 1 indicating diabetic (268 examples), and 0 indicating non-diabetic (500 examples). In *Chapter 3, Deep Learning with Keras*, we built Keras models to perform classification on this dataset. We trained and evaluated the models using training set/test set splitting and reported the test error rate. In this activity, we are going to use what we learned in this topic to train and evaluate a deep learning model using k-fold cross-validation. We will use the model that resulted in the best test error rate from the previous activity. The goal is to compare the cross-validation error rate with the training set/test set approach error rate:

1. Import the necessary libraries. Load the dataset from the **data** subfolder of the **Lesson04** folder from GitHub using **data=numpy.loadtxt("./data/pima-indians-diabetes.csv", delimiter=",")**. Store the training data in **X** using **X = data[:,0:8]**, and store the class labels in **y** using **y = data[:,8]**. Print the number of examples in the dataset, the number of features available, and the possible values for the class labels.

2. Define the function that returns the Keras model. The Keras model will be a deep neural network with 2 hidden layers, the first hidden layer of size 16 and the second hidden layer of size 8, and use the ReLU activation function to perform the classification. Use the following values for the hyperparameters:

   optimizer = 'adam', loss = 'binary_crossentropy', metrics = ['accuracy']

3. Build the scikit-learn interface for the Keras model with **epochs=300** and **batch_size=5**. Define the cross-validation iterator as **StratifiedKFold** with **k=5**. Perform k-fold cross-validation on the model and store the scores.

4. Print the accuracy for each iteration/fold, plus the overall cross-validation accuracy and its associated standard deviation.

5. Compare this result with the result from *Activity 4, Diabetes Diagnosis with Neural Networks* of *Chapter 3, Deep Learning with Keras*.

The accuracy resulted from training set/test set approach performed in *Activity 4,* *Diabetes Diagnosis with Neural Networks of Chapter 3, Deep Learning with Keras,* was 76.623%, which is higher than the accuracy we achieved when performing 5-fold cross-validation on the same deep learning model and the same dataset. The reason for this difference is that the test error rate resulting from training set/test set approach was computed by only including a subset of the data points in the model's evaluation. On the other hand, the test error rate here is computed by including all the data points in the evaluation, and therefore this estimation of the model's performance is more accurate and more robust.

In this activity, we used cross-validation to perform model evaluation on a problem involving a real dataset. Improving model evaluation is not the only purpose of using cross-validation, and it can be used to select the best model or parameters for a given problem as well.

> **Note**
>
> The solution for this activity can be found on page 315.

Model Selection with Cross-validation

Cross-validation provides us with a robust estimation of model performance on unseen examples. For this reason, it can be used to decide between two models for a particular problem or to decide which model parameters (or hyperparameters) to use for a particular problem. In these cases, we would like to find out which model or which set of model parameters/hyperparameters results in the lowest test error rate. Therefore, we will select that model or that set of parameters/hyperparameters for our problem.

In this section, you are going to practice using cross-validation for this purpose. You will learn how to define a set of hyperparameters for your deep learning model and then write user-defined functions in order to perform cross-validation on your model for each of the possible combinations of hyperparameters. You will then observe which combination of hyperparameters leads to the lowest test error rate, and that combination will be your choice for your final model.

Cross-Validation for Model Evaluation versus Model Selection

In this section, we are going to go deeper into what it means to use cross-validation for model evaluation versus model selection. We learned so far that evaluating a model on the training set results in an underestimation of the model's error rate on unseen examples, splitting the dataset into a training set and a test set gives us a more accurate estimation of the model's performance but suffers from high variance, and lastly, cross-validation results in a much more robust and accurate estimation of the model's performance on unseen examples. An illustration of the error rate estimations resulting from these three approaches for model evaluation is shown in Figure 4.9.

The figure shows the case where the error rate estimation in the training set/test set approach is slightly lower than the cross-validation estimation. However, it is important to remember that the training set/test set error rate can be higher than the cross-validation estimation error rate as well, depending on what data is included in the test set (hence the high variance problem). On the other hand, the error rate resulting from evaluation on the training set is always lower than the other two approaches.

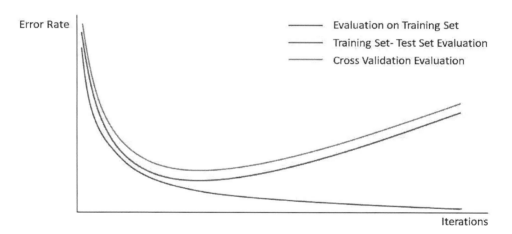

Figure 4.9: Illustration of the error rate estimations resulting from the three approaches to model evaluation

We have established that cross-validation leads to the best estimation of a model's performance on independent data examples. Knowing this, we can use cross-validation to decide which model to use for a particular problem. For example, if we have four different models and we would like to decide which one is a better fit for a particular dataset, we can train and evaluate each of the four models using cross-validation and choose the model with the lowest cross-validation error rate as our final model for the dataset. Figure 4.10 shows an illustration of the cross-validation error rate associated with four hypothetical models. It can be concluded from the figure that Model 1 is the best fit for the problem, while Model 4 is the worst choice. These four models could be deep neural networks with a different number of hidden layers and a different number of units in their hidden layers.

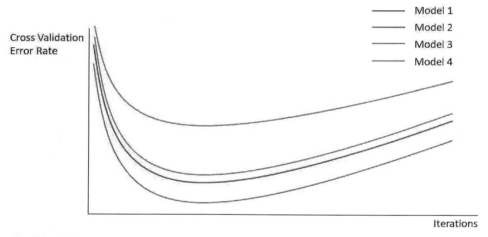

Figure 4.10: Illustration of cross-validation error rates associated with four hypothetical models

After we have found out which model is the best fit for a particular problem, the next step is choosing the best set of parameters or hyperparameters for that model. We discussed before that when building a deep neural network, several hyperparameters need to be selected for the model, and several choices are available for each of these hyperparameters. These hyperparameters include the type of activation function, loss function, and optimizer, plus the number of epochs and batch size. We can define the set of possible choices for each of these hyperparameters and then implement the model along with cross-validation to find the best combination of hyperparameters. An illustration of the cross-validation error rates associated with four different sets of hyper parameters for a hypothetical deep learning model is shown in Figure 4.11. It can be concluded from the figure that Set 1 is the best choice for this model.

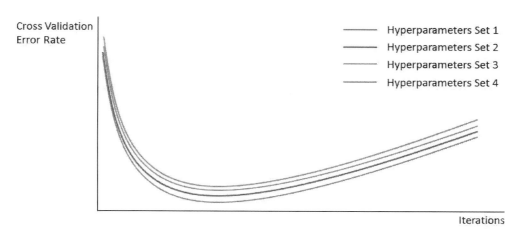

Figure 4.11: Illustration of cross-validation error rates associated with four different sets of hyper parameters for a hypothetical deep learning model

Exercise 13: Write User-Defined Functions to Implement Deep Learning Models with Cross-Validation

In this exercise, you will learn how to use cross-validation for the purpose of model selection.

Let's first execute the following code block to generate a simulated dataset of 500 data points of a regression problem, where each data point has 2 feature values. Similar to the previous exercises, let's assume that this dataset contains the changes in a company's stock price over 500 days. The two features included in the dataset are the changes of the stock price in the two previous trading days, and the output is the change of the stock price for today. The goal is to build a model to predict how much the stock price of this company will change on a specific day, based on the changes in the two previous trading days:

```
# create some simulated regression data

import numpy

from sklearn.datasets import make_regression

X, y = make_regression(n_samples=500, n_features=2, n_informative=2,
noise=5, random_state=0)

# Print the sizes of the dataset

print("Number of Examples in the Dataset = ", X.shape[0])

print("Number of Features for each example = ", X.shape[1])

# print output range

print("Output Range = [%f, %f]" %(min(y), max(y)))
```

Following is the code to implement the exercise:

1. Define three functions to return three Keras models. The first model should have one hidden layer of size 4, the second model should have one hidden layer of size 8, and the third model should have 2 hidden layers, the first layer of size 16, and second layer of size 8. Use ReLU activation function for all the hidden layers. The goal is to find out which of these three models leads to the lowest cross-validation error rate:

```python
# Defne the Keras models
from keras.models import Sequential
from keras.layers import Dense

def build_model_1():
    # build the Keras model_1
    model = Sequential()
    model.add(Dense(4, input_dim=2, activation='relu'))
    model.add(Dense(1))
    # Compile the model
    model.compile(loss='mean_squared_error', optimizer='adam')
    # return the model
    return model

def build_model_2():
    # build the Keras model_2
    model = Sequential()
    model.add(Dense(8, input_dim=2, activation='relu'))
    model.add(Dense(1))
    # Compile the model
    model.compile(loss='mean_squared_error', optimizer='adam')
    # return the model
    return model

def build_model_3():
    # build the Keras model_3
    model = Sequential()
    model.add(Dense(16, input_dim=2, activation='relu'))
    model.add(Dense(8, activation='relu'))
    model.add(Dense(1))
    # Compile the model
    model.compile(loss='mean_squared_error', optimizer='adam')
    # return the model
    return model
```

2. Write a loop to build the Keras wrapper and perform 3-fold cross-validation on the three models. Store the scores for each model:

```
# define a seed for random number generator so the result will be
reproducible
seed = 1
numpy.random.seed(seed)
# perform cross-validation on each model
from keras.wrappers.scikit_learn import KerasRegressor
from sklearn.model_selection import KFold
from sklearn.model_selection import cross_val_score
results =[]
models = [build_model_1, build_model_2, build_model_3]
# loop over three models
for m in range(len(models)):
    model = KerasRegressor(build_fn=models[m], epochs=300, batch_size=10,
verbose=0)
    kf = KFold(n_splits=3)
    result = cross_val_score(model, X, y, cv=kf)
    results.append(result)
```

3. Print the final cross-validation error rate for each of the models to find out which model has a lower error rate:

```
# print the cross-validation scores
print("Cross-validation Loss for Model 1 =", abs(results[0].mean()))
print("Cross-validation Loss for Model 2 =", abs(results[1].mean()))
print("Cross-validation Loss for Model 3 =", abs(results[2].mean()))
```

4. Here's an example output:

```
Cross Validation Loss for Model 1 = 4039.4971624321684
Cross Validation Loss for Model 2 = 189.19754301641356
Cross Validation Loss for Model 3 = 26.400964782187724
```

Figure 4.12: Final cross-validation error rates of all the three models

Model 3 results in the lowest error rate, so we will use it in the next steps.

5. Use cross-validation again in order to decide on the number of epochs and batch size for the model that resulted in the lowest cross-validation error rate. Write the code to perform 3-fold cross-validation on every possible combination of **epochs** and **batch-size** in the ranges **epochs=[300, 350]** and **batch_size=[10, 15]** and store the scores:

```
# define a seed for random number generator so the result will be
reproducible
numpy.random.seed(seed)
results =[]
epochs = [300, 350]
batches = [10, 15]

# Loop over pairs of epochs and batch_size
for e in range(len(epochs)):
    for b in range(len(batches)):
        model = KerasRegressor(build_fn= build_model_3, epochs= epochs[e],
batch_size= batches[b], verbose=0)
        kf = KFold(n_splits=3)
        result = cross_val_score(model, X, y, cv=kf)
        results.append(result)
```

> **Note**
>
> The preceding code block uses two **for** loops to perform 3-fold cross-validation for all possible combinations of **epochs** and **batch_size**. Since there are two choices for each of them, four different pairs are possible and therefore cross-validation will be performed four times.

6. Print the final cross-validation error rate for each of the **epochs/batch_size** pairs to find out which pair has the lowest error rate:

```
# Print cross-validation score for each possible pair of epochs, batch_
size
c = 0
for e in range(len(epochs)):
    for b in range(len(batches)):
        print("batch_size =", batches[b],", epochs =", epochs[e], ", Test
Loss =", abs(results[c].mean()))
        c += 1
```

7. Here's an example output:

```
batch_size = 10 , epochs = 300 , Test Loss = 26.264930088328608
batch_size = 15 , epochs = 300 , Test Loss = 28.685517518077663
batch_size = 10 , epochs = 350 , Test Loss = 25.695710466310718
batch_size = 15 , epochs = 350 , Test Loss = 25.761238063949587
```

Figure 4.13: Cross-validation losses for each pair of epochs and batch_size

As you can see the performance for **epochs=350** and **batch_size=10**, and for **epochs=350** and **batch_size=15** are almost the same. Therefore, we choose **epochs=350** and **batch_size=15** in the next step to speed up the process.

8. Use cross-validation again in order to decide on the activation function for the hidden layers and the optimizer for the model from **activations = ['relu', 'tanh']** and **optimizers = ['sgd', 'adam', 'rmsprop']**. Remember to use the best pair of **batch_size** and **epochs** from the previous step:

```
# Modify build_model_3 function
def build_model_3(activation='relu', optimizer='adam'):
    # build the Keras model_3
    model = Sequential()
    model.add(Dense(16, input_dim=2, activation=activation))
    model.add(Dense(8, activation=activation))
    model.add(Dense(1))
    # Compile the model
    model.compile(loss='mean_squared_error', optimizer=optimizer)
    # return the model
    return model


results =[]
activations = ['relu', 'tanh']
optimizers = ['sgd', 'adam', 'rmsprop']

#Define a seed for the random number generator so the result will be
reproducible
numpy.random.seed(seed)
# Loop over pairs of activation and optimizer
for o in range(len(optimizers)):
    for a in range(len(activations)):
        optimizer = optimizers[o]
        activation = activations[a]
        model = KerasRegressor(build_fn= build_model_3, epochs=350, batch_
```

```
        size=15, verbose=0)
            kf = KFold(n_splits=3)
            result = cross_val_score(model, X, y, cv=kf)
            results.append(result)
```

> **Note**
>
> Notice that we had to modify the **build_model_3** function by passing the
> **activation**, the **optimizer**, and their default values as arguments of the function.

9. Print the final cross-validation error rate for each pair of **activation** and **optimizer** to find out which pair has the lower error rate:

```
# Print cross-validation score for each possible pair of optimizer,
activation
c = 0
for o in range(len(optimizers)):
    for a in range(len(activations)):
        print("activation = ", activations[a],", optimizer = ",
optimizers[o], ", Test Loss = ", abs(results[c].mean()))
        c += 1
```

10. Here's the output:

```
activation =  relu , optimizer =  sgd , Test Loss =   27.48036775127323
activation =  tanh , optimizer =  sgd , Test Loss =   25.692216749794227
activation =  relu , optimizer =  adam , Test Loss =   27.608108422119944
activation =  tanh , optimizer =  adam , Test Loss =   26.73038675214977
activation =  relu , optimizer =  rmsprop , Test Loss =   26.72362163875697
activation =  tanh , optimizer =  rmsprop , Test Loss =   25.832545044784336
```

Figure 4.14: Cross-validation losses for each pair of optimizer and activation functions

11. The **activation='tanh'** and **optimizer='sgd'** pair results in the lowest error rate. Also, the result for the **activation='tanh'** and **optimizer='rmsprop'** pair is almost as good. Therefore, we can use either of the optimizers in the final model in order to predict how much the stock price of this company will change on a specific day.

Now you are ready to practice model selection using cross-validation on a problem involving a real dataset. In Activity 6, you will practice these steps further by implementing them by yourself on a classification problem with the diabetes dataset.

> **Note**
>
> Activities 2 and 3 involve performing k-fold cross-validation several times, and therefore the steps may take several minutes to complete. If it is taking too long to complete, you may want to try speeding up the process by decreasing the number of folds or the number of epochs or increasing the batch sizes. Obviously, if you do so, you will get different results from **expected outputs**, but the same principles still apply for selecting the model and hyperparameters.

Activity 6: Model Selection Using Cross-Validation for the Diabetes Diagnosis Classifier

In this activity, we are going to improve our classifier for the diabetes dataset by using cross-validation for model selection and hyperparameter selection:

1. Import the required packages. Load the dataset from the **data** subfolder of **Lesson04** folder from GitHub using **data=numpy.loadtxt("./data/pima-indians-diabetes.csv", delimiter=",")**. Store the training data in **X** using **X = data[:,0:8]**, and store the class labels in **y** using **y = data[:,8]**.

2. Define three functions each returning a different Keras model. The first Keras model will be a deep neural network with three hidden layers all of size 4 and ReLU activation functions. The second Keras model will be a deep neural network with two hidden layers, the first layer of size 16 and the second later of size 8, and ReLU activation functions. The third Keras model will be a deep neural network with two hidden layers both of size 8, and a ReLU activation function. Use the following values for the hyperparameters:

    ```
    optimizer = 'adam', loss = 'binary_crossentropy', metrics = ['accuracy']
    ```

3. Write the code to loop over the three models and perform 5-fold cross-validation on each of them (use **epochs=300** and **batch_size=5** in this step). Store all the cross-validation scores in a list and then print the results. Which model results in the best accuracy?

> **Note**
>
> Steps 3, 4, and 5 of this activity involve performing 5-fold cross-validation 3, 4, and 6 times, respectively. Therefore, they may take some time to complete.

4. Write the code to use **epochs = [250, 300]** and **batches = [5, 10]** values for **epochs** and **batch_size**. Perform 5-fold cross-validation for each possible pair on the Keras model that resulted in the best accuracy from step 3. Store all the cross-validation scores in a list and then print the results. Which **epochs** and **batch_size** pair results in the best accuracy?

5. Write the code to use **optimizers = ['rmsprop', 'adam','sgd']** and **activations = ['relu', 'tanh']** values for **optimizer** and **activation**. Perform 5-fold cross-validation for each possible pair on the Keras model that resulted in the best accuracy from step 3. Use the **batch_size** and **epochs** values that resulted in the best accuracy from step 4. Store all the cross-validation scores in a list and then print the results. Which **optimizer** and **activation** pair results in the best accuracy?

> **Note**
>
> Please note that there is randomness associated with initializing weights and biases in a deep neural network, and also with selecting examples to include in each fold when performing k-fold cross-validation. Therefore, you might get a completely different result if you run the exact same code twice. For this reason, it is important to set up seeds when building and training neural networks, and when performing cross-validation. By doing this, you can make sure that you are repeating the exact same neural network initialization and the exact same training sets and test sets when you re-run the code.

In this activity, you learned how to use cross-validation to evaluate deep neural networks in order to find the model that results in the lowest error rate for a **classification problem**. You also learned how to improve a given classification model by using cross-validation in order to find the best set of hyperparameters for it.

> **Note**
>
> The solution for this activity can be found on page 317.

Activity 7: Model Selection Using Cross-validation on the Boston House Prices Dataset

In this activity, you are going to practice model selection using cross-validation one more time. Here we are going to use **the Boston Housing Dataset** to build a model that predicts house prices in the suburbs of Boston given properties such as the number of bedrooms and their distance from employment centers.

The dataset can be loaded in scikit-learn using `sklearn.datasets.load_boston()`. It contains 506 house prices and for each of them, 13 attributes/features are included in the dataset. The goal is to build a deep neural network that receives the 13 features and predicts the price of the house. Since the output is a number, this is a regression problem:

1. Import all the required packages.

2. Print the input and output sizes to check the number of examples in the dataset and the number of features for each example. Also, you can print the range of the output (the output in this dataset represents the median value of owner-occupied homes in thousands of dollars).

3. Define three functions, each returning a different Keras model. The first Keras model will be a shallow neural network with 1 hidden layer of size 10 and a ReLU activation function. The second Keras model will be a deep neural network with 2 hidden layers of size 10 and a ReLU activation function in each layer. The third Keras model will be a deep neural network with 3 hidden layers of size 10 and a ReLU activation function in each layer.

Use the following values as well:

```
optimizer = 'adam', loss = 'mean_squared_error'
```

> **Note**
>
> Steps 4, 5, and 6 of this activity involve performing 5-fold cross-validation 3, 4, and 3 times, respectively. Therefore, they may take some time to complete.

4. Write the code to loop over the three models and perform 5-fold cross-validation on each of them (use **epochs=100** and **batch_size=5** in this step). Store all the cross-validation scores in a list and then print the results. Which model results in the lowest test error rate?

5. Write the code to use **epochs = [80, 100]** and **batches = [5, 10]** values for **epochs** and **batch_size**. Perform 5-fold cross-validation for each possible pair on the Keras model that resulted in the lowest test error rate from step 4. Store all the cross-validation scores in a list and then print the results. Which **epochs** and **batch_size** pair results in the lowest test error rate?

6. Write the code to use **optimizers = ['rmsprop', 'sgd', 'adam']** and perform 5-fold cross-validation for each possible optimizer on the Keras model that resulted in the lowest test error rate from step 4. Use the **batch_size** and **epochs** values that resulted in the lowest test error rate from step 5. Store all the cross-validation scores in a list and then print the results. Which **optimizer** results in the lowest test error rate?

In this activity, you learned how to use cross-validation to evaluate deep neural networks in order to find the model that results in the lowest error rate for a **regression problem**. Also, you learned how to improve a given regression model by using cross-validation in order to find the best set of hyperparameters for it.

> **Note**
>
> The solution for this activity can be found on page 322.

Summary

In this chapter, you learned about cross-validation, which is one of the most important resampling methods. It results in the best estimation of model performance on independent data. You learned about the basics of cross-validation and its two different variations, along with a comparison of them. You also learned about the Keras wrapper with scikit-learn, which is a very helpful tool that allows scikit-learn methods and functions such as performing cross-validation to be easily applied to Keras models. You learned the step-by-step process of implementing cross-validation in order to evaluate Keras deep learning models using the Keras wrapper with scikit-learn. Lastly, you learned that cross-validation estimations of model performance can be used to decide among different models for a particular problem or to decide about parameters (or hyperparameters) for a particular model. You practiced using cross-validation for this purpose by writing user-defined functions in order to perform cross-validation on different models or different possible combinations of hyperparameters and selecting the model or the set of hyperparameters that leads to the lowest test error rate for your final model.

In the next chapter, you will learn that what we did here in order to find the best set of hyperparameters for our model is, in fact, a technique called **hyperparameter tuning** or **hyperparameter optimization**. Also, you will learn how to perform hyperparameter tuning in scikit-learn by using a method called **grid search** and without the need to write user-defined functions to loop over possible combinations of hyperparameters.

5

Improving Model Accuracy

Learning Objectives

By the end of this chapter, you will be able to:

- Explain the concept of regularization
- Explain the procedures of different regularization techniques
- Apply L1 and L2 regularization to improve accuracy
- Apply dropout regularization to improve accuracy
- Describe grid search and random search hyperparameter optimizers in scikit-learn
- Use hyperparameter tuning in scikit-learn to improve model accuracy

In this chapter, we will learn about the concept of regularization and different regularization techniques. We will then use regularization to improve accuracy. We will also learn how to use hyperparameter tuning to improve model accuracy.

Introduction

Deep learning is not only about building neural networks, training them using an available dataset, and reporting the **model accuracy**. It involves trying to understand your model and the dataset, as well as moving beyond a basic model by improving it in many aspects. In this chapter, you will learn about two very important groups of techniques for improving machine learning models in general, and deep learning models in particular. These techniques are regularization methods and hyperparameter tuning.

Regarding **regularization** methods, we'll first answer the questions of why we need them and how they help. We'll then introduce two of the most important and most commonly used regularization techniques. You'll learn in great detail about parameter regularization and its two variations, **L1** and **L2** norm regularizations. You will then learn about a regularization technique, specifically designed for neural networks, called **dropout regulation**. You will also practice implementing each of these techniques on Keras models by completing activities that involve real-life datasets. We'll end the regularization discussion by briefly introducing some other regularization techniques that you may find helpful later in your work.

We will talk about the importance of **hyperparameter tuning**, especially for deep learning models, exploring how tuning the values of hyperparameters can dramatically affect model accuracy, as well as how it is extremely challenging to tune the many hyperparameters that require tuning when building deep neural networks. You will learn about two very helpful methods in scikit-learn that you can use for performing hyperparameter tuning on Keras models. You will learn about the benefits and drawbacks of each method, and how to combine them in order to gain the most from those methods. Lastly, you will practice implementing hyperparameter tuning for Keras models using scikit-learn optimizers by completing an activity.

Regularization

Since deep neural networks are highly flexible models, overfitting is an issue that can often arise when training them. Therefore, one very important part of becoming a deep learning expert is knowing how to detect overfitting, and subsequently how to address the overfitting problem in your model. Regularization techniques are an important group of methods specifically aimed at reducing overfitting in machine learning models. Understanding regularization techniques thoroughly and being able to apply them to your deep neural networks is an essential step toward building deep neural networks in order to solve real-life problems. In this section, you will learn about the underlying concepts of regularization, providing you with the foundation required for the following sections, where you will learn how to implement various types of regularization methods using Keras.

The Need for Regularization

The main goal of machine learning is to build models that perform well on not only the examples they are trained on, but also new examples that were not included in training. A good machine learning model is one that finds the form and the parameters of the true underlying process/function producing the training examples, but does not capture the noise associated with individual training examples. Such a machine learning model can generalize well to new examples produced by the same process later. The approaches we've discussed before – such as splitting a dataset into a training set and a test set, and cross-validation – were all designed to estimate the generalization ability of a trained model. In fact, the term used to refer to a test set error and cross-validation error is "generalization error." This simply means the error rate on examples that were not used in training. Once again, the main goal of machine learning is to build models with low generalization error rates.

In *Chapter 3, Deep Learning with Keras*, we discussed two very important issues with machine learning models: the issues of overfitting and underfitting. We stated that underfitting is the scenario where the estimated model is not flexible/complex enough to capture all the relations and patterns associated with the true process. This is a model with **high bias** and is detected when the training error is high. On the other hand, overfitting is the scenario when the model used for estimating the true process is too flexible/complex. This is a model with **high variance** and is diagnosed when there is a large gap between the training error and the generalization error. An overview of these scenarios for a binary classification problem is shown in the following figure:

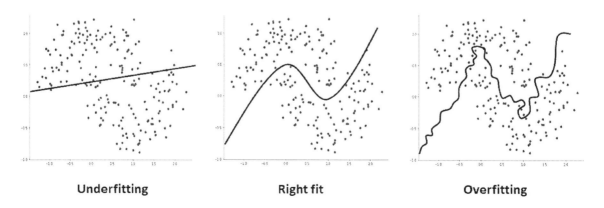

| Underfitting | Right fit | Overfitting |

Figure 5.1 Overview of three different models with different levels
of flexibility applied to the same dataset

Underfitting is a less problematic issue than overfitting. In fact, underfitting can be fixed easily by making the model more flexible/complex. In deep neural networks, this means changing the architecture of the network, making the network larger by adding more layers to it, or increasing the number of units in the layers. Similarly, there are simple solutions for addressing overfitting, such as making the model less flexible/complex (again, by changing the architecture of the network) or providing the network with more training examples. However, making the network less complex sometimes comes at the cost of a dramatic increase in bias or training error rate. The reason for this is that, most of the time, the cause of overfitting is not the flexibility of the model but too few training examples. On the other hand, providing more data examples in order to decrease overfitting is not always possible. As a result, finding ways to reduce the generalization error while keeping model complexity and the number of training examples fixed is both important and challenging. That is why we need regularization techniques when building highly flexible machine learning models such as deep neural networks.

That is why we need regularization techniques when building highly flexible machine learning models, such as deep neural networks, to suppress the flexibility of the model so that it cannot overfit to individual examples.

Reducing Overfitting with Regularization

Regularization methods try to modify the learning algorithm in a way that reduces the variance of the model. By decreasing the variance, regularization techniques intend to reduce the generalization error while not increasing the training error (or, at least, not increasing the training error drastically).

Regularization methods provide some kind of restriction that helps with the stability of the model. There are several ways that this can be achieved. One of the most common ways of performing regularization on deep neural networks is by putting some type of penalizing term on weights, therefore keeping the weights small. Keeping the weights small makes the network less sensitive to noise in individual data examples. Weights in a neural network are, in fact, the coefficients that determine how small or big an effect each processing unit will have on the final output of the network. If the units have large weights, it means that each of them will have a significant influence on the output. Combining all the large influences caused by each processing unit will result in many fluctuations in the final output. On the other hand, keeping the weights small reduces the amount of influence each unit will have on the final output. Indeed, by keeping the weights near zero, some of the units will have almost no effect on the output. Training a large neural network where each unit has little or no effect on the output is the equivalent of training a much simpler network, and so variance and overfitting are reduced. An illustration of such a case is shown in the following figure:

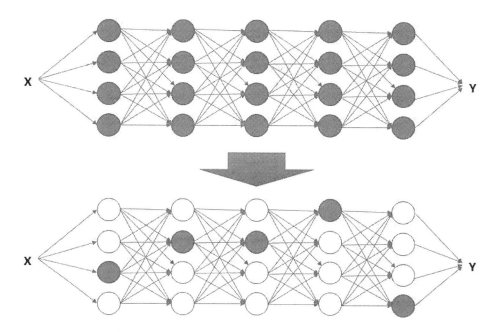

Figure 5.2. Schematic view of how regularization zeroes out the effect of some units in a large network. In the bottom network, white units have near-zero effect on the output

So far, we have learned about the concepts behind regularization. In the next section, we will look at the most common methods of regularization for deep learning models, along with how to implement them in Keras.

L1 and L2 Regularization

The most common type of regularization for deep learning models is the one that keeps the weights of the network small. This type of regularization is called **weight regularization** and has two different variations: **L2 regularization** and **L1 regularization**. In this section, you will learn about these regularization methods in detail, along with how to implement them in Keras. Additionally, you will practice applying them to real-life problems and observe how they can improve the performance of a model.

L1 and L2 Regularization Formulation

In weight regularization, a penalizing term is added to the loss function. This term is either L2 norm (the sum of the squared values) of the weights, or L1 norm (the sum of the absolute values) of the weights. If L1 norm is used, then it will be called **L1 regularization**. If L2 norm is used, then it will be called **L2 regularization**. In each case, the sum is multiplied by a hyperparameter called a **regularization parameter** (*lambda*).

Therefore, for L1 regularization, the formula is as follows:

Loss function = Old loss function + lambda * sum of absolute values of the weights

And for L2 regularization, the formula is as follows:

Loss function = Old loss function + lambda * sum of squared values of the weights

Lambda can take any value between 0 and 1, where *lambda=0* means no penalty at all (equivalent to a network with no regularization), and *lambda=1* means full penalty.

Like every other hyperparameter, the right value for *lambda* can be selected by trying out different values and observing which value provides a lower generalization error. In fact, a good practice is to start with a network with no regularization and observe the results. Then, perform regularization with increasing values of lambda, as in 0.001, 0.01, 0.1, 0.5, ..., and observe the results in each case in order to figure out how much penalizing on the weights values is suitable for a particular problem.

In each iteration of the optimization algorithm with regularization, the weights (w) become smaller and smaller. That is why weight regularization is commonly referred to as **weight decay**.

So far, we have only discussed regularizing weights in a deep neural network. However, you need to keep in mind that the same procedure can be applied to biases as well. More precisely, we can update the loss function again by adding a bias penalizing term to it as well, and therefore keep values of biases small during the training of a neural network.

> **Note**
>
> If you perform regularization by adding two terms to the loss function, one for penalizing weights and one for penalizing biases, then we call it **parameter regularization** instead of weight regularization.

However, regularizing bias values is not done very commonly in deep learning. The reason for this is that weights are much more important parameters of neural networks. In fact, usually, adding another term to regularize biases will not change the results dramatically in comparison to regularizing only weight values.

L2 regularization is the most common regularizations technique used in machine learning in general. The difference between L1 regularization and L2 regularization is that L1 results in a more sparse weights matrix, meaning there are more weights equal to zero, and therefore more nodes that are completely removed from the network. L2 regularization, on the other hand, is more subtle. It decreases the weights drastically, but at the same time leaves you with fewer weights equal to 0. It is also possible to perform both L1 and L2 regularization at the same time.

Now that you have learned about how L1 and L2 regularization work, you are ready to move on to implementing L1 and L2 regularization on deep neural networks in Keras.

L1 and L2 Regularization Implementation in Keras

Keras provides a regularization API, which can be used to add penalizing terms to the loss function in order to regularize weights or biases in each layer of a deep neural network. In order to define the penalty term or **regularizer**, you need to define the desired regularization method under `keras.regularizers`.

For example, to define an L1 **regularizer** with *lambda=0.01*, you can write this:

```
from keras.regularizers import l1
keras.regularizers.l1(0.01)
```

Similarly, to define an L2 **regularizer** with *lambda=0.01*, you can write this:

```
from keras.regularizers import l2
keras.regularizers.l2(0.01)
```

Finally, to perform both L1 and L2 **regularizers** with *lambda=0.01*, you can write this:

```
from keras.regularizers import l1_l2
keras.regularizers.l1_l2(l1=0.01, l2=0.01)
```

Each of these **regularizers** can be later applied to weights and/or biases in a layer. For example, if we would like to apply L2 regularization (with *lambda=0.01*) on both the weights and biases of a dense layer with eight nodes, we can write this:

```
from keras.layers import Dense
from keras.regularizers import l2
model.add(Dense(8, kernel_regularizer=l2(0.01), bias_regularizer=l2(0.01)))
```

We will practice implementing L1 and L2 regularization further in *Activity* 8, in which you will apply regularization on the deep learning model for the diabetes dataset and observe how the results change in comparison to previous activities on this dataset.

> **Note**
>
> All activities will be developed in the Jupyter Notebook. Please download the GitHub repository with all the prepared templates from https://github.com/TrainingByPackt/Applied-Deep-Learning-with-Keras/tree/master/Lesson05.

Activity 8: Weight Regularization on a Diabetes Diagnosis Classifier

We learned about the diabetes dataset in the activities of previous chapters. The dataset consists of information for 768 patients, and for each patient, 8 different measurements are available, as well as a class label, which can only take two values: **1** indicating diabetic (268 examples), and **0** indicating non-diabetic (500 examples). In this activity, you will build a Keras model to perform classification on this dataset according to the network architecture and hyperparameter values that we achieved in previous chapters. The goal is to apply different types of weight regularization on the model and observe how each type changes the result.

In this activity, we will use the training set/test set approach to perform evaluation for two reasons. First, since we are going to try several different regularizers, performing cross-validation will take a long time. Second, we would like to plot the trends in training error and test error in order to understand, in a visual way, how regularization prevents the model from overfitting to data examples.

Here are the steps you need to complete in this activity:

1. Load the dataset from the **data** subfolder of **Lesson05** from GitHub using `data=numpy.loadtxt("./data/pima-indians-diabetes.csv", delimiter=",")`. Store the training data in **X** using `X = data[:,0:8]`, and the class labels in **y** using `y = data[:,8]`. Split the dataset into a training set and a test set using the **sklearn. model_selection.train_test_split** method. Hold back 30% of the data examples for the test set.

2. Define a Keras model with two hidden layers of size 8 to perform the classification. Use these values for the hyperparameters: `activation='relu'`, `loss='binary_crossentropy'`, `optimizer='sgd'`, `metrics=['accuracy']`, `batch_size=10`, and `epochs=300`.

3. Train the model on the training set, and evaluate with the test set. Store the training loss and test loss at every iteration. After training is complete, plot the trends in training error and test error (change the limits of the vertical axis to (0, 1), so you can better observe the changes in losses). What is the minimum error rate on the test set?

4. Add L2 regularizers with *lambda*=0.01 to the hidden layers of your model and repeat the training. After training is complete, plot the trends in training error and test error. What is the minimum error rate on the test set?

5. Repeat the previous step for *lambda*=0.1 and *lambda*=0.5, train the model for each value of *lambda*, and report the results. Which value of *lambda* is a better choice for performing L2 regularization on this deep learning model and this dataset?

6. Repeat the previous step, this time with L1 regularizers for *lambda*=0.01 and *lambda*=0.1, train the model for each value of *lambda*, and report the results. Which value of *lambda* is a better choice for performing L1 regularization on this deep learning model and this dataset?

7. Add L1_L2 regularizers with L1 *lambda* equal to 0.01 and L2 *lambda*=0.1 to the hidden layers of your model and repeat the training. After training is complete, plot the trends in training error and test error. What is the minimum error rate on the test set?

In this activity, you practiced implementing L1 and L2 **weight regularizations** for a real-life problem and compared the results of the regularized model with those of a model without any regularization.

> **Note**
>
> The solution for this activity can be found on page 327.

Dropout Regularization

In this section, you will learn about how dropout regularization works, how it helps with reducing overfitting, and how to implement it using Keras. Lastly, you will have the chance to practice what you have learned about dropout by completing an activity involving a real-life dataset.

Principles of Dropout Regularization

Dropout regularization works by randomly removing nodes from a neural network during training. More precisely, dropout sets up a probability on each node that determines the chance of that node being included in the training at each iteration of the learning algorithm. Imagine we have a large neural network where a dropout chance of 0.5 is assigned to each node. Therefore, at each iteration, the learning algorithm flips a coin for each node to decide whether that node will be removed from the network or not. An illustration of such a process is shown in the following figure. This process is repeated at each iteration; this means that at each iteration, randomly selected nodes are removed from the network, and so the parameter-updating process is done on a different and, of book, smaller network. For example, the network shown at the bottom of Figure 5.3 will be used for one iteration of the training only. For the next iteration, some other randomly selected nodes will be crossed out from the top network, and therefore the resulting network from removing those nodes will be different from the bottom network in the figure.

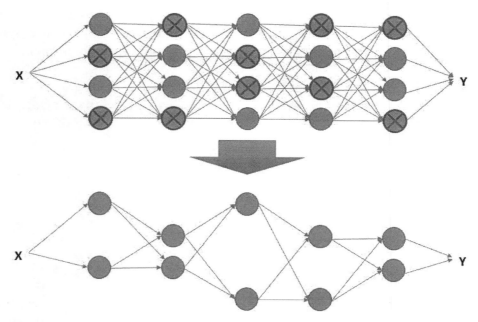

Figure 5.3: Illustration of removing nodes from a deep neural network in dropout regularization

When some nodes are chosen to be removed/ignored in an iteration of a learning algorithm, it means that they won't participate in the parameter-updating process at all in that iteration. More precisely, the forward propagation to predict the output, the loss computation, and the backpropagation to compute the derivatives are all to be done on the smaller network with some nodes removed. Consequently, parameter updating will be done only on the nodes that are present in the network in that iteration, and the weights and biases of removed nodes won't be updated.

However, it is important to keep in mind that to evaluate the performance of the model on the test set or hold-out set, the original complete network is always used. If we perform the evaluation of a network with random nodes deleted from it, noise will be introduced to the results, and this is not desirable.

In **dropout** regularization, **training** is always performed on the networks that result from randomly selected nodes removed from the original network. **Evaluation** is always performed using the original network.

Reducing Overfitting with Dropout

In this section, we are going to discuss the concepts behind using dropout as a regularization method. As discussed before, the goal of regularization techniques is to prevent a model from overfitting data. Therefore, we are going to look at explanations of how randomly removing a portion of nodes from a neural network helps to reduce variance and overfitting. The most obvious explanation is that by removing nodes from a network, we are performing training on a smaller network in comparison to the original network. As you learned before, a smaller neural network provides less flexibility, and therefore the chance of the network overfitting to data is lower.

There is another reason why dropout regularization does such a good job of reducing overfitting: by randomly removing inputs at each layer in a deep neural network, the overall network becomes less sensitive to single inputs. We know that during training a neural network, the weights are updated in a way that the final model will fit to the training examples. By removing some of the weights from the training process at random, dropout forces other weights to participate in learning the patterns related to the training examples at that iteration, and therefore the final weight values will be better spread out. In other words, instead of some weights updating too much in order to fit to some input values, all the weights learn to participate in learning those input values and, consequently, overfitting decreases. This is why performing dropout results in a much more robust model in comparison to simply using a smaller network. In fact, dropout regularization usually tends to work better on larger networks. Now that you have learned all about the underlying procedure of dropout and the reasons behind its effectiveness, we can move on to implementing dropout regularization in Keras.

Exercise 14: Dropout Implementation in Keras

Dropout regularization is provided as a core layer in Keras. As such, you can add dropout to your model in the same way that you would add layers to your network. When defining a dropout layer in Keras, you need to provide the **rate** hyperparameter as an argument. **rate** can take any value between 0 and 1, and determines the portions of input units to be removed/ignored. In this exercise, you will learn the step-by-step process of implementing a Keras deep learning model with dropout layers.

First, execute the following code block to generate a simulated dataset of 400 data points of two classes, where each data example has 10 feature values. Also, split the dataset into a training set and a test set:

```
# create some simulated classification data
import numpy
numpy.random.seed(1)
from sklearn.datasets import make_classification
X, y = make_classification(n_samples=400, n_features=10, n_classes=2)


# Split the dataset into training set and test set with a 0.7-0.3 ratio
from sklearn.model_selection import train_test_split
X_train, X_test, y_train, y_test = train_test_split(X, y, test_size=0.3,
random_state=0)
```

Let's assume that this dataset represents a real-life scenario involving a binary classification problem. For example, the dataset may consist of the credit card history for 400 individuals. The 10 features included in the dataset may represent information such as payment history, length of credit history, and recent activity for each of the individuals. The output classes represent the likelihood of default and can take either 0 or 1; output=0 means that the individual will pay their credit card debt, and output=1 means that the individual will default. A company that issues some type of credit card is interested in building a model using this dataset in order to predict whether a potential customer has a high chance of defaulting. Now, let's go through the steps:

1. Import all the necessary dependencies. Build a three-layer Keras model without dropout regularization, train the model, and print the error rate on the test set:

    ```
    #Define your model
    from keras.models import Sequential
    from keras.layers import Dense, Activation
    ```

```
numpy.random.seed(1)

model = Sequential()
model.add(Dense(16, activation='relu', input_dim=10))
model.add(Dense(8, activation='relu'))
model.add(Dense(4, activation='relu'))
model.add(Dense(1, activation='sigmoid'))
```

2. Choose the loss function as binary cross-entropy and the optimizer as **sgd** and train the model for 300 epochs with batch_size=5 on the training set. Then evaluate the trained model on the test set:

```
model.compile(optimizer='sgd', loss='binary_crossentropy')
# train the model
model.fit(X_train, y_train, epochs=300, batch_size=5, verbose=0)
# evaluate on test set
print("Test Loss =", model.evaluate(X_test, y_test))
```

Here's the expected output:

```
120/120 [==============================] - 0s 308us/step
Test Loss = 0.37075048089027407
```

Figure 5.4: Error rate of the test set

Therefore, the test error rate for predicting whether an individual will default on their credit card or not after training the model for 300 epochs is equal to 37.07%.

3. Add dropout regularization of **rate=0.5** to the first hidden layer of your model and repeat the training and evaluation:

```
# define the keras model with dropout in the first hidden layer
from keras.layers import Dropout
numpy.random.seed(1)

model = Sequential()
model.add(Dense(16, activation='relu', input_dim=10))
model.add(Dropout(0.5))
model.add(Dense(8, activation='relu'))
model.add(Dense(4, activation='relu'))
model.add(Dense(1, activation='sigmoid'))
```

```
model.compile(optimizer='sgd', loss='binary_crossentropy')
# train the model
model.fit(X_train, y_train, epochs=300, batch_size=5, verbose=0)
# evaluate on test set
print("Test Loss =", model.evaluate(X_test, y_test))
```

Here's the expected output:

```
120/120 [==============================] - 0s 492us/step
Test Loss = 0.16076135536034902
```

Figure 5.5: Error rate of the test set with dropout regularization rate=0.5 added in the first hidden layer

After adding dropout regularization with **rate=0.5** to the first layer of the network, the test error rate is reduced from 37.07% to 16.08%.

4. Add dropout layers with **rate=0.2** to the second layer and third layer of the model from the previous step and repeat the training and evaluation:

```
# define the keras model with dropout in all hidden layers
numpy.random.seed(1)

model = Sequential()
model.add(Dense(16, activation='relu', input_dim=10))
model.add(Dropout(0.5))
model.add(Dense(8, activation='relu'))
model.add(Dropout(0.2))
model.add(Dense(4, activation='relu'))
model.add(Dropout(0.2))
model.add(Dense(1, activation='sigmoid'))

model.compile(optimizer='sgd', loss='binary_crossentropy')
# train the model
model.fit(X_train, y_train, epochs=300, batch_size=5, verbose=0)
# evaluate on test set
print("Test Loss =", model.evaluate(X_test, y_test))
```

Here's the expected output:

```
120/120 [==============================] - 0s 650us/step
Test Loss = 0.14980176190535227
```

Figure 5.6: Error rate of the test set with dropout regularizations of rate=0.5 added in the first hidden layer, rate=0.2 added in the second and third hidden layers

By keeping the dropout regularization of **rate=0.5** in the first layer while adding dropout regularizations of **rate=0.2** to the second and third layers, the test error rate is reduced from 16.08% to 14.98%.

As you saw in this exercise, you can also apply dropout with different rates to the different layers depending on how much overfitting you think can happen in those layers. Usually, we prefer not to perform dropout on the input layer and output layer. Regarding the hidden layers, we need to tune the **rate** values and observe the results in order to decide what value is best suited to a particular problem. In the following activity, you will practice implementing deep learning models along with dropout regularization in Keras on the Boston Housing dataset.

Activity 9: Dropout Regularization on Boston Housing Dataset

In *Activity 7 of Chapter 4, Evaluating your Model with Cross Validation with Keras Wrappers*, you used the Boston housing dataset in order to build a model for predicting house prices in the suburbs of Boston given properties of the houses, such as the number of bedrooms, their distance from employment centers, the neighborhood crime rate, and so on. The dataset contains 506 house prices, and for each of them, 13 attributes/features are included in the dataset.

In this activity, you will start with the model from *Activity 7 of Chapter 4, Evaluating your Model with Cross Validation with Keras Wrappers*. You will use the training set/test set approach to train and evaluate the model, plot the trends in training error and the generalization error, and observe the model overfitting to data examples. You will then attempt to improve model performance by addressing the overfitting issue through the use of dropout regularization. You will particularly try to find out which layers you should add dropout regularization to and what **rate** value will improve this specific model the most. Here are the steps you need to complete:

1. Load the dataset using **sklearn.datasets.load_boston()**. The dataset is also stored in the **data** subfolder of **Lesson05** GitHub repository. Split the dataset into a training set and a test set with a 3.7 ratio. Scale the training examples to have a mean equal to 0 and a variance equal to 1. Apply the same scaling to the test data examples.

2. Define a Keras model with 2 hidden layers of size 10 to predict the house prices. Use these values for the hyperparameters: **activation='relu'**, **loss='mean_squared_error'**, **optimizer='rmsprop'**, **batch_size=5**, and **epochs=150**.

3. Train the model on the training set, then evaluate on the test set. Store the training loss and test loss at every iteration. After training is completed, plot the trends in training error and test error. What are the lowest error rates on the training set and the test set?

4. Add dropout regularization with `rate=0.2` to the first hidden layer of your model and repeat the training (since training with dropout takes longer, train for 200 epochs). After training is completed, plot the trends in training error and test error. What are the lowest error rates on the training set and the test set?

5. Repeat the previous step, this time adding dropout regularization with `rate=0.2` to both hidden layers of your model, train the model, and report the results.

6. Repeat the previous step, this time with `rate=0.1`, train the model, and report the results.

7. Which dropout regularization has resulted in the best performance on this deep learning model and this dataset so far?

In this activity, you learned how to implement dropout regularization in Keras and practiced it on a problem involving the Boston Housing dataset. Dropout regularization is specifically designed for the purpose of reducing overfitting in neural networks and works by randomly removing nodes from a neural network during the training. This procedure results in a neural network with well spread out weight values, which leads to less overfitting to individual data examples.

> **Note**
>
> The solution for this activity can be found on page 337.

Other Regularization Methods

In this section, you will learn briefly about some other regularization techniques that are commonly used and have been shown to be effective in deep learning. It is important to keep in mind that regularization is a wide-ranging and active research field in machine learning. As a result, covering all available regularization methods in one chapter is not possible (and most likely not necessary, especially in a book on applied deep learning). Therefore, in this section, we will briefly cover three more regularization methods, called **early stopping**, **data augmentation**, and **adding noise**. You will learn briefly about their underlying ideas, and you'll gain a few tips and recommendations on how to use them.

Early Stopping

We discussed earlier in this chapter that the main assumption in machine learning is that there is a true function/process that produces training examples. However, this process is unknown and there is no explicit way to find it. Not only is there no way to find the exact underlying process – choosing a model with the right level of flexibility or complexity for estimating the process is challenging as well. Therefore, one good practice is to select a highly flexible model, such as a deep neural network, to model the process and monitor the training process carefully. By monitoring the training process, we can train the model just enough for it to capture the form of the true process, and we can stop the training right before it starts to overfit to individual data examples. This is the underlying idea behind early stopping. We discussed the idea of early stopping briefly before in the *Model Evaluation* section of *Chapter 3, Deep Learning with Keras*. We stated there that by monitoring and observing the changes in training error and test error during training, we can determine how little training is too little and how much training is too much. Figure 5.7 shows a view of the changes in training error and test error when a highly flexible model is trained on a dataset. As can be seen from the figure, the training needs to stop in the region labeled **Right Fit** to avoid overfitting:

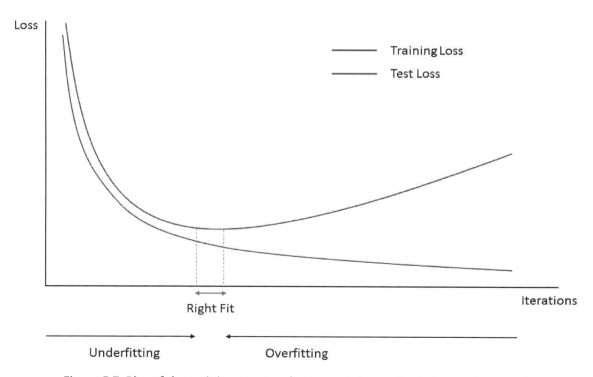

Figure 5.7: Plot of the training error and test error during the training of a model

In *Chapter 3, Deep Learning with Keras,* we practiced storing and plotting changes in training error and test error in order to identify overfitting happening. You learned that you can provide a validation set or test set when training a Keras model and store the metrics values for each of them at each epoch of training by writing this:

```
history=model.fit(X_traing, y_train, validation_data=(X_test, y_test),
epochs=epochs)
```

Here, you are going to learn how to implement early stopping in Keras. This means forcing the Keras model to stop the training when a desired metric, for example, the test error rate, is not improving anymore. In order to do so, you need to define an **EarlyStopping()** callback and provide it as an argument to **model.fit()**.

When defining an **EarlyStopping()** callback, you need to provide it with the right arguments. The first argument is **monitor**, which determines what metric will be monitored during training for the purpose of performing early stopping. Usually, **monitor='val_loss'** is a good choice, meaning that we would like to monitor the test error rate. Also, depending on what argument you have chosen for **monitor**, you need to set the **mode** argument to either **'min'** or **'max'**. If the metric is error/loss, we would like to minimize it. For example, the following code block defines an **EarlyStopping()** callback that monitors the test error during training and detects if it is not decreasing anymore:

```
from keras.callbacks import EarlyStopping
es_callback = EarlyStopping(monitor='val_loss', mode='min')
```

If there are a lot of fluctuations or noise in the error rates, it is probably not a good idea to stop the training at the first epoch of not improving. For this reason, we can set the **patience** argument to a number of epochs in order to give the early stopping method some time to monitor the desired metric for a longer while before stopping the training process:

```
es_callback = EarlyStopping(monitor='val_loss', mode='min', patience=20)
```

We also can modify the **EarlyStopping()** callback in order to stop the training if a minimum of improvement in the **monitor** metric has not happened in the past epoch, or the **monitor** metric has reached a baseline level:

```
es_callback = EarlyStopping(monitor='val_loss', mode='min', min_delta=1)
es_callback = EarlyStopping(monitor='val_loss', mode='min', baseline=0.2)
```

After you are done with defining the `EarlyStopping()` callback, you can provide it as a `callbacks` argument to `model.fit()` and train the model. The training will automatically stop according to the `EarlyStopping()` callback:

```
history=model.fit(X_traing, y_train, validation_data=(X_test, y_test),
epochs=epochs, callbacks=[es_callback])
```

Exercise 15: Implementing Early Stopping in Keras

In this exercise, you will learn how to implement early stopping on a Keras deep learning model. In order to do so, let's first execute the following code block to generate a simulated dataset of 400 data points of two classes, where each data example has 10 feature values, and also split the dataset into a training set and a test set. Similar to what we did in the previous exercise, we assume that this dataset contains the credit card history for 400 individuals. The 10 features included in the dataset may represent information such as payment history, length of credit history, and recent activity for each of the individuals. The output classes represent the likelihood of defaulting and can take either 0 or 1; output=0 means that the individual will pay their credit card debt, and output=1 means that the individual will default. The goal is to build a model in order to predict whether an individual who has applied for a new credit card has a high chance of defaulting:

```
# create some simulated classification data

import numpy

numpy.random.seed(1)

from sklearn.datasets import make_classification

X, y = make_classification(n_samples=400, n_features=10, n_classes=2)


# Split the dataset into training set and test set with a 0.7-0.3 ratio

from sklearn.model_selection import train_test_split

X_train, X_test, y_train, y_test = train_test_split(X, y, test_size=0.3,
random_state=0)
```

Now, let's go through the steps:

1. Import all the necessary dependencies. Build a three-layer Keras model without early stopping, train the model for 300 epochs, and plot the trends in training error and test error:

```
#Define your model
from keras.models import Sequential
from keras.layers import Dense, Activation

numpy.random.seed(1)

model = Sequential()
model.add(Dense(16, activation='relu', input_dim=10))
model.add(Dense(8, activation='relu'))
model.add(Dense(4, activation='relu'))
model.add(Dense(1, activation='sigmoid'))
```

2. Choose the **loss** function as binary cross-entropy and the optimizer as SGD, train the model for 300 epochs with batch_size=5, while storing the training error and the test error at every iteration:

```
model.compile(optimizer='sgd', loss='binary_crossentropy')
# train the model
history = model.fit(X_train, y_train, validation_data=(X_test, y_test),
epochs=300, batch_size=5, verbose=0)
```

3. Import the required packages for plotting:

```
import matplotlib.pyplot as plt
import matplotlib
%matplotlib inline
```

4. Plot the training error and test error:

```
matplotlib.rcParams['figure.figsize'] = (10.0, 8.0)
plt.plot(history.history['loss'])
plt.plot(history.history['val_loss'])
plt.ylim(0,1)
plt.ylabel('loss')
plt.xlabel('epoch')
plt.legend(['train loss', 'test loss'], loc='upper right')
```

Here's the expected output:

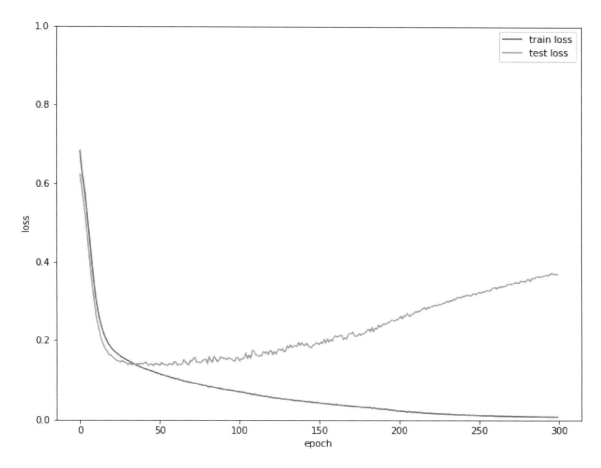

Figure 5.8: Plot of training error and test error during the training
of the model without early stopping

As you can see from the plot, training the model for 300 epochs results in a large gap between the training error and test error, which is indicative of overfitting.

5. Repeat the previous steps while adding **es_callback = EarlyStopping(monitor='val_loss', mode='min')** to the training. Repeat step 3 to plot the training error and test error:

```
#Define your model with early stopping on test error
from keras.callbacks import EarlyStopping
numpy.random.seed(1)

model = Sequential()
model.add(Dense(16, activation='relu', input_dim=10))
model.add(Dense(8, activation='relu'))
model.add(Dense(4, activation='relu'))
model.add(Dense(1, activation='sigmoid'))
#  Choose the loss function to be binary cross entropy and the optimizer
to be SGD for training the model
model.compile(optimizer='sgd', loss='binary_crossentropy')
# define the early stopping callback
es_callback = EarlyStopping(monitor='val_loss', mode='min')
# train the model
history=model.fit(X_train, y_train, validation_data=(X_test, y_test),
epochs=300, batch_size=5, callbacks=[es_callback], verbose=0)
```

Here's the expected output:

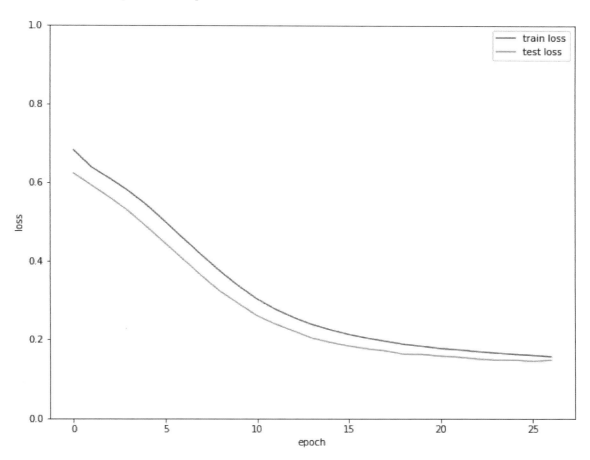

Figure 5.9: Plot of training error and test error during the training
of the model with early stopping (patience=0)

By adding the early stopping callback with `patience=0` to the model, the training
process automatically stops after about 25 epochs.

6. Repeat the previous step while adding **patience=10** to your early stopping callback. Repeat step 3 to plot the training error and test error:

```
#Define your model with early stopping on test error with patience=10
from keras.callbacks import EarlyStopping
numpy.random.seed(1)

model = Sequential()
model.add(Dense(16, activation='relu', input_dim=10))
model.add(Dense(8, activation='relu'))
model.add(Dense(4, activation='relu'))
model.add(Dense(1, activation='sigmoid'))
# Choose the loss function to be binary cross entropy and the optimizer to
be SGD for training the model
model.compile(optimizer='sgd', loss='binary_crossentropy')
# define the early stopping callback
es_callback = EarlyStopping(monitor='val_loss', mode='min', patience=10)
# train the model
history=model.fit(X_train, y_train, validation_data=(X_test, y_test),
epochs=300, batch_size=5, callbacks=[es_callback], verbose=0)
```

Here's the expected output:

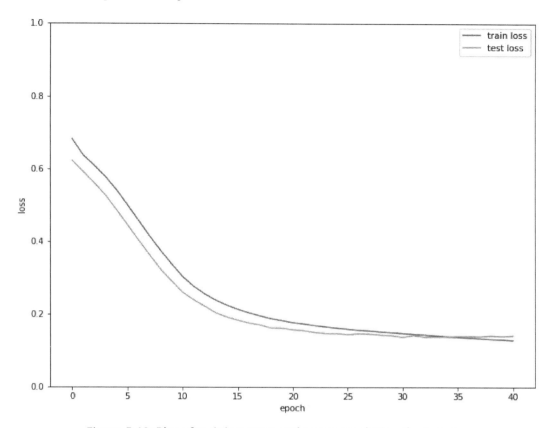

Figure 5.10: Plot of training error and test error during the training
of the model with early stopping (patience=10)

By adding the early stopping callback with **patience=10** to the model, the training
process automatically stops after about 40 epochs.

Data Augmentation

Data augmentation is a regularization technique that tries to address overfitting by training the model on more training examples in an inexpensive way. In data augmentation, the available data is transformed in different ways and then fed to the model as new training data. This type of regularization has been shown to be effective, especially for some specific applications, such as object detection/recognition in computer vision and speech processing. For example, in computer vision applications, you can simply double or triple the size of your training dataset by adding mirrored versions and rotated versions of each image to the dataset. The new training examples generated by these transformations are obviously not as good as original training examples. However, they are shown to improve the model in terms of overfitting.

One challenging aspect of performing data augmentation is choosing the right transformations to be performed on data. Transformations need to be selected carefully depending on the type of dataset and the application.

Adding Noise

The underlying idea behind regularizing a model by adding noise to the data is the same as that for data augmentation regularization. Training a deep neural network on a small dataset increases the chance of the network memorizing single data examples as opposed to capturing the relations between inputs and outputs. This will result in poor performance on new data later, which is indicative of the model overfitting to the training data. In contrast, training a model on a large dataset increases the chance of the model capturing the true underlying process instead of memorizing single data points, and therefore reduces the chances of overfitting.

One way to expand the training data and reduce overfitting is to generate new data examples by injecting noise into the available data. This type of regularization has been shown to reduce overfitting to an extent that is comparable to weight regularization techniques. By adding different versions of a single example to the training data (each created by adding a small amount of noise to the original example), we can ensure that the model will not fit to the noise in the data. Additionally, increasing the size of the training dataset by including these modified examples provides the model with a better representation of the underlying data generation process, and increases the chance of the model learning the true process.

In deep learning applications, you can improve model performance by adding noise to the weights or activations of the hidden layers, or gradients of the network, or even to the output layer, as well as adding noise to the training examples (input layer). Deciding where to add noise in a deep neural network is another challenge that needs to be addressed by trying different networks and observing the results.

In Keras, you can easily define noise as a layer and add it to your model. For example, to add Gaussian noise with standard deviation of 0.1 (the mean is equal to 0) to your model; you can write this:

```
from keras.layers import GaussianNoise

model.add(GaussianNoise(0.1))
```

The code given here will add Gaussian noise to the outputs/activations of the first hidden layer of the model:

```
model = Sequential()

model.add(Dense(4, input_dim=30, activation='relu'))

model.add(GaussianNoise(0.01))

model.add(Dense(4, activation='relu'))

model.add(Dense(4, activation='relu'))

model.add(Dense(1, activation='sigmoid'))
```

In this section, you learned briefly about three regularization methods: early stopping, data augmentation, and adding noise. In addition to their basic concepts and procedures, you also learned about how they reduce overfitting and were given some tips and recommendations on how to use them.

Hyperparameter Tuning with scikit-learn

Hyperparameter tuning is a very important technique for improving the performance of deep learning models. In *Chapter 4, Evaluating your Model with Cross Validation with Keras Wrappers*, you learned about using a Keras wrapper with scikit-learn, which allows for Keras models to be used in a scikit-learn workflow. As a result, different general machine learning and data analysis tools and methods available in scikit-learn can be applied to Keras deep learning models. Among those methods are scikit-learn hyperparameter optimizers. In the previous chapter, you learned how to perform hyperparameter tuning by writing user-defined functions to loop over possible values for each hyperparameter. In this section, you will learn how to perform it in a much easier way by using various hyperparameter optimization methods available in scikit-learn. You will also get to practice applying those methods by completing an activity involving a real-life dataset.

Grid Search with scikit-learn

So far, we have established that building deep neural networks involves making decisions about several hyperparameters. The list of hyperperparameters includes the number of hidden layers, the number of units in each hidden layer, the activation function for each layer, the loss function for the network, and the type of optimizer and its parameters, the type of regularizer and its parameters, the batch size, the number of epochs, and others. We also observed that different values of hyperparameters can affect the performance of a model significantly. Therefore, finding the best values for hyperparameters is one of the most important and challenging parts of becoming a deep learning expert. Since there are no absolute rules for picking the hyperparameters that work for every dataset and every problem, deciding the values of hyperparameters needs to be done through trial and error for each particular problem. This process of training and evaluating models with different hyperparameters and deciding about the final hyperparameters based on model performance is called **hyperparamer tuning** or **hyperparameter optimization**.

Having a range or a set of possible values for each hyperparameter that we are interested in tuning can create a grid such as the one shown in Figure 5.11. Therefore, hyperparameter tuning can be seen as a grid search problem; we would like to try every cell in the grid (every possible combination of hyperparameters) and find the one cell that results in the best performance for the model:

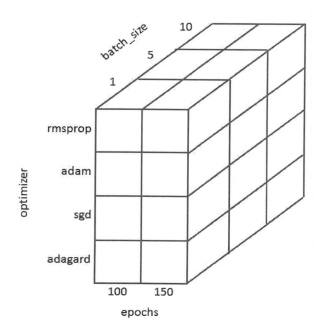

Figure 5.11: A hyperparameter grid created by some values for optimizer, batch_size, and epochs

scikit-learn provides a parameter optimizer called **GridSearchCV()** to perform this exhaustive grid search. **GridSearchCV()** receives the model as the **estimator** argument, and the dictionary containing all possible values for the hyperparameters as the **param_grid** argument. It then goes through every point in the grid, performs cross-validation on the model using the hyperparameter values at that point, and returns the best cross-validation score along with the values of the hyperparameters that led to that score.

You learned in the previous chapter that in order to use Keras models in scikit-learn, you need to first define a function that returns a Keras model. For example, the code block given here defines a Keras model that we would like to perform hyperparameter tuning on later:

```
from keras.models import Sequential
from keras.layers import Dense
def build_model():
    model = Sequential(optimizer)
    model.add(Dense(10, input_dim=13, activation='relu'))
    model.add(Dense(10, activation='relu'))
    model.add(Dense(1))
    model.compile(loss='mean_squared_error', optimizer= optimizer)
    return model
```

The next step would be to define the grid of parameters. For example, say we would like to tune over **optimizer=['rmsprop', 'adam', 'sgd', 'adagrad']**, **epochs = [100, 150]**, **batch_size = [1, 5, 10]**. Therefore, we write this:

```
optimizer = ['rmsprop', 'adam', 'sgd', 'adagrad']
epochs = [100, 150]
batch_size = [1, 5, 10]

param_grid = dict(optimizer=optimizer, epochs=epochs, batch_size= batch_size)
```

Now that the hyperparameter grid is created, we can create the wrapper to build the interface for the Keras model and use it as an estimator to perform the grid search:

```
from keras.wrappers.scikit_learn import KerasRegressor
model = KerasRegressor(build_fn=build_model, verbose=0)


from sklearn.model_selection import GridSearchCV
grid_search = GridSearchCV(estimator=model, param_grid=param_grid, cv=10)
results = grid_search.fit(X, y)
```

The code block given here goes exhaustively through every cell in the grid and performs 10-fold cross-validation using hyperparameter values in each cell (here it performs 10-fold cross-validation 4*2*3=24 times). It then returns the cross-validation score for each of these 24 cells, along with the one that resulted in the best score.

> **Note**
>
> Performing k-fold cross-validation on many possible combinations of hyperparameters sure takes a long time. For this reason, you can parallelize the process by passing the **n_jobs=-1** argument to **GridSearchCV()**, which results in using every processor available to perform the grid search. The default value for this argument is **n_jobs=1**, which means no parallelization.

Randomized Search with scikit-learn

As you may have realized, an exhaustive grid search may not be the best choice for tuning the hyperparameters of a deep learning model, as it is not very efficient. There are many hyperparameters in deep learning, and especially if you would like to try a large range of values for each, an exhaustive grid search would simply take too long to complete. An alternative way to perform hyperparameter optimization is to perform random sampling on the grid and perform k-fold cross-validation only on some randomly selected cells. scikit-learn provides an optimizer called **RandomizedSearchCV()** to perform random search for the purpose of hyperparameter optimization.

For example, we can change the code from the previous section from an exhaustive grid search to a random search, as follows:

```
from keras.wrappers.scikit_learn import KerasRegressor
model = KerasRegressor(build_fn=build_model, verbose=0)


from sklearn.model_selection import RandomizedSearchCV
grid_search = RandomizedSearchCV(estimator=model, param_distributions=param_
grid, cv=10, n_iter=12)
results = grid_search.fit(X, y)
```

Notice that **RandomizedSearchCV()** requires the extra **n_iter** argument, which determines how many random cells must be selected. This indeed determines how many times k-fold cross-validation will be performed. Therefore, by choosing a smaller number, fewer hyperparameter combinations will be considered and the method will take less time to complete. Also, please note that the **param_grid** argument is changed to **param_distributions** here. The **param_distributions** argument can take a dictionary with parameter names as keys, and either lists of parameters or distributions as values for each key.

It could be argued that **RandomizedSearchCV()** is not as good as **GridSearchCV()**, as it does not consider all the possible values and combinations of values for hyperparameters, which is reasonable. As a result, one smart way of performing hyperparameter tuning for deep learning models is to start with either **RandomizedSearchCV()** on many hyperparameters, or **GridSearchCV()** on fewer hyperparameters with larger gaps between them. This can help figure out which hyperparameters are more important than others in terms of their influence on model performance. It can also help narrow the range for important hyperparameters. Then, you can complete your hyperparameter tuning by performing **GridSearchCV()** on the smaller number of hyperparameters and the smaller ranges for each of them. This is called the **coarse-to-fine** approach to hyperparameter tuning.

Now you are ready to practice implementing hyperparameter tuning using scikit-learn optimizers in some activity. In this activity, you will try to improve your model for the diabetes dataset by tuning the hyperparameters.

Activity 10: Hyperparameter Tuning on the Diabetes Diagnosis Classifier

We learned about the diabetes dataset in the activities of previous chapters. The dataset consists of information for 768 patients, and for each patient, 8 different measurements are available, as well as a **class** label that can only take two values: **1**, indicating diabetic (268 examples), and **0**, indicating non-diabetic (500 examples). In this activity, you will build a Keras model similar to those in the previous activities; only this time, you will add regularization methods to your model as well. Then, you will use scikit-learn optimizers to perform tuning on the model hyperparameters, including the hyperparameters of the regularizers. Here are the steps you need to complete in this activity:

1. Load the dataset from the **data** subfolder of **Lesson05** folder from GitHub using `data=numpy.loadtxt("./data/pima-indians-diabetes.csv", delimiter=",")`. Store the training data in **X** using `X = data[:,0:8]`, and the class labels in **y** using `y = data[:,8]`.

2. Define a function that returns a Keras model with two hidden layers of size 8 with L2 weight regularizations. Use these values as the hyperparameters for your model: `activation='relu'`, `loss='binary_crossentropy'`, `optimizer='sgd'`, `metrics=['accuracy']`. Also, make sure to pass the L2 `lambda` hyperparameter as an argument to your function, so we can tune it later.

3. Create the wrapper for your Keras model and perform `GridSearchCV()` on it using `cv=5`, and add the following values in the parameter grid: `lambda_parameter = [0.01, 0.5, 1]`, `epochs = [350, 400]`, `batch_size = [10]`. This might take some time to process. Once the random search is complete, print the accuracy and the hyperparameters of the best cross-validation score. You can also print every other cross-validation score, along with the hyperparameters that resulted in that score.

4. Repeat the previous step, this time using `GridSearchCV()` on a narrower range with `lambda_parameter = [0.001, 0.01, 0.05, 0.1]`, `epochs = [400]`, and `batch_size = [10]`. It might take some time to process.

5. Repeat the previous step, removing L2 regularizers from your Keras model and instead adding dropout regularization with the **rate** parameter at each hidden layer. Perform `GridSearchCV()` on the model using the following values in the parameter grid and print the results: `rate = [0, 0.2, 0.4]`, `epochs = [350, 400]`, `batch_size = [10]`.

6. Repeat the previous step using `rate = [0.0, 0.05, 0.1]` and `epochs=[400]`.

In this activity, we learned how to implement hyperparameter tuning on a Keras model with regularizers to perform classification using a real-life dataset. We learned how to use scikit-learn optimizers to perform tuning on model hyperparameters, including the hyperparameters of the regularizers.

> **Note**
>
> The solution for this activity can be found on page 344.

Summary

In this chapter, you learned about two very important groups of techniques for improving the accuracy of your deep learning models: regularization techniques and hyperparameter-tuning techniques. You learned about how regularization helps address the overfitting problem, and had an introduction to different regularization methods. Among those methods, L1 and L2 norm regularization and dropout regularization were covered in detail, since they are very important, commonly used regularization techniques. You also learned about the importance of hyperparameter tuning for machine learning models and saw how performing hyperparameter tuning is highly challenging for deep learning models in particular. You learned how to perform hyperparameter tuning on Keras models more easily using scikit-learn optimizers.

In the next chapter, you will learn about the limitations of accuracy metrics when evaluating model performance. You will also learn about other metrics, such as precision, sensitivity, specificity, and AUC-ROC score, including how to use them in order to better understand how poor or good your model's performance is.

Model Evaluation

Learning Objectives

By the end of this chapter, you will be able to:

- Explain model evaluation, accuracy, null accuracy, and the limitations of accuracy

- Explain imbalanced datasets and confusion matrices

- Evaluate sensitivity, specificity, precision, FPR, ROC curves, and AUC scores

- Evaluate the classification threshold

In this chapter, we will learn how to evaluate a model using accuracy. We will evaluate the model with sensitivity, specificity, precision, FPR, ROC curves, and AUC curves. Lastly, we will apply a classification threshold on the model.

Introduction

In this chapter, we will learn about some different evaluation techniques other than **accuracy**. For any data scientist, the first step after building a model is to evaluate it, and the easiest way to evaluate a model is through its accuracy. However, in real-world scenarios, we often deal with datasets where accuracy is not the best evaluation technique. This chapter explores core concepts such as imbalanced datasets and how different evaluation techniques can be used to work through these imbalanced datasets. The chapter begins with an introduction to accuracy and its limitations. It then explores the concepts of null accuracy, imbalanced datasets, sensitivity, specificity, precision, false positives, ROC curves, and AUC scores.

Accuracy

To understand accuracy properly, first let's explore **model evaluation**. Model evaluation is an integral part of the model development process. Once you build your model and execute it, the next step is to evaluate your model. A model is built on a **training dataset**, and evaluating a model's performance on the same training dataset is a bad practice in data science. Once a model is trained on a training dataset, it should be evaluated on a dataset that is completely different from the training dataset. This dataset is known as the **test dataset**. The objective should always be to build a model that generalizes, which means the model should produce similar (but not the same) results, or relatively similar results, on any dataset. This can only be achieved if we evaluate the model on data that is unknown to it.

The model evaluation process requires a metric that can quantify a model's performance. The simplest metric for model evaluation is accuracy. Accuracy is the fraction of predictions that our model gets right. This is the formula for calculating accuracy:

Accuracy = (Number of correct predictions) / (Total number of predictions)

For example, if we have 10 records and 7 are predicted correctly, then we say that the accuracy of our model is 70%. This is calculated as 7/10 = 0.7 or 70 %.

Null accuracy is accuracy that can be achieved by predicting the most frequent class. If we don't run an algorithm and just predict accuracy based on the most frequent outcome, then the accuracy calculated based on this prediction is known as null accuracy.

Null accuracy = (Total number of instances of frequently occurring class) / (Total number of instances)

Take a look at this example:

10 actual outcomes: [1,0,0,0,0,0,0,0,1,0].

Prediction: [0,0,0,0,0,0,0,0,0,0]

Null accuracy = 8/10 = 0.8 or 80%

So, our null accuracy is 80%, meaning we are correct 80% of the time. That means we have achieved 80% accuracy without running an algorithm. Always remember that when null accuracy is high, it means that the distribution of response variables is skewed in favor of the frequently occurring class.

Let's work on an exercise to find the null accuracy of a dataset. The null accuracy of a dataset can be found by using the `value_count` function in the pandas library. The `value_count` function returns a series containing counts of unique values.

> **Note**
>
> All the Jupyter notebooks for the exercises and activities in this chapter are available on GitHub at https://github.com/TrainingByPackt/Applied-Deep-Learning-with-Keras/tree/master/Lesson06.

Exercise 16: Calculating Null Accuracy on a Dummy Healthcare Dataset

We have a dummy healthcare dataset that has `patient id` and `diagnosis` columns. The `diagnosis` column shows whether the patient has been diagnosed with flu. Rows with a `diagnosis` value of 1 mean the patient has flu, and 0 means the patient does not have flu. Find the null accuracy of the dataset:

1. Open a Jupyter notebook. Import all the required libraries and load the `Flu.csv` file from the GitHub repository:

```
# Import the pandas library
import pandas as pd
#Load the Flu.csv file from GitHub
df= pd.read_csv("Flu.csv")
df.head()
```

This is the output of the preceding code:

	patient id	diagnosis
0	1001	1
1	1002	1
2	1003	1
3	1004	0
4	1005	1

Figure 6.1: Data exploration of the Flu.csv dataset

2. Use the built-in **value_count** function from the pandas library to get the distribution for data of the **diagnosis** column. The **value_count** function shows the total instances of unique values:

```
df.diagnosis.value_counts()
```

```
1    96
0     4
Name: diagnosis, dtype: int64
```

Figure 6.2: Output of value_count function

3. Use the **head** function with the **value_count** function to find the null accuracy. The **head(1)** function fetches the most frequent class and the **len** function returns the total number of instances:

```
df.diagnosis.value_counts().head(1)/len(df.diagnosis)
```

```
1    0.96
Name: diagnosis, dtype: float64
```

Figure 6.3: Null Accuracy of Flu.csv dataset

The calculated null accuracy of the dataset is 96%.

We can see that our dataset has a very high null accuracy of 96%. So, if we just make a dumb model that predicts the majority class for all outcomes, our model will be 96% accurate. We will see in *Activity 11, Computing the Accuracy and Null Accuracy of a Neural Network When We Change the Train/Test Split*, how null accuracy changes as we change the test/train split.

Advantages and Limitations of Accuracy

The a Advantages of accuracy are as follows:

- **Easy to use**: Accuracy is very easy to compute and understand as it is just a simple fraction formula.

- **Popular compared to other techniques**: Since it is the easiest metric to compute, it is the most popular. It is also universally accepted as the first step of evaluating a model. Most introductory books on data science also teach accuracy as an evaluation metric.

- **Good for comparing different models**: Suppose you are trying to solve a problem with different models. You can always trust the model that gives the highest accuracy.

The limitations of accuracy are as follows:

- **No representation of response variable distribution**: Accuracy doesn't give us any idea about the distribution of the response/dependent variable. If we get an accuracy of 80% in our model, we have no idea how the response variable is distributed and what the null accuracy of the dataset is. If the null accuracy of our dataset is above 70%, then an 80% accurate model is pretty useless.

- **Type 1 and type 2 errors**: Accuracy also gives no information about the type 1 and type 2 errors of the model. A type 1 error is when a class is negative and we have predicted it as positive, and a type 2 error is when a class is positive and we have predicted it as negative. We will be studying both these errors later in this chapter.

Imbalanced Datasets

Imbalanced datasets are a distinct case for classification problems where the class distribution varies between the classes. In such datasets, one class is overwhelmingly dominant. In other words, the null accuracy of an imbalanced dataset is very high. Consider an example of credit card fraud. If we have a dataset of credit card transactions, then we will find that, of all the transactions, a very miniscule number of transactions were fraudulent and the majority of transactions were normal transactions. If 1 represents a fraudulent transaction and 0 represents a normal transaction, then there will be many 0s and hardly any 1s. The null accuracy of the dataset may be more than 99%. This means the majority class (in this case, 0) is overwhelmingly greater than the minority class (in this case, 1). Such sets are imbalanced datasets. The following figure shows a generalized scatter plot of an imbalanced dataset, where the stars represent the minority class and the circles represent the majority class:

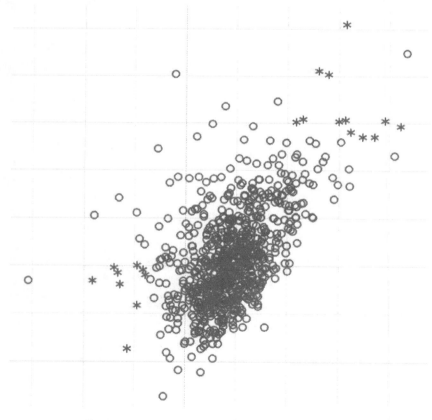

Figure 6.4: A general imbalanced dataset scatter plot

Working with Imbalanced Datasets

In machine learning, there are two ways of overcoming the shortcomings of imbalanced datasets, which are as follows:

- **Sampling techniques**: One way we can mitigate the imbalance of a dataset is by using special sampling techniques with which we can select our training and testing data in such a way that there is adequate representation of all classes. There are many such techniques, such as oversampling the minority class, which means we take more samples from the minority class; or we could under -sample the majority class, which means we take a smaller sample from the majority class. However, if the data is highly imbalanced with null accuracies above 90%, then no sampling techniques will give the correct representation of the actual data and we might get results that overfit. So, the best way is to modify our evaluation techniques.

- **Modifying model evaluation techniques**: When working with highly imbalanced datasets, it is better to modify model evaluation techniques. This is the most robust method to get good results. There are many evaluation metrics other than accuracy that can be modified to evaluate a model. To learn all those techniques, it is important to understand the concept of a **confusion matrix**.

Confusion Matrix

A confusion matrix describes the performance of the classification model. In other words, confusion matrix is a way to summarize classifier performance. The following figure shows a basic representation of a confusion matrix:

Figure 6.5: Basic representation of a confusion matrix

The following code is an example of a confusion matrix:

```
from sklearn.metrics import confusion_matrix
cm=confusion_matrix(y_test,y_pred_class)
print(cm)
```

The following figure shows the output of the preceding code:

```
array([[89,  2],
       [13,  4]], dtype=int64)
```

Figure 6.6: Example confusion matrix

These are the meanings of the abbreviations used in the preceding figure:

- **TN (True negative)**: This is the count of outcomes that were originally negative and were predicted negative.

- **FP (False positive)**: This is the count of outcomes that were originally negative but were predicted positive. This error is also called a **type 1 error**

- **FN (False negative)**: This is the count of outcomes that were originally positive but were predicted negative. This error is also called a **type 2 error**.

- **TP (True positive)**: This is the count of outcomes that were originally positive and were predicted as positive.

The aim of all machine learning and deep learning algorithms is to maximize TN and TP and minimize FN and FP. This is example code that calculates TN, FP, FN, and TP:

```
##True Negative
TN=cm[0,0]
##False Negative
FN=cm[1,0]
##False Positives
FP=cm[0,1]
##True Positives
TP=cm[1,1]
```

> **Note**
>
> Accuracy does not help us understand type 1 and type 2 errors.

Metrics Computed from a Confusion Matrix

The metrics that can be derived from a confusion matrix are sensitivity, specificity, precision, false positive rate, ROC, and AUC:

- **Sensitivity**: This is the number of positive predictions divided by the total actual number of positives. Sensitivity is also known as recall, or true positive. In our case, it is the total number of patients classified as 1 divided by the total number of patients who are actually 1:

  $Sensitivity = TP \ / \ (TP+FN)$

  Sensitivity means how often the prediction is correct when the actual value is positive. In cases such as patient re-admission, we need our model to be highly sensitive. We need 1 to be predicted as 1. If a 0 is predicted as 1, it is acceptable, but if a 1 is predicted as 0, it means a patient who was re-admitted is predicted as not re-admitted, and this will cause severe penalties for the hospital.

- **Specificity**: This is the number of negative predictions divided by the total number of actual negatives. To use the previous example, it would be re-admission predicted as 0 divided by the total number of patients who were actually 0. Specificity is also known as the true negative rate:

  $Specificity=TN \ / \ (TN+FP)$

  Specificity means how often the prediction is correct when the actual value is negative. There are cases, such us spam email detection, where we need our algorithm to be more specific. The model predicts 1 when an email is spam and 0 when it isn't. We want the model to predict 0 as always 0, because if a non-spam email is classified as spam, important emails may end up in the spam folder. Sensitivity can be compromised here because some spam emails may arrive in our inbox, but non-spam emails should never go to the spam folder.

> **Note**
>
> As discussed earlier, whether a model should be sensitive or specific totally depends on the business problem.

- **Precision**: This is the true positive prediction divided by the total number of positive predictions. Precision means how often are we correct when the value predicted is positive:

Precision= TP / (TP+FP)

- **False Positive Rate (FPR)**: The FPR is calculated as the ratio between the number of false positive events and the total number of actual negative events. FPR means when the actual value is negative, how often are we incorrect? FPR is also equal to 1 - specificity.

False positive rate= FP / (FP+TN)

- **Receiver Operating Characteristic (ROC) curve**: Another important way to evaluate a classification model is by using an ROC curve. An ROC curve is a plot between the true positive rate (sensitivity) and the FPR (1–specificity). The following figure shows an example of an ROC curve:

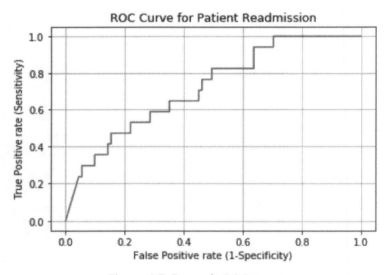

Figure 6.7: Example ROC curve

To decide which ROC curve is the best among multiple curves, we need to look at the empty space on the upper left of the curve. The smaller the space, the better the result. The following figure shows an example of multiple ROC curves:

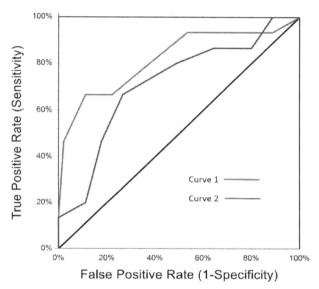

Figure 6.8: Example of multiple ROC curve

> **Note**
>
> The red curve is better than the blue curve because it leaves less space in the upper-left corner.

The ROC curve of a model tells us the relationship between sensitivity and specificity.

- **Area Under Curve (AUC):** This is the area under the ROC curve. Sometimes, AUC is also written as AUROC, meaning the area under the ROC curve. Basically, AUC is a numeric value that represents the area under an ROC curve. The larger the area under the ROC, the better, and the bigger the AUC score, the better. *Figure 6.8* shows us an example of an AUC.

In *Figure* 6.8, the AUC of the red curve is greater than the AUC of the blue curve, which means the AUC of the red curve is better than the AUC of the blue curve. There is no standard rule for the AUC score, but here are some generally acceptable values and how they relate to model quality:

AUC Score	Model Quality
0.9 to 1	Excellent
0.8 to o.9	Good
0.7 to 0.8	Fair
0.6 to 0.7	Poor
0.5 to 0.6	Fail

Figure 6.9: General acceptable AUC score

Now that we are done understanding the theory behind the various metrics, let's do some activities and exercises to implement what we have learned.

Exercise 17: Computing Accuracy and Null Accuracy with Healthcare Data

Predict which patients will be readmitted to hospital within 30 days after getting discharged. We have a healthcare dataset of patients admitted to hospital who were later discharged. What the hospital is trying to do is predict whether a patient is likely to be readmitted to the hospital within 30 days of discharge. If patients above a certain percentage of cases are re-admitted within 30 days of discharge, then the hospital may face penalties and fines from the government. So, the objective of the hospital is to predict which patients are probable candidates for being re-admitted within 30 days of discharge. This way, the hospital can provide special care for those patients and avoid their re-admission, and also provide high-quality care for their patients, which should be their primary concern

> **Note**
>
> The dataset can be downloaded from the GitHub repository at https://github.com/TrainingByPackt/Applied-Deep-Learning-with-Keras/tree/master/Lesson06/data.

Here is a snapshot of the metadata that we will be using in the exercise:

S.No.	Variable Name	Description	Type
1	Patient_id	Patient Identification	Categorical
2	Age	Age of Patient	Numeric
3	Admission_type	Category in which Patient was admitted	Categorical
4	PreExistingDisease	Whether Patient suffers from a Pre Existing Disease	Numeric
5	PreviousSurgery	Whether Patient has undergone previous surgery	Numeric
6	Gender	Gender of Patient	Categorical
7	Smoker	Whether the Patient is a smoker	Numeric
8	Homeless	Whether the patient has shelter	Numeric
9	DaysinHospital	Number of Days the Patient spent in hospital before	Numeric
10	Readmitted	Whether the patient is readmitted to hospital	Numeric

Figure 6.10: Metadata of the patient re-admission dataset

> **Note**
>
> The dark gray shade (S.No. 10) in *Figure 6.10* differentiates the response variable for the explanatory variables.

> **Note**
>
> Throughout this exercise, you may get slightly different results due to the random nature of the internal mathematical operations.

Data preprocessing and exploratory data analysis:

1. Import the required libraries. Load and explore the dataset:

```
#import the libraries
import numpy as np
import pandas as pd
#Load the Data
patient_data=pd.read_csv("Health_Data.csv")
##use the head function to get a glimpse data
patient_data.head()
```

The following figure shows the output of the preceding code:

	Patient_id	Age	Admission_type	PreExistingDisease	PreviousSurgery	Gender	Smoker	Homeless	DaysinHospital	Readmitted
0	1	33	Urgent	Y	0	M	1	0	1	0
1	2	34	Emergency	N	0	M	1	0	22	0
2	3	88	Trauma	Y	1	M	1	1	100	1
3	4	56	Elective	Y	0	M	1	0	2	0
4	5	45	Trauma	Y	0	M	1	0	34	0

Figure 6.11: First five rows of the patient re-admission dataset

2. Describe the numeric and categorical values in the dataset:

```
#Summary of Numerical Data
patient_data.describe()
```

The following figure shows the output of the preceding code:

	Patient_id	Age	PreviousSurgery	Smoker	Homeless	DaysinHospital	Readmitted
count	357.00000	357.000000	357.000000	357.000000	357.000000	357.000000	357.000000
mean	179.00000	42.574230	0.341737	0.596639	0.378151	43.182073	0.193277
std	103.20126	29.274624	0.474957	0.491261	0.485606	47.362609	0.395423
min	1.00000	0.000000	0.000000	0.000000	0.000000	1.000000	0.000000
25%	90.00000	14.000000	0.000000	0.000000	0.000000	12.000000	0.000000
50%	179.00000	35.000000	0.000000	1.000000	0.000000	32.000000	0.000000
75%	268.00000	67.000000	1.000000	1.000000	1.000000	55.000000	0.000000
max	357.00000	96.000000	1.000000	1.000000	1.000000	352.000000	1.000000

Figure 6.12: Numerical metadata of the patient re-admission dataset

3. Summarize the categorical data by using the **describe** function:

```
#Summary of Categorical Data
patient_data.describe(include=['object'])
```

The following figure shows the output of the preceding code:

	Admission_type	PreExistingDisease	Gender
count	357	357	357
unique	5	2	2
top	Urgent	N	F
freq	131	228	186

Figure 6.13: Categorical metadata of the patient re-admission dataset

Note that the **Admission_type** column has 5 unique types, while the **PreExistingDisease** and **Gender** columns have 2 unique types.

4. Separate the independent and dependent variables. Since column 0, which is the **patient_id** column, does not add any value, we discard that column. Columns 1 to 8 are independent variables, and the last column is the dependent variable:

```
mydata=pd.read_csv("Health_Data.csv")
X=mydata.iloc[:,1:9]
y=mydata.iloc[:,9]
```

> **Note**
>
> Independent variables are also known as explanatory variables, and dependent variables are also knows as response variables. Also remember that indexing in Python starts from 0.

5. Explore **X** using the **head** function:

```
X.head()
```

The following figure shows the output of the preceding code:

	Age	Admission_type	PreExistingDisease	PreviousSurgery	Gender	Smoker	Homeless	DaysinHospital
0	33	Urgent	Y	0	M	1	0	1
1	34	Emergency	N	0	M	1	0	22
2	88	Trauma	Y	1	M	1	1	100
3	56	Elective	Y	0	M	1	0	2
4	45	Trauma	Y	0	M	1	0	34

Figure 6.14: The first 5 rows of the X variable of the patient re-admission dataset

6. Explore **y** using the **head** function:

    ```
    y.head()
    ```

    The following figure shows the output of the preceding code:

    ```
    0    0
    1    0
    2    1
    3    0
    4    0
    Name: Readmitted, dtype: int64
    ```

    Figure 6.15: The first 5 rows of the y variable of the patient re-admission dataset

7. Create dummy variables for the categorical variables. Note that the input should all be numeric variables. Use the **get_dummies** function from pandas to create dummy variables. Note that we need to create dummies for the categorical variables:

    ```
    ##New Admission type
    A_type=pd.get_dummies(X.iloc[:,1],drop_first=True,prefix='Atype')
    ##New Gender
    New_gender=pd.get_dummies(X.iloc[:,4],drop_first=True,prefix='Gender')
    ##New Pre Existing Disease Variable
    Pre_exdis=pd.get_dummies(X.iloc[:,2],drop_first=True,prefix='PreExistDis')
    ```

8. Drop the original categorical variables and replace them with the transformed numeric dummy variables:

    ```
    ## Drop the original categorical columns
    X.drop(['Admission_
    type','PreExistingDisease','Gender'],axis=1,inplace=True)
    ##Concat the new transformed data to X DataFrame
    X=pd.concat([X,A_type,New_gender,Pre_exdis],axis=1)
    ```

9. Take a look at the new transformed data:

    ```
    X.head()
    ```

The following figure shows the output of the preceding code:

	Age	PreviousSurgery	Smoker	Homeless	DaysinHospital	Atype_Emergency	Atype_Newborn	Atype_Trauma	Atype_Urgent	Gender_M	PreExistDis_Y
0	33	0	1	0	1	0	0	0	1	1	1
1	34	0	1	0	22	1	0	0	0	1	0
2	88	1	1	1	100	0	0	1	0	1	1
3	56	0	1	0	2	0	0	0	0	1	1
4	45	0	1	0	34	0	0	1	0	1	1

Figure 6.16: The first five rows of the X variable

10. Split the data into test and train sets by using the **train_test_split** function from the scikit-learn library. To make sure we all get the same results, set the **random_state** parameter to 110. The data is split with a 70:30 ratio, meaning 70% of the data is training data and the remaining 30% is testing data:

```
from sklearn.model_selection import train_test_split
xtrain,xtest,ytrain,ytest= train_test_split(X, y, test_size=0.30, random_state=110)
```

> Note
>
> If you use a different **random_state**, you may get a different test-train split, which may yield slightly different results.

11. Scale the data using the **StandardScaler** function:

```
##Initialize StandardScaler
from sklearn.preprocessing import StandardScaler
sc=StandardScaler()
#Transform the training data
xtrain=sc.fit_transform(xtrain)
xtrain=pd.DataFrame(xtrain,columns=xtest.columns)
#Transform the testing data
xtest=sc.transform(xtest)
xtest=pd.DataFrame(xtest,columns=xtrain.columns)
```

> Note
>
> The **sc.fit_transform()** function transforms the data, and the data is also converted to a NumPy array. We may need the data for further analysis in the DataFrame objects, so the **pd.DataFrame()** function reconverts data into a DataFrame.

12. Now convert the DataFrame to NumPy again by using the **values** function:

```
#Convert DataFrame to NumPy array
x_train=xtrain.values
x_test=xtest.values
y_train=ytrain.values
y_test=ytest.values
```

> **Note**
>
> As a best practice, we should have training and testing data in NumPy and a DataFrame. We mostly use NumPy objects, but we may need DataFrame objects in some scenarios, which we will cover later in the chapter.

13. Show the new transformed data using the **head** method:

```
xtrain.head()
```

The following figure shows the output of the preceding code:

Age	PreviousSurgery	Smoker	Homeless	DaysinHospital	Atype_Emergency	Atype_Newborn	Atype_Trauma	Atype_Urgent	Gender_M	PreExistDis_Y
1.415411	1.340803	0.792118	1.210515	1.883715	-0.363068	-0.303488	1.835326	-0.739313	-0.911527	1.306339
1.583479	1.340803	0.792118	1.210515	1.069799	-0.363068	-0.303488	1.835326	-0.739313	-0.911527	1.306339
0.675914	-0.745822	0.792118	1.210515	-0.453684	-0.363068	-0.303488	-0.544862	1.352607	1.097060	-0.765498
0.306166	-0.745822	-1.262438	-0.826095	-0.244988	2.754307	-0.303488	-0.544862	-0.739313	-0.911527	-0.765498
-1.071987	-0.745822	0.792118	-0.826095	-0.912816	-0.363068	-0.303488	-0.544862	-0.739313	1.097060	-0.765498

Figure 6.17: Transformed data in the training dataset

This completes the data preprocessing part of the exercise. Now build a neural network and calculate the accuracy.

14. Now, import the libraries that are required for creating the neural network architecture:

```
##Import the relevant Keras libraries
from keras.models import Sequential
from keras.layers import Dense
from keras.layers import Dropout
```

15. Initiate the **Sequential** class:

```
##Initiate the Model with Sequential Class
model=Sequential()
```

16. Add the first **Dense** layer and the **Dropout** layer. We have set the **Dropout** rate as `0.3`:

```
## Add the 1st dense layer and Dropout Layer
model.add(Dense(units=6,activation='relu',kernel_
initializer='uniform',input_dim=11))
model.add(Dropout(rate=0.3))
```

> **Note**
>
> Here, **units=6** indicates the output. The output dim is the average of input and output. In our case, the average of 11 inputs and 1 output will be the output dim.

17. Add the first **Dense** layer and the **Dropout** layer. We have set the **Dropout** rate as `0.3`. Here, **Dropout** is used to avoid overfitting:

```
##Add the 2nd dense Layer and Dropout Layer
model.add(Dense(units=6,activation='relu',kernel_initializer='uniform'))
model.add(Dropout(rate=0.3))
```

18. Add an output **Dense** layer with a `sigmoid` activation function:

```
##Add Output Dense Layer
model.add(Dense(units=1,activation='sigmoid',kernel_
initializer='uniform'))
```

> **Note**
>
> Since the output is binary, we are using the **sigmoid** function. If the output is multiclass (that is, more than two classes), then the **softmax** function should be used.

19. Compile the network and fit the model. The metric used here is accuracy:

```
#Compile the Model
model.compile(optimizer='adam',loss='binary_
crossentropy',metrics=['accuracy'])
```

> **Note**
>
> The metric's name, which in our case is accuracy, is defined in the preceding code.

20. Fit the model with 100 epochs and a batch size of 20:

```
#Fit the Model
model.fit(x_train,y_train,epochs=100,batch_size=20)
```

21. Create two prediction variables, **y_pred_class** and **y_pred_prob**:

```
#y_pred_class is the predcition and y_pred_prob is probabilities of the
prediction
y_pred_class=model.predict(x_test)
y_pred_prob=model.predict_proba(x_test)
```

Two prediction variables are created here. One is the normal prediction class, and the other is the probability of prediction. **y_predict_proba** will be used to adjust thresholds later in the chapter.

22. Explore the predicted class:

```
##Explore the y_pred_class
y_pred_class[:5]
```

The following figure shows the output of the preceding code:

```
array([[0.070409  ],
        [0.00045063],
        [0.05486067],
        [0.03846052],
        [0.01186392]], dtype=float32)
```

Figure 6.18: Values of the predicted y_pred_class

> **Note**
>
> **y_pred_class** contains the probabilities of prediction.

23. Set the threshold for class prediction. Any values that are above the threshold 0.5 will be 1, and values below 0.5 will be 0:

```
##Set threshold all values above threshold are 1 and #below 0
y_pred_class=y_pred_class>0.5
```

24. Print the predicted class after setting the threshold:

```
## false means 0 and true means 1
print(y_pred_class[:5])
```

The following figure shows the output of the preceding code:

```
[[False]
 [False]
 [False]
 [False]
 [False]]
```

Figure 6.19: Values of the predicted class as Booleans

Any value greater than the threshold, which here is 0.5, will belong to class 1, which is the positive class, that is, the patient will be re-admitted. Anything below the 0.5 threshold will belong to class 0, the negative class, which means the patient will not be re-admitted. Here, false means **y_pred_class<0.5** and true means **y_pred_class>0.5**.

25. Print the predictor class as an integer by using the **astype** function:

```
y_pred_class.astype(int)[:5]
```

The following figure shows the output of the preceding code:

```
array([[0],
       [0],
       [0],
       [0],
       [0]])
```

Figure 6.20: Values of the predicted class in Integer

26. Calculate the accuracy by using the **accuracy_score** function from scikit-learn:

```
from sklearn.metrics import accuracy_score
accuracy_score(y_test,y_pred_class)
```

The following figure shows the output of the preceding code:

```
0.8703703703703703
```

Figure 6.21: Final calculated accuracy

The model returns accuracy of 87.03 %. But is it good enough? We can get the answer to this only by comparing it with the null accuracy.

Compute the null accuracy:

1. Null accuracy can be calculated using the **value_count** function of the pandas library, which was used in *Exercise 16, Calculating Null Accuracy on a Dummy Healthcare Dataset*, of this chapter:

   ```
   # Use the value_count function to calculate distinct class values
   ytest.value_counts()
   ```

   The following figure shows the output of the preceding code:

   ```
   0    91
   1    17
   Name: Readmitted, dtype: int64
   ```

   Figure 6.22: Final calculated accuracy

   > **Note**
   >
   > **ytest** is used here, not **y_test**. A pandas series is needed for the **value_count** method to work. Out of the total 108 values in **ytest**, 91 values are 0s and 17 values are 1s.

2. Calculate the null accuracy:

   ```
   ##use head function and divide it by lenght of ytest
   ytest.value_counts().head(1)/len(ytest)
   ```

   The following figure shows the output of the preceding code:

   ```
   0    0.842593
   Name: Readmitted, dtype: float64
   ```

   Figure 6.23: Output showing the null accuracy

So, we have obtained the null accuracy of the model, and as we conclude this exercise, the following points must be noted: the accuracy of our model is 87%, approximately. Under ideal conditions, 87% accuracy is good accuracy, but not here, because the null accuracy is very high. The null accuracy of our model is 84%. Since the null accuracy of the model is so high, an accuracy of 87% is not significant, and accuracy in such cases is not the correct metric with which to evaluate an algorithm.

Now let's go through an exercise on computing the accuracy and null accuracy of the neural network model when we change the train/test split.

Activity 11: Computing the Accuracy and Null Accuracy of a Neural Network When We Change the Train/Test Split

A train/test split is a random sampling technique. In this activity, we will see that our null accuracy and accuracy will be affected by changing the train/test split. To implement this, the part of the code where the train/test split was defined has to be changed. We will use the same dataset that we used in *Exercise 17, Computing Accuracy and Null Accuracy with Healthcare Data*. Follow these steps to perform the activity:

1. Import all the necessary dependencies and load the dataset.

2. Look for the dependent and independent variables. Filter out the useless columns, such as **patient_id**. This column is useless because it does not affect the dependent variable in any way.

3. Create dummy variables for the categorical variables. Note that the input should all be numeric variables. Then, drop the original categorical variables and replace them with the transformed numeric dummy variables.

4. Change **test_size** and **random_state** from 0.30 to 0.25 and 110 to 500, respectively. Scale the data using the **StandardScaler** function. Now convert the DataFrame to NumPy again using the **values** function.

5. Import the libraries required to build a neural network architecture and initiate the **Sequential** class.

6. Add the first **Dense** layer and the **Dropout** layer. We have set the **Dropout rate** to 0.3. Perform this step twice to avoid overfitting. Then, add an output **Dense** layer with the **sigmoid** activation function.

7. Compile the network and then fit the model using accuracy. Fit the model with 100 epochs and a batch size of 20.

8. Create two prediction variables, **y_pred_class** and **y_pred_prob**.

9. Set the threshold for class prediction. Any values that are above the threshold (0.5) will be 1, and values below 0.5 will be 0. Calculate the accuracy using the **accuracy_score** function from scikit-learn.

10. Calculate the null accuracy using the pandas **value_count** function.

> **Note**
>
> In this activity, you may get slightly different results due to the random nature of internal mathematical operations.

> **Note**
>
> The solution for this activity can be found on page 349.

Activity 12: Derive and Compute Metrics Based on a Confusion Matrix

Continuing with the same patient re-admission data, derive the sensitivity, specificity, precision, and FPR of the neural network model. Also adjust the threshold value and re-compute the sensitivity and specificity:

1. Compile and run the ANN as shown in *Exercise 17, Computing Accuracy and Null Accuracy with Healthcare Data*, and then continue with the next step.

2. Compute a confusion matrix using scikit-learn by using the **confusion_matrix** function.

3. Calculate the true negative, false negative, false positive, and true positive.

4. Calculate the sensitivity, specificity, precision, and FPR with the use of the confusion matrix.

5. Adjust the threshold by giving a different value to **y_pred_class**.

6. Once the threshold is adjusted, re-compute the sensitivity, specificity, precision, and FPR, and note the difference.

7. Visualize the data distribution. Plot a histogram for our predicted probabilities to see why the decrease in the threshold value increases the sensitivity. Recall that we created the **y_pred_prob** variable to predict the probabilities of the classifier.

> **Note**
>
> You may get slightly different results due to the random nature of internal mathematical operations.

> **Note**
>
> The solution for this activity can be found on page 354.

Exercise 18: Calculate the ROC and AUC Curves

Use the patient re-admission data and calculate the ROC curve and AUC Curve. Also define a function with which we can check the values of sensitivity and specificity for a given threshold:

1. Open a Jupyter notebook and run the code from *Exercise 17, Computing Accuracy and Null Accuracy with Healthcare Data*:

> **Note**
>
> The full code to execute step 1 is in the **Lesson06/Exercise18.ipynb** file.

```
import numpy as np
import pandas as pd

#Load the Data
patient_data=pd.read_csv("Health_Data.csv")

//[...]

# Use the value_count function to calculate distinct class values
ytest.value_counts()

##use head function and divide it by lenght of ytest
print("Null Accuracy:",ytest.value_counts().head(1)/len(ytest))
```

https://bit.ly/2GlivKp

2. Import **roc_curve** from scikit-learn and run the following code:

```
from sklearn.metrics import roc_curve
fpr,tpr,thresholds=roc_curve(y_test,y_pred_prob)
```

fpr =False Positive rate (1- specificity)

tpr = True Positive rate (sensitivity)

thresholds = the threshold value of **y_pred_prob**

> **Note**
>
> The second parameter for the ROC curve is **y_pred_prob**, not **y_pred**.

3. Run the following code to plot the ROC curve using **matplotlib.pyplot**:

```
import matplotlib.pyplot as plt
plt.plot(fpr,tpr)
plt.title("ROC Curve for Patient Readmission")
plt.xlabel("False Positive rate (1-Specificity)")
plt.ylabel("True Positive rate (Sensitivity)")
plt.grid(True)
plt.show()
```

The following figure shows the output of the preceding code:

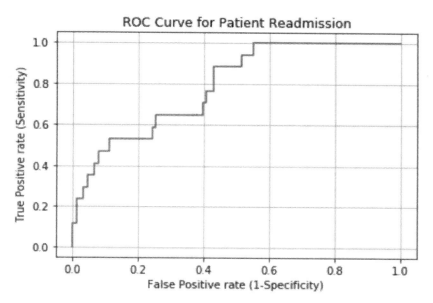

Figure 6.24: ROC curve of the patient re-admission dataset

4. The ROC curve does not show how sensitivity and specificity change with the threshold. To check what the sensitivity and specificity would be for a given threshold, we can write a user-defined function:

```
def optimum_threshold(my_threshold):
    print ("Sensitivity:",tpr[thresholds>my_threshold][-1])
    print ("Specificity:",1-fpr[thresholds>my_threshold][-1])
```

We create an **optimum_threshold** function with the **my_threhold** variable. Sensitivity is calculated as the true positive rate using **tpr[thresholds>my_threshold] [-1]**. It selects the last value of the **tpr** array, which is actually the highest value, since **tpr** are arranged in ascending order. **1-fpr** will give the sensitivity and **1-fpr[thresholds>my_threshold][-1]** will fetch the highest **fpr** value, and subtracting the highest **fpr** value from 1 will fetch the lowest specificity.

5. Calculate the sensitivity and specificity for the different threshold values. Make sure you execute each value one at a time to get the results. Calculate the sensitivity and specificity with a threshold value of 0.3:

```
optimum_threshold(0.3)
```

This is the output of the preceding code:

```
Sensitivity: 0.47058823529411764
Specificity: 0.9230769230769231
```

Figure 6.25: Sensitivity and specificity at a threshold value of 0.3

Calculate the sensitivity and specificity at a threshold value of 0.5:

```
optimum_threshold(0.5)
```

The following is the output of the preceding code:

```
Sensitivity: 0.23529411764705882
Specificity: 0.989010989010989
```

Figure 6.26: Sensitivity and specificity at a threshold value of 0.5

Calculate the sensitivity and specificity at a threshold value of 0.03:

```
optimum_threshold(0.03)
```

The following is the output of the preceding code:

```
Sensitivity: 1.0
Specificity: 0.4505494505494505
```

Figure 6.27: Sensitivity and specificity at a threshold value of 0.03

Calculate the sensitivity and specificity at a threshold value of 0.1:

```
optimum_threshold(0.1)
```

The following is the output of the preceding code:

```
Sensitivity: 0.6470588235294118
Specificity: 0.7472527472527473
```

Figure 6.28: Sensitivity and specificity at a threshold value of 0.1

Note

When the threshold value is 0.03, sensitivity is 1 and specificity is 0.4. Recall that this is what we just learned from the ROC curve.

6. Last is the AUC score, which is calculated as follows:

```
from sklearn.metrics import roc_auc_score
roc_auc_score(y_test,y_pred_prob)
```

The following is the output of the preceding code:

```
0.7899159663865547
```

Figure 6.29: AUC score

The AUC score of 78.9% suggests that our model is fair, as per the general acceptable AUC score shown in *Figure 6.9*.

In this exercise, we learned how to calculate an ROC and AUC curve with the healthcare dataset. We also learned how specificity and sensitivity change with different threshold values.

Summary

In this chapter, we learned about model evaluation and accuracy. We learned how accuracy is not the most appropriate technique for evaluation when our dataset is imbalanced. We also learned how to compute a confusion matrix using scikit-learn and how to derive other metrics, such as sensitivity, specificity, precision, and false positive rate. Finally, we learned how to use threshold values to adjust metrics and how ROC curves and AUC scores help us evaluate our models. It is very common to deal with imbalanced datasets in real-life problems. Problems such as credit card fraud detection, disease prediction, and spam email detection all have imbalanced data in different proportions.

Computer Vision with Convolutional Neural Networks

Learning Objectives

By the end of this chapter, you will be able to:

- Explain computer vision
- Explain the architecture of a convolutional neural network
- Perform max pooling, flattening, feature mapping, and feature detection
- Explain image augmentation
- Build image processing applications and classify images

In this chapter, we will learn about the architecture of neural networks and perform techniques such as max pooling, flattening, feature mapping, and feature detection. We will also learn about image augmentation and how to build image processing applications and classify images.

Introduction

Computer vision is one of the most important concepts in machine learning and artificial intelligence. With the wide use of smart phones for capturing, sharing, and uploading images every day, the amount of data generated through images is increasing exponentially. So, the need for experts specializing in the field of computer vision is at an all-time high. Industries such as the health care industry are on the verge of a revolution due to the progress made in the field of medical imaging. This chapter introduces you to computer vision and the various industries in which computer vision is used. You will also learn about **Convolutional Neural Networks** (**CNNs**), which are the most widely used neural networks for image processing. Like neural networks, CNNs are also made up of neurons. The neurons receive inputs that are processed using weighted sums and activation functions. However, unlike ANNs, which use vectors as inputs, a CNN uses images as its input. In this chapter, we will be studying CNNs in greater detail, along with the associated concepts of max pooling, flattening, feature maps, and feature selection. We will use Keras as a tool to run image processing algorithms on real-life images.

Computer Vision

To understand computer vision, let's first understand what human vision is. Human vision is the ability of the human eye and brain to see and recognize objects. Computer vision is the process of giving a machine a similar, if not better, understanding of seeing and identifying objects in the real world. It is fairly simple for a human eye to precisely identify whether an animal is a tiger or a lion. But it takes a lot of training for a computer system to understand such objects distinctly. Computer vision can also be defined as building mathematical models that can mimic the function of a human eye and brain. Basically, it is about training computers to understand and process images and videos.

Computer vision is an integral part of many cutting-edge areas of robotics: health care and medical (X-ray, MRI scans, CT scans, and so on), drones, self-driving cars, sports and recreation, and so on. Almost all business need computer vision to run successfully. Imagine the large amount of data generated by CCTV footage across the world, the number of pictures our smart phones capture each day, the number of videos shared on internet sites such as YouTube on a daily basis, and the pictures we share on popular social networking sites such as Facebook and Instagram. All of this generates huge volumes of image data. To process and analyze this data and make computers more intelligent in terms of processing, this data requires high-level experts who specialize in computer vision. Computer vision is a highly lucrative field in machine learning.

Convolutional Neural Networks

When you talk about computer vision, you talk about CNNs in the same breath. A CNN is a class of deep neural network that is mostly used in the field of computer vision and imaging. CNNs are used to identify images, cluster them by their similarity, and implement object recognition within scenes. A CNN has different layers, namely the input layer, the output layer, and multiple hidden layers. These hidden layers of a CNN consist of fully connected layers, convolutional layers, a RELU layer as an activation function, normalization layers, and pooling layers. On a very simple level, CNNs help to identify images and label them appropriately; for example, a tiger image will be identified as a tiger:

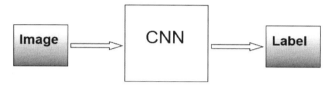

Figure 7.1: A Generalized CNN

An example of a CNN classifying a tiger:

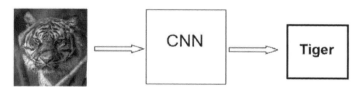

Figure 7.2: CNN classifying a tiger

Architecture of a CNN

The main components of a CNN architecture are as follows:

1. Input image
2. Convolutional layer
3. Pooling layer
4. Flattening

Input Image

An **input image** forms the first component of a CNN architecture. An image can be of any type: a human, an animal, scenery, a medical X-ray image, and so on. Each image is converted into a mathematical matrix of zeros and ones. At a very high level, the following figure explains how a computer views an image of the letter T. All the blocks that have a value of one represent the data, while the zeros represents blank space:

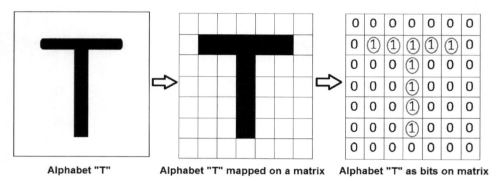

Figure 7.3: Matrix for the letter 'T'

Convolution Layer

The **convolution layer** is the place where the image processing starts. A convolution layer consists of two steps:

1. Feature detector or filter

2. Feature map

Feature detector or filter: This is a matrix or pattern that you put on an image to transform it into a feature map:

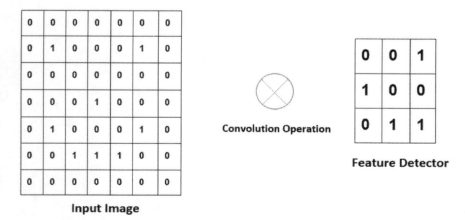

Figure 7.4: Feature detector

Now, as highlighted, this feature detector is put (superimposed) on the original image and the computation is done on the corresponding elements. The computation is done by multiplying the corresponding elements shown as follows. This process is repeated for all cells. This results in a new processed image – (0x0+0x0+0x1) + (0x1+1x0+0x0) + (0x0+0x1+0x1) = 0:

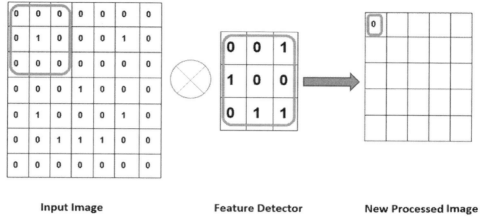

Input Image   Feature Detector   New Processed Image

Figure 7.5: Feature detector masked in image

Feature Map: This is the reduced image that is produced by the convolution of an image and feature detector. We have to put the feature detector on all possible locations of the original image and derive a smaller image from it; that derived image is the feature map of the input image:

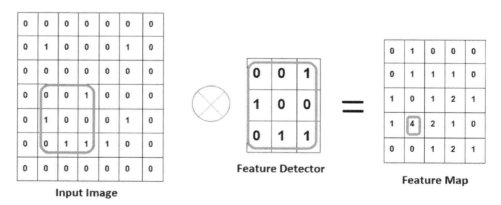

Input Image   Feature Detector   Feature Map

Figure 7.6: Feature map

Note

Here, the feature detector is the filter and the feature map is the reduced image. Some information is lost while reducing the image.

In an actual CNN, a number of feature detectors are used to produce a number of feature maps, as shown in the following figure:

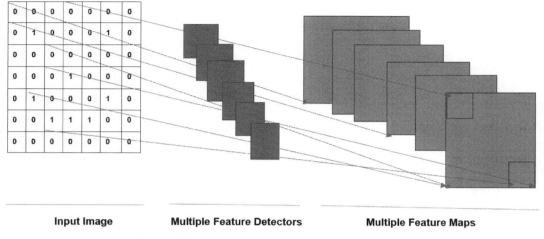

Input Image   **Multiple Feature Detectors**   **Multiple Feature Maps**

Figure 7.7: Multiple feature detectors and maps

Pooling Layer

The **pooling layer** helps in ignoring the less important data in the image and further reduces the image, while preserving its important features. Consider the example of the following three images, which have four cats:

Figure 7.8: Example cat images

To identify whether the image has a cat in it or not, the neural network analyzes the picture. It may look at ear shape, eye shape, and so on. At the same time, the image consists of lots of features that are not related to cats. The tree and leaves in the first two images are useless in the identification of the cat. The pooling mechanism helps the algorithm understand which part of the image is relevant and which is irrelevant.

The feature map derived from the convolution layer is passed through a pooling layer to further reduce the image, preserving the most relevant part of the image. The pooling layer consists of functions such as max pooling, min pooling, and average pooling. What it means is that we select a matrix size, say 2x2, and we scan the feature map and select the maximum number from the 2x2 matrix fitting in that block. The following figure gives a clear idea of how max pooling works. Refer to the colors – the max number in each of the colored boxes from the feature map are selected in the pooled feature map:

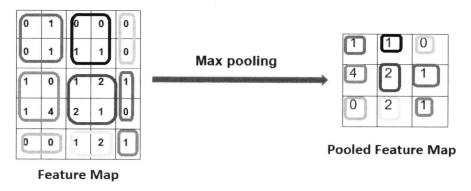

Figure 7.9: Pooling

Consider the case of the box that has number four in it. Let's assume that number four represents the ears of a cat, while the blank space around the ears is zero and one. So, we ignore the zero and one of that block and only select four. The following is example code for adding a pooling layer; here, **Maxpool2D** is used for max pooling, which helps to identify the most important features:

```
classifier.add(MaxPool2D(2,2))
```

Flattening

Flattening is that part of a CNN where the image is made ready to use as an input to an ANN. As the name suggests, the pooled image is flattened and converted into a single column. Each row is made into a column and stacked one over another. We have converted a 3x3 matrix into a 1xn matrix, where n, in our case, is 9:

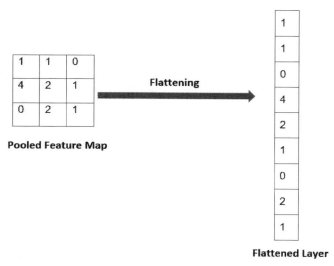

Figure 7.10: Flattening

In real time, we have a number of pooled feature maps, and we flatten them in a single column. This single column is used as an input for an ANN. The following image shows a number of pooled layers flattened into a single column:

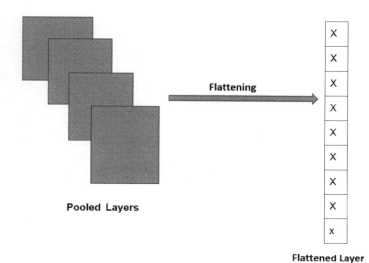

Figure 7.11: Pooling and flattening

The following is example code for adding a flattening layer; here **Flatten** is used for flattening the CNN:

```
classifier.add(Flatten())
```

Now, let's look at the overall structure of a CNN in a single figure:

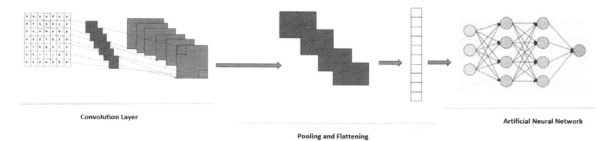

Figure 7.12: CNN architecture

The following is example code to add the first layer to a CNN:

```
classifier.add(Conv2D(32,3,3,input_shape=(64,64,3),activation='relu'))
```

32,3,3 refers to the fact that there are 32 feature detectors of size 3x3. As a best practice, always start with 32, and then you can add 64 or 128 later.

Input_shape: Since all images are of different shapes and sizes, this **input_image** converts all images into a uniform shape and size. **(64,64)** is the dimension of the converted image. It can be set to 128 or 256, but if you are working on a CPU on a

laptop, it is advisable to use 64x64. The last argument, **3**, is used because the image is a colored image (coded in red, blue, green, or RGB). If the image is black and white, the argument can be set to one. The activation function used is Relu.

> **Note**
>
> We are using Keras with TensorFlow as the backend in this book. If the backend is Theano, then **input_image** will be coded as (3,64,64).

The last step is to fit the data created. Here is the code to do so:

```
classifier.fit_generator(training_set,
steps_per_epoch = 5000,
epochs = 25,
validation_data = test_set,
validation_steps = 1000)
```

> **Note**
>
> **steps_per_epoch** is the number of training images. **validation_steps** is the number of test images.

Image Augmentation

The word **augmentation** means the action or process of making or becoming greater in size or amount. **Image** or **data augmentation** works in a similar manner. Image/data augmentation creates many batches of our images. Then, it applies random transformations on random images inside the batches. Data transformation can be rotating images, shifting them, flipping them, and so on. By applying this transformation, we get more diverse images inside the batches, and we also have much more data than we had originally.

A cylinder can be rotated from different angles and seen differently. In the following figure, a single cylinder is seen from five different angles. So, we have effectively created five different images from a single image:

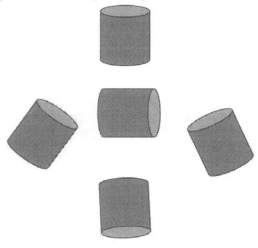

Figure 7.13: Image augmentation of a cylinder

The following is example code of image augmentation; here, the **ImageDataGenerator** class is used for processing. **shear_range**, **zoom_range**, and **horizontal_flip** are all used for the transformation of images:

```
from keras.preprocessing.image import ImageDataGenerator


train_datagen = ImageDataGenerator(rescale = 1./100,
                                   shear_range = 0.3,
                                   zoom_range = 0.3,
                                   horizontal_flip = False)
test_datagen = ImageDataGenerator(rescale = 1./100)
```

Advantages of Image Augmentation

Image augmentation is an important part of processing images:

- **Reducing overfitting**: It helps reduce overfitting by creating multiple versions of the same image by slicing and dicing it across all angles.

- **Increases the quantity of images**: A single image acts as multiple images. So, essentially, the dataset has less images, but each image can be converted into multiple images with image augmentation. Image augmentation will increase the number of images and each image will be treated differently by the algorithm.

- **Easy to predict new images**: Imagine that a single image of a football is looked at from different angles and each angle is considered a distinct image. This will mean that the algorithm will be more accurate at predicting new images:

Figure 7.14: Image augmentation of an image of a ball

Now that we have learned the concepts and theory behind computer vision with CNNs, let's work on some practical examples.

We will first start with a simple CNN, then we will tweak our CNN by permutation and combinations of the following:

1. Adding more CNN layers

2. Adding more ANN layers

3. Changing the optimizer function

4. Changing the activation function

Exercise 19: Build a CNN and Identify Images of Cats and Dogs

We have images of cats and dogs, which are divided into training and testing sets, and we have to build a CNN that identifies whether an image is a cat or a dog.

> **Note**
>
> All the exercises and activities will be developed in the Jupyter Notebook. Please download the GitHub repository with all the prepared templates from https://github.com/TrainingByPackt/Applied-Deep-Learning-with-Keras/tree/master/Lesson07.

Before we start on the following steps, ensure that you have downloaded the image datasets from the GitHub repository to your own working directory. You will need a **training_set** folder to train your model, and a **test_set** folder to test your model. Each of these folders will contain a **cats** folder, containing cat images, and a **dogs** folder, containing dog images.

The steps for completing this exercise are as follows:

1. Import the libraries and classes:

```
#Import the Libraries

from keras.models import Sequential
from keras.layers import Conv2D
from keras.layers import MaxPool2D
from keras.layers import Flatten
from keras.layers import Dense
```

2. Now, initiate the model with the **Sequential** class:

```
#Initiate the classifier
classifier=Sequential()
```

3. Add the first layer of the CNN:

```
classifier.add(Conv2D(32,3,3,input_shape=(64,64,3),activation='relu'))
```

32,3,3 shows that there are 32 feature detectors of 3x3 size.

4. Now, add the pooling layer with the image size as 2x2:

```
classifier.add(MaxPool2D(2,2))
```

5. The final step of building the CNN is flattening:

```
classifier.add(Flatten())
```

6. Add the first **Dense** layer of the ANN. Here, 128 is the output of the number of nodes. As a best practice, 128 is good to get started. **Activation** is **relu**. As a best practice, a power of two is preferred:

```
classifier.add(Dense(128,activation='relu'))
```

7. Add the output layer of the ANN. This is a binary classification problem, so the output is **1** and the activation is **sigmoid**:

```
classifier.add(Dense(1,activation='sigmoid'))
```

8. The next step is to compile the network:

```
#Compile the network
classifier.compile(optimizer='adam',loss='binary_
crossentropy',metrics=['accuracy'])
```

9. The following code will scale and transform the images, making them ready for processing:

```
from keras.preprocessing.image import ImageDataGenerator

train_datagen = ImageDataGenerator(rescale = 1./255,
                                    shear_range = 0.2,
                                    zoom_range = 0.2,
                                    horizontal_flip = True)
test_datagen = ImageDataGenerator(rescale = 1./255)
```

10. Create a training set from the **training set** folder. **'../dataset/training_set'** is the folder where our data is placed. Our CNN model has an image size of 64x64, so the same size should be passed here too. **batch_size** is the number of images in a single batch, which is 32. **Class_mode** is set to **binary**, as we are working on binary classifiers:

```
training_set = train_datagen.flow_from_directory('../dataset/training_set',
target_size = (64, 64),
batch_size = 32,
class_mode = 'binary')
```

11. Create the test set:

```
test_set = test_datagen.flow_from_directory('../dataset/test_set',
target_size = (64, 64),
batch_size = 32,
class_mode = 'binary')
```

12. Finally, fit the data. **steps_per_epoch** is **10000**, as there are 10,000 images in the training set. **validation_steps** is **2500** as the test set has 2,500 images. The following step might take more time to execute:

```
classifier.fit_generator(training_set,
steps_per_epoch = 10000,
epochs = 2,
validation_data = test_set,
validation_steps = 2500)
```

The following figure is the output of the preceding code:

```
10000/10000 [==============================] - 3402s 340ms/step - loss: 0.4650 - acc: 0.7760 - val_loss:
0.5276 - val_acc: 0.7712
Epoch 2/2
10000/10000 [==============================] - 3222s 322ms/step - loss: 0.3349 - acc: 0.8527 - val_loss:
0.5961 - val_acc: 0.7719
```

Figure 7.15: Accuracy of the model

The accuracy on the validation set is 77.19 %.

Note

To get more accurate results, try increasing the number of epochs to about 25. This will increase the time taken to process the data, and the total time is dependent on the configuration of your machine.

This completes the exercise on processing images and identifying the contents of the images. An important thing to remember here is that this is robust code for any binary classification problem in computer vision. This means that the code remains the same even if the image data changes.

Activity 13: Amending our Model with Multiple Layers and the Use of SoftMax

Since we have run a CNN model successfully, the next logical step is to try and improve the performance of our algorithm. There are many ways to improve the performance, and one of the most straightforward ways is by adding multiple ANN models, which we will learn about in this activity. We will also change the activation from sigmoid to SoftMax. We can then compare the result with the earlier activity. Follow these steps to complete the activity:

1. To build a CNN import library and create a **Sequential** class, import **Conv2D**, **MaxPool2D**, **Flatten**, and **Dense**. **Conv2D** is used to build the convolution layer. Since our pictures are in 2D, we have used 2D here. Similarly, **Maxpool2D** is used for max pooling, **Flatten** is used for flattening the CNN, and **Dense** is to add a fully connected CNN to an ANN.

2. Start building a CNN architecture using the preceding libraries. After adding the first layer, add two additional layers to your CNN.

3. Add a pooling and flattening layer to it, which will serve as the input for the ANN.

4. Build a fully connected ANN whose inputs will be the output of the CNN. After adding the first layer of your ANN, add three additional layers. For the output layer of your ANN, use the SoftMax activation function.

5. Perform image augmentation to process and transform the data. The **ImageDataGenerator** class is used for processing. **shear_range**, **zoom_range**, and **horzintal_flip** are all used for the transformation of images.

6. Create the training and test set data. Lastly, fit the data created.

> **Note**
>
> The solution for this activity can be found on page 361.

Let's change the activation function back, and then check the accuracy.

Exercise 20: Amending our model by reverting to the Sigmoid activation function

We will rebuild our model but revert the activation function from SoftMax back to sigmoid. We can then compare the accuracy to our previous model:

1. Import the libraries and classes:

    ```
    #Import the Libraries

    from keras.models import Sequential
    from keras.layers import Conv2D
    from keras.layers import MaxPool2D
    from keras.layers import Flatten
    from keras.layers import Dense
    ```

2. Now, initiate the model with the **Sequential** class:

    ```
    #Initiate the classifier
    classifier=Sequential()
    ```

3. Add the first layer of the CNN:

    ```
    classifier.add(Conv2D(32,3,3,input_shape=(64,64,3),activation='relu'))
    classifier.add(Conv2D(32, (3, 3), activation = 'relu'))
    classifier.add(Conv2D(32, (3, 3), activation = 'relu'))
    ```

4. Now, add the pooling layer with the image size as 2x2:

    ```
    classifier.add(MaxPool2D(2,2))
    ```

5. Add one more **Conv2D** and pooling layer to supplement it:

    ```
    classifier.add(Conv2D(32, (3, 3), activation = 'relu'))
    classifier.add(MaxPool2D(pool_size = (2, 2)))
    ```

6. The final step of building the CNN is flattening:

    ```
    classifier.add(Flatten())
    ```

7. Add the first **Dense** layer of the ANN. Here, **128** is the output of the number of nodes. As a best practice, 128 is good to get started. **Activation** is **relu**. As a best practice, a power of two is preferred. Add multiple layers:

    ```
    classifier.add(Dense(128,activation='relu'))
    classifier.add(Dense(128,activation='relu'))
    classifier.add(Dense(128,activation='relu'))
    ```

8. Add the output layer of the ANN. This is a binary classification problem, so the output is one and the activation is **sigmoid**:

```
classifier.add(Dense(1,activation='sigmoid'))
```

9. The next step is to compile the network:

```
classifier.compile(optimizer='adam',loss='binary_
crossentropy',metrics=['accuracy'])
```

10. The following code will scale and transform the images, making them ready for processing:

```
from keras.preprocessing.image import ImageDataGenerator

train_datagen = ImageDataGenerator(rescale = 1./255,
                                   shear_range = 0.2,
                                   zoom_range = 0.2,
                                   horizontal_flip = True)

test_datagen = ImageDataGenerator(rescale = 1./255)
```

11. Create a training set from the **training set** folder. **../dataset/training_set** is the folder where our data is placed. Our CNN model has an image size of 64x64, so the same size should be passed here too. **batch_size** is the number of images in a single batch, which is 32. **class_mode** is binary as we are working on binary classifiers:

```
training_set = train_datagen.flow_from_directory('../dataset/training_set',
target_size = (64, 64),
batch_size = 32,
class_mode = 'binary')
```

12. Create the test set:

```
test_set = test_datagen.flow_from_directory('../dataset/test_set',
target_size = (64, 64),
batch_size = 32,
class_mode = 'binary')
```

13. Finally, we will fit the data. **steps_per_epoch** is **10000** as there are 10,000 images in training set. **validation_steps** is **2500** as the test set has 2,500 images:

```
classifier.fit_generator(training_set,
steps_per_epoch = 10000,
epochs = 2,
validation_data = test_set,
validation_steps = 2500)
```

The following figure shows the output of the preceding code:

```
10000/10000 [==============================] - 11256s 1s/step - loss: 0.3756 - acc: 0.8255 - val_loss: 0.4191 - val_acc: 0.83
30
Epoch 2/2
10000/10000 [==============================] - 19370s 2s/step - loss: 0.2071 - acc: 0.9146 - val_loss: 0.3951 - val_acc: 0.85
62
```

Figure 7.16: Accuracy of the model

The accuracy of the model is over 85%, which is clearly greater than the accuracy of the model we built in the last exercise. This shows the importance of activation functions. Just changing the output activation function from SoftMax to sigmoid increased the accuracy from 50% to 85%.

> **Note**
>
> In a binary classification problem (in our case, cats versus dogs), it is always better to use sigmoid as the activation function at the output.

Exercise 21: Changing the Optimizer from Adam to SGD

In this exercise, we will amend the model again by changing the optimizer to SGD. We can then compare the accuracy to our previous models:

1. Import the libraries and classes:

```
#Import the Libraries

from keras.models import Sequential
from keras.layers import Conv2D
from keras.layers import MaxPool2D
from keras.layers import Flatten
from keras.layers import Dense
```

2. Now, initiate the model with the **Sequential** class:

    ```
    #Initiate the classifier
    classifier=Sequential()
    ```

3. Add the first layer of the CNN:

    ```
    classifier.add(Conv2D(32,3,3,input_shape=(64,64,3),activation='relu'))
    ```

4. Now, add the pooling layer with the image size as 2x2:

    ```
    classifier.add(MaxPool2D(2,2))
    ```

5. Add one more **Conv2D** and pooling layer to supplement it:

    ```
    classifier.add(Conv2D(32, (3, 3), input_shape = (64, 64, 3), activation =
    'relu'))
    ```

6. Add a **Flatten** layer to complete the CNN architecture:

    ```
    classifier.add(Flatten())
    ```

7. Add the first **Dense** layer of ANN:

    ```
    classifier.add(Dense(128,activation='relu'))
    ```

8. Add three more dense layers to the network:

    ```
    classifier.add(Dense(128,activation='relu'))
    classifier.add(Dense(128,activation='relu'))
    classifier.add(Dense(128,activation='relu'))
    ```

9. Add the output layer of ANN:

    ```
    classifier.add(Dense(1,activation='softmax'))
    ```

10. The next step is to compile the network:

    ```
    classifier.compile(optimizer='SGD',loss='categorical_
    crossentropy',metrics=['accuracy'])
    ```

11. The following code will scale and transform the images, making them ready for processing:

```
from keras.preprocessing.image import ImageDataGenerator

train_datagen = ImageDataGenerator(rescale = 1./255,
                                   shear_range = 0.2,
                                   zoom_range = 0.2,
                                   horizontal_flip = True)
test_datagen = ImageDataGenerator(rescale = 1./255)
```

12. Create a training set from the **training_set** folder:

```
training_set = train_datagen.flow_from_directory('../dataset/training_set',
target_size = (64, 64),
batch_size = 32,
class_mode = 'binary')
```

13. Create the test set from the **test-set** folder:

```
test_set = test_datagen.flow_from_directory('../dataset/test_set',
target_size = (64, 64),
batch_size = 32,
class_mode = 'binary')
```

14. Finally, fit the data. **steps_per_epoch** is **10000** as there are 10,000 images in training set. **validation_steps** is **2500** as the test set has 2,500 images:

```
classifier.fit_generator(training_set,
steps_per_epoch = 10000,
epochs = 2,
validation_data = test_set,
validation_steps = 2500)
```

The following figure shows the output of the preceding code:

```
10000/10000 [==============================] - 11600s 1s/step - loss: 0.5766 - acc: 0.6839 - val_loss: 0.4443 - val_acc: 0.79
05
Epoch 2/2
10000/10000 [==============================] - 19013s 2s/step - loss: 0.3952 - acc: 0.8206 - val_loss: 0.3875 - val_acc: 0.82
43
```

Figure 7.17: Accuracy of the model

The accuracy is 83.90%, as we have used multiple ANNs and the optimizer as SGD optimizer.

So, we have worked with a number of different permutations and combinations of our model. It seems the best accuracy for this dataset can be obtained by:

1. Adding multiple CNN layers.

2. Adding multiple ANN layers.

3. Having the activation as sigmoid.

4. Having the optimizer as adam.

5. Increasing the epoch size to about 25 (this takes a lot of computational time – make sure you have a GPU to do this). This will increase the accuracy of your predictions.

Finally, we will go ahead and predict a new unknown image, passing it to the algorithm and validating whether the image is correctly classified.

Exercise 22: Classifying a New Image

In this exercise, we will try to classify a new image. The image is not exposed to the algorithm, so this will be the test of our algorithm. You can run any of the algorithms in this chapter (although the one that gets the highest accuracy is preferred), and then use the model to classify the image.

> **Note**
>
> The image for use in this exercise can be found in the GitHub repository at https://github.com/TrainingByPackt/Applied-Deep-Learning-with-Keras/tree/master/Lesson07.

Before we start on the following steps, ensure you have downloaded `test_image_1` from the GitHub repository to your own working directory. This exercise follows on directly from the previous exercises, so ensure that you have one of the algorithms from this chapter ready to run in your workspace.

The steps for completing this exercise are as follows:

1. Load the image. `'../test/test_image_1.jpg'` is the path of the test image. Please change the path to where you have saved the dataset in your system:

```
new_image = image.load_img('../test/test_image_1.jpg', target_size = (64,
64))
```

2. Process the image:

```
new_image = image.img_to_array(new_image)
new_image = np.expand_dims(new_image, axis = 0)
```

3. Predict the new image:

```
result = classifier.predict(new_image)
```

4. The **prediction** method will output the image as **1** or **0**. To map **1** and **0** to **Dog** or **Cat** use the **class_indices** method with an **if…else** statement, as follows:

```
training_set.class_indices
if result[0][0] == 1:
    prediction = 'It is a Dog'
else:
    prediction = 'It is a Cat'

print(prediction)
```

The following figure shows the output of the preceding code:

It is a Dog

Figure 7.18: Image classification of a dog image

test_image_1 is a dog's image (you can see this by viewing the image for yourself), and was correctly predicted to be a dog by the model.

In this exercise, we trained our model then gave the model an image of a dog, and we found out that the algorithm is classifying the image correctly. You can train the model on any type of image by using the same process. For example, if you train the model with scans of lung infections and healthy lungs, then the model will be able to classify whether a new scan represents an infected lung or a healthy lung.

Activity 14: Classify a New Image

In this activity, you will try to classify another new image, as done in the preceding exercise. The image is not exposed to the algorithm, so this will be the test of our algorithm. You can run any of the algorithms in this chapter (although the one that gets the highest accuracy is preferred) and then use the model to classify your images. The steps to implement the activity are as follows:

1. Run any one of the algorithms from this chapter.

2. Load the image (**test_image_2**) from your directory.

3. Process the image using the algorithm.

4. Predict the subject of the new image. You can view the image yourself to check whether the prediction is correct.

> **Note**
>
> The image for use in this activity can be found in the GitHub repository at https://github.com/TrainingByPackt/Applied-Deep-Learning-with-Keras/tree/master/Lesson07.

Before starting, ensure you have downloaded **test_image_2** from the GitHub repository to your own working directory. This activity follows on directly from the previous exercises, so please ensure that you have one of the algorithms from this chapter ready to run in your workspace.

> **Note**
>
> The solution for this activity can be found on page 363.

Summary

In this chapter, we studied why we need computer vision and how it works. We understood why computer vision is one of the hottest fields in machine learning. Then, we worked with convolutional neural networks, their architecture, and how we can build CNNs in real-life applications. We also tried to improve our algorithms by adding more ANN and CNN layers and by changing activation and optimizer functions. We also tried different activation functions and loss functions. In the end, we were able to successfully classify new images of cats and dogs through the algorithm. Remember, the images of dogs and cats can be substituted with any other images, such as tigers and deer, or MRI scans of brains with and without a tumor. Any binary-classification computer-imaging problem can be solved with the same approach.

In the next chapter, we will study an even more efficient technique for working on computer vision, which is less time-consuming and easier to implement.

8

Transfer Learning and Pre-Trained Models

Learning Objectives

By the end of this chapter, you will be able to:

- Explain transfer learning and pre-trained models
- Apply feature extraction to pre-trained models
- Use pre-trained models for image classification
- Apply fine-tuning to pre-trained models

In this chapter, we will learn about transfer learning and pre-train sets. Then, we will apply feature extraction to pre-trained models. We will use these pre-trained models to classify images. Lastly, we will apply fine tuning on pre-trained models.

Introduction

In the previous chapter, we learned how to create a **convolutional neural network (CNN)** from scratch with Keras. However, in real-world projects, you almost never code a convolutional neural network from scratch. You always tweak and train them as per the requirement. This book introduces you to the important concepts of **transfer learning** and **pre-trained networks**, also known as pre-trained models, which are used in the industry. This is an advanced level of machine learning, so this chapter assumes that you have adequate knowledge of neural networks and CNNs. We will use images and, rather than building a CNN from scratch, we will match these images on pre-trained models to try to classify them. We will also tweak our models to make them more flexible. The models we will use here are VGG16 and ResNet50, which we will discuss further in the chapter. Before starting to work on pre-trained models, we need to understand about transfer learning.

Pre-Trained Sets and Transfer Learning

Humans are trained to learn by experience. We tend to use the knowledge we gain in one situation in similar situations we face in the future. Suppose you want to learn how to drive an SUV. You have never driven an SUV; all you know is how to drive a small hatchback car.

The dimensions of the SUV are considerably larger than the hatchback, so navigating the SUV in traffic will surely be a challenge. Still, some basic systems, such as the clutch, accelerator, and brakes, remain similar to that of the hatchback. So, knowing how to drive a hatchback will surely be of great help to you when you starting to learn to drive the SUV. All the knowledge that you acquired while driving a hatchback can be used when you are learning to drive a big SUV.

This is precisely what transfer learning is. By definition, transfer learning is a concept in machine learning in which we store and use knowledge gained in one activity while learning another similar activity. The hatchback-SUV model perfectly fits the definition.

Suppose we want to know whether a picture is of a dog or cat, we can have two approaches. One is building a deep-learning model from scratch and then passing on the new pictures to the networks. Another option is to use a pre-trained deep-learning neural network model that has already been built by using cats, and dogs' images, instead of creating a neural network from scratch. Using the pre-trained model saves us computational time and resources. There can be some unforeseen advantages of using a pre-trained network. For example, almost all pictures of dogs and cats will have some more objects in the picture, such as trees, sky, and furniture. We can even use this pre-trained network to identify objects such as trees, sky, and furniture.

So, a pre-trained network is a saved network (a neural network in the case of deep learning) that was trained on a very large dataset, mostly on image classification problems. To work on a pre-trained network, we need to understand the concepts of feature extraction and fine-tuning.

Feature Extraction

To understand feature extraction, we first need to revisit the architecture of a convolutional neural network.

You may recall that the full architecture of a CNN, at a high level, consists of:

- A convolution layer
- A pooling and flattening Layer
- An Artificial Neural Network (ANN)

The following figure shows a complete CNN architecture:

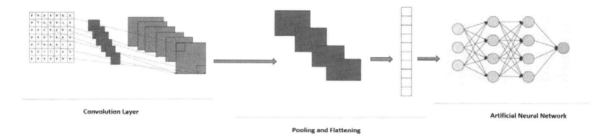

Convolution Layer

Pooling and Flattening

Artificial Neural Network

Figure 8.1: CNN Architecture

Now, let's divide this architecture into two parts. The first part contains everything but the ANN, and the second part only contains the ANN. The following figure shows a split CNN architecture:

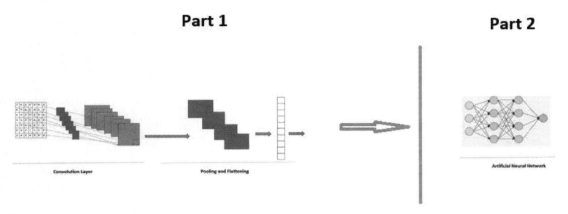

Figure 8.2: CNN split architecture: convolutional base and classifier

The first part is called a **convolutional base** and the second part is called the **classifier**.

In feature extraction, we keep reusing the convolutional base and the classifier is changed. So, we preserve the learnings of the convolutional layer and we can pass different classifiers on top of the convolutional layer. A classifier can be dog versus cat, bikes versus cars, or even medical X-ray images to classify tumors, infections, and so on. The following figure shows some convolutional base layers used for different classifiers:

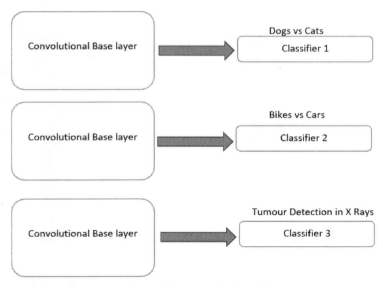

Figure 8.3: Reusable convolutional base layer

The obvious next question is, can't we reuse the classifier too, like the base layer? The general answer is no. The reason is that learning from the convolutional base is likely to be more generic and therefore more reusable. But, the learning of the classifier is mostly specific to the classes on which the model was trained. So, it is advisable to reuse only the convolutional base layer and not the classifier.

The amount of generalized learning from a convolutional base layer depends on the depth of the layer. For example, in the case of a cat, the initial layers of the model learn about general traits such as edges and the background, while the higher layers may learn more about specific details such as eyes, ears, or the shape of the nose. So, if your new dataset is something very different from the original dataset, for example, if you wish to identify fruit instead of cats, then it is better to only use some initial layers of the base convolutional base layer rather than using the whole layer.

Freezing convolutional layers: One of the most important features of pre-trained learning is to understand the concept of freezing some layers of a pre-trained network. Freezing essentially means that we stop the process of the weight updating of some convolutional layers. Since we are using a pre-trained network, it is important to understand that we will need the information stored in the initial layers of the network. If that information is updated in training a network, we might lose some generic concepts learned and stored in the pre-trained network. If we add a classifier (CNN), many dense layers on top of the network are randomly initialized, and there may be cases where, due to back propagation, the learning of the initial layers of the network will be totally destroyed.

To avoid this information decay, we freeze some layers. This is done by making the layers non-trainable.

Fine-Tuning a Pre-Trained Network

Fine-tuning means tweaking our neural network in such a way that it becomes more relevant to the task at hand. We can freeze some of the initial layers of the network so that we don't lose information stored in those layers. The information stored there is generic and of useful. However, if we can freeze those layers while our classifier is learning and then unfreeze them, we can tweak them a little so that they fit even better to the problem at hand. Suppose we have a pre-trained network that identifies animals. However, if we want to identify specific animals, such as dogs and cats, then we can tweak the layers a little bit so that they can learn how dogs and cats look. This is like using the whole pre-trained network and then adding a new layer that consists of images of dogs and cats. We will be doing a similar activity by using a pre-built network and adding a classifier on top of it, which will be trained on pictures of dogs and cats.

There is a three-point system to work with fine-tuning:

- Add a classifier (ANN) on top of a pre-trained system.
- Freeze the convolutional base and train the network.
- Train the added classifier and the un-frozen part of the convolutional base jointly.

The ImageNet Dataset

In real practical work experience, you almost never need to build a base convolutional model on your own. You will always use pre-trained models. But, where do you get the data from. For visual computing, the answer is ImageNet. The ImageNet dataset is a large visual database that is used in visual object recognition. It consists more of than 14 million labelled images with object names. ImageNet contains more than 20,000 categories.

Some Pre-Trained Networks in Keras

These pre-trained networks can be thought of as the base convolutional layers. You use these networks and fit a classifier (ANN):

- VGG16
- Inception V3
- Xception
- ResNet50
- Mobilenet

Different vendors have created the preceding pre-trained networks. For example, ResNet50 was created by Microsoft, and Inception V3 and MobileNet were created by Google. In this chapter, we will be working with VGG16 and ResNet50.

> **Note**
>
> All the exercises and activities will be developed in the Jupyter Notebook. Please download the GitHub repository with all the prepared templates from https:// github.com/TrainingByPackt/Applied-Deep-Learning-with-Keras/tree/master/ Lesson08.

Exercise 23: Identify an Image Using the VGG16 Network

We have a picture of a man wearing a suit. We will use the VGG16 Network to process and identify the image. Before completing the following steps, ensure you have downloaded the **man_in_suit** image from GitHub and saved it to your working directory:

1. Import the libraries:

```
import numpy as np
from keras.applications.vgg16 import VGG16
from keras.preprocessing import image
from keras.applications.vgg16 import preprocess_input
```

2. Initiate the model:

```
classifier = VGG16()
```

> **Note**
>
> The last layer of predictions (Dense) has 1,000 values. This means that VGG16 has a total of 1,000 labels and our image will be one out of those 1,000 labels.

3. Load the image. **'../Data/Prediction/man_in_suit.jpg'** is the path of the image on our system; it will be different on your system:

```
new_image= image.load_img('../Data/Prediction/man_in_suit.jpg', target_
size=(224, 224))
new_image
```

The following figure shows the output of the preceding code:

Figure 8.4: Man in a suit

The target size should be 224x224 as VGG16 accepts only **(224,224)**.

4. Change the image to an array by using the **img_to_array** function:

```
transformed_image= image.img_to_array(new_image)
transformed_image.shape
```

The following figure shows the output of the preceding code:

(224, 224, 3)

Figure 8.5: Shape of the image

5. To process the image further, it has to be in a four-dimensional form for VGG16. So, we need to expand the dimension of the image as follows:

```
transformed_image=np.expand_dims(transformed_image,axis=0)
transformed_image.shape
```

The following figure shows the output of the preceding code:

(1, 224, 224, 3)

Figure 8.6: New shape of the image after expanding to four-dimensions

6. Preprocess the image:

```
transformed_image=preprocess_input(transformed_image)
transformed_image
```

The following figure shows the output of the preceding code:

```
array([[[[ -45.939003,   -37.779   ,   -36.68    ],
         [ -46.939003,   -34.779   ,   -31.68    ],
         [ -44.939003,   -33.779   ,   -28.68    ],
         ...,
         [ -99.939   ,   -99.779   ,   -62.68    ],
         [ -98.939   ,   -94.779   ,   -62.68    ],
         [ -94.939   ,   -89.779   ,   -59.68    ]],

        [[ -46.939003,   -38.779   ,   -37.68    ],
         [ -47.939003,   -35.779   ,   -32.68    ],
         [ -45.939003,   -34.779   ,   -29.68    ],
```

Figure 8.7: A screenshot of image preprocessing

7. Create the predictor variable:

```
y_pred= classifier.predict(transformed_image)
y_pred
```

8. Check the shape of the image. It should be of the (1,1000) shape. It's 1000 because ImageNet database has 1,000 categories of images. The predictor variable shows the probability of our image being one of those images:

```
y_pred.shape
```

The following figure shows the output of the preceding code:

(1, 1000)

Figure 8.8: Verifying the shape of the image

9. Select the top five probabilities of what our image is:

```
from keras.applications.vgg16 import decode_predictions
decode_predictions(y_pred,top=5)
```

The following figure shows the output of the preceding code:

```
[[('n04350905', 'suit', 0.82904965),
  ('n04591157', 'Windsor_tie', 0.06311033),
  ('n04479046', 'trench_coat', 0.021564618),
  ('n10148035', 'groom', 0.018631358),
  ('n03594734', 'jean', 0.013046923)]]
```

Figure 8.9: Selected top five probabilities of our image

The first column of the array is the internal code number. The second is the possible label and the third is the probability of the image being the label.

10. Make the predictions in human-readable form. We extract the most probable label from the output as follows:

```
label = decode_predictions(y_pred)
# Most likely result is retrived, for example highest probability
decoded_label = label[0][0]
# The classification is printed
print('%s (%.2f%%)' % (decoded_label[1], decoded_label[2]*100 ))
```

The following figure shows the output of the preceding code:

```
suit (82.90%)
```

Figure 8.10: Final prediction

We predicted an image that says, with 82.9% probability, that the picture is of a suit. Clearly, higher accuracy here means a relatively similar object to our picture is present in the ImageNet database, and our algorithm has done a fantastic job.

Activity 15: Use the VGG16 Network to Train a Deep Learning Network to Identify Images

You are given an image of a cat. Use the VGG16 network to predict the image. Before you start, ensure that you have downloaded the image (**test_image_1**) to your working directory. To complete the activity, follow these steps:

1. Import the required libraries along with the VGG16 network.

2. Initiate the pre-trained VGG16 model.

3. Load the image that is to be classified.

4. Preprocess the image by applying the transformations.

5. Create a predictor variable to predict the image.

6. Label the image and classify it.

> **Note**
>
> The solution for this activity can be found on page 365.

Exercise 24: Classification of Images That Are Not Present in the ImageNet Database.

Now, let's work with an image that is not part of the 1,000 labels in our VGG16 network. This is a pyramid image, and there are pyramid labels in our pre-trained network. Let's see what results we get:

1. Import the libraries:

```
import numpy as np
from keras.applications.vgg16 import VGG16
from keras.preprocessing import image
from keras.applications.vgg16 import preprocess_input
```

2. Initiate the model:

```
classifier = VGG16()
print(classifier.summary())
```

`classifier.summary()` shows us the architecture of the network. The following are the points to be noted: it has a four-dimensional input shape (None, 224,224,3) and it has three convolutional layers. The following figure shows the last four layers of the output:

```
flatten (Flatten)              (None, 25088)              0

fc1 (Dense)                    (None, 4096)               102764544

fc2 (Dense)                    (None, 4096)               16781312

predictions (Dense)            (None, 1000)               4097000
================================================================
Total params: 138,357,544
Trainable params: 138,357,544
Non-trainable params: 0
```

None

Figure 8.11: Summary of the image using the VGG16 classifier

Note

The last layer of predictions (Dense) has 1,000 values. This means that VGG16 has a total of 1,000 labels and our image will be one out of those 1,000 labels.

3. Load the image. `'../Data/Prediction/pyramid.jpg'` is the path of the image on our system. It will be different on your system:

```
new_image= image.load_img('../Data/Prediction/pyramid.jpg', target_size=(224, 224))
new_image
```

The following figure shows the output of the preceding code:

Figure 8.12: Sample pyramid image for prediction

The target size should be 224x224 as VGG16 accepts only **(224,224)**.

4. Change the image to an array by using the **img_to_array** function:

```
transformed_image= image.img_to_array(new_image)
transformed_image.shape
```

5. To process this image further, it has to be in a four-dimensional form for VGG16. So, we need to expand the dimension of the image as follows:

```
transformed_image=np.expand_dims(transformed_image,axis=0)
transformed_image.shape
```

6. Pre-process the image:

```
transformed_image=preprocess_input(transformed_image)
transformed_image
```

The following figure shows the output of the preceding code:

```
array([[[[ 97.061   ,  86.221   ,  89.32    ],
         [ 96.061   ,  85.221   ,  88.32    ],
         [ 97.061   ,  86.221   ,  89.32    ],
         ...,
         [ 58.060997,  44.221   ,  46.32    ],
         [ 60.060997,  46.221   ,  49.32    ],
         [ 62.060997,  48.221   ,  51.32    ]],

        [[ 96.061   ,  86.221   ,  87.32    ],
         [103.061   ,  93.221   ,  94.32    ],
         [101.061   ,  91.221   ,  92.32    ],
         ...,
         [ 53.060997,  39.221   ,  41.32    ],
         [ 54.060997,  40.221   ,  43.32    ],
         [ 56.060997,  42.221   ,  45.32    ]],

        [[ 90.061   ,  79.221   ,  80.32    ],
         [ 93.061   ,  82.221   ,  83.32    ],
         [ 97.061   ,  86.221   ,  87.32    ],
         ...,
         [ 53.060997,  39.221   ,  41.32    ],
         [ 53.060997,  39.221   ,  42.32    ],
         [ 55.060997,  41.221   ,  44.32    ]],
```

Figure 8.13: Screenshot showing a few instances of image preprocessing

7. Create the predictor variable:

```
y_pred= classifier.predict(transformed_image)
y_pred
```

The following figure shows the output of the preceding code:

```
array([[6.13451618e-08, 9.75525950e-07, 4.23466957e-07, 5.22295409e-07,
        2.26427446e-07, 4.08960545e-07, 8.66295579e-07, 1.99088731e-06,
        9.83872042e-07, 1.87045271e-06, 9.84587359e-07, 8.44672172e-08,
        1.31816194e-06, 4.18820719e-06, 4.55754019e-07, 2.52440918e-06,
        3.59976610e-07, 3.55078873e-06, 6.29364467e-06, 4.82221765e-07,
        5.24750067e-06, 4.71067506e-06, 5.39780331e-06, 1.63588666e-05,
        2.44527882e-06, 4.22415205e-08, 2.27910576e-07, 1.11375300e-06,
        1.03393978e-08, 1.13393249e-07, 2.39346463e-07, 1.01789595e-07,
        9.19396754e-08, 3.22333079e-07, 5.48555772e-06, 1.41607882e-06,
        8.38057701e-07, 3.51283305e-08, 1.58944644e-07, 7.19306399e-07,
        3.76838727e-07, 6.94572506e-08, 3.25316455e-06, 5.40365409e-06,
        6.90626905e-07, 2.25816081e-07, 3.57748632e-07, 3.28104562e-07,
        7.43478097e-08, 1.68728732e-07, 4.62492039e-07, 1.85900024e-06,
        5.65942315e-08, 7.96408699e-08, 2.39774499e-06, 2.32500685e-08,
        1.33880562e-07, 2.34648169e-07, 1.61747039e-06, 1.20090021e-07,
        4.84484588e-07, 1.26489539e-07, 2.07566416e-07, 4.36104770e-08,
        4.60033256e-08, 1.26742279e-07, 1.65323354e-06, 1.22634185e-06,
        2.25393947e-07, 6.22100379e-06, 6.65404158e-08, 9.87853355e-08,
        1.05115632e-07, 6.00570684e-06, 3.70224797e-07, 2.26105058e-07,
        3.88955323e-06, 3.91333970e-06, 7.21313597e-07, 1.06073662e-06,
```

Figure 8.14: Creating the predictor variable

8. Check the shape of the image. It should be of the (1,1000) shape. 1000 because, as mentioned previously, the Imagenet database has 1,000 categories of images. The predictor variable shows the probabilities of our image being one of those images. The following figure shows the output of the preceding code:

```
y_pred.shape
```

$$(1, 1000)$$

Figure 8.15: Expected shape of the image

9. Out of the 1,000 labels that the VGG16 network has, the following code will select the top five probabilities of what our image label is:

```
from keras.applications.vgg16 import decode_predictions
decode_predictions(y_pred,top=5)
```

The following figure shows the output of the preceding code:

```
[[('n02793495', 'barn', 0.27790722),
  ('n03028079', 'church', 0.25305647),
  ('n02825657', 'bell_cote', 0.13496666),
  ('n03837869', 'obelisk', 0.07406475),
  ('n09193705', 'alp', 0.05210917)]]
```

Figure 8.16: Top five probabilities of what our image can be

The first column of the array is an internal code number. The second is the label, and the third is the probability of the image being the label.

10. Make the predictions in human-readable form. We extract the most probable label from the output as follows:

```
label = decode_predictions(y_pred)
# Most likely result is retrieved, for example highest probability
decoded_label = label[0][0]
# The classification is printed
print('%s (%.2f%%)' % (decoded_label[1], decoded_label[2]*100 ))
```

The following figure shows the output of the preceding code:

```
barn (27.79%)
```

Figure 8.17: Final prediction of the image

So, you can see that the network predicted that our image was a barn, with close to 28% accuracy. Clearly, the image is not a barn, but a pyramid; out of all the labels that the VGG16 network contains, a barn is the closest thing to a pyramid. The following image is that of a barn:

Figure 8.18: Barn

To avoid such outputs, we could freeze the existing layer of VGG16 and add our own layer. We could add a layer that has images of barns and pyramids, so that we can obtain a better output.

To understand this in detail, let's work on a different example, where we freeze the last layer of the network and add our own layer with images of cats and dogs. This will help the network improve its accuracy in classifying images of cats and dogs.

If you have a large number of barn and pyramid images, you could perform a similar task to improve the model's ability to classify barns and pyramids. You could then test it be rerunning the previous exercise.

Exercise 25: Fine-Tune the VGG16 Model

Let's work on an exercise to fine-tune the VGG 16 model. In this exercise, we will freeze the network and remove the last layer of VGG16, which has 1,000 labels in it. After removing the last layer, we will build a new dog-cat classifier ANN, as done in *Chapter 7, Computer Vision with Convolutional Neural Networks*, and will connect this ANN to VGG16 instead of the original one with 1,000 labels. Essentially, what we will do is replace the last layer of VGG16 with a user-defined layer.

Before we start on the following steps, ensure you have downloaded the image datasets from the GitHub repository to your own working directory. You will need a **training_set** folder and a **test_set** folder to test your model. Each of these folders will contain a **cats** folder, containing cat images, and a **dogs** folder, containing dog images.

The steps for completing this exercise are as follows:

> **Note**
>
> Unlike the original new model, which had 1,000 labels (100 different object categories), this new fine-tuned model will only have images of dogs or cats. So, whatever image you provide as an input to the model, it will categorize it as a dog or cat based on its prediction probability.

1. Import the libraries:

    ```
    import numpy as np
    import keras
    from keras.layers import Dense
    ```

2. Initiate the model:

    ```
    vgg_model=keras.applications.vgg16.VGG16()
    ```

3. Check the model summary:

    ```
    vgg_model.summary()
    ```

    The following figure shows the output of the preceding code:

fc1 (Dense)	(None, 4096)	102764544
fc2 (Dense)	(None, 4096)	16781312
predictions (Dense)	(None, 1000)	4097000

    ```
    =================================================================
    Total params: 138,357,544
    Trainable params: 138,357,544
    Non-trainable params: 0
    ```

Figure 8.19: Model summary after initiating the model

4. Remove the last layer:

```
last_layer = str(vgg_model.layers[-1])

classifier= keras.Sequential()
for layer in vgg_model.layers:
    if str(layer) != last_layer:
        classifier.add(layer)
```

> **Note**
>
> Code explanation: we have created a new model name's classifier instead of **vgg_model**. All layers, except the last layer of **vgg_model**, have been included in the classifier.

5. Recheck the summary:

```
classifier.summary()
```

The following figure shows the output of the preceding code:

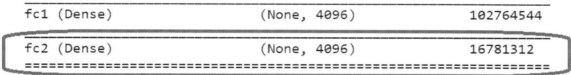

```
fc1 (Dense)                     (None, 4096)                 102764544
_____
fc2 (Dense)                     (None, 4096)                  16781312
========================================================================
Total params: 134,260,544
Trainable params: 134,260,544
Non-trainable params: 0
```

Figure 8.20: Rechecking the summary after removing the last layer

The last layer of prediction (**Dense**) has been deleted.

6. Freeze layers by making the model non-trainable:

```
for layer in classifier.layers:
    layer.trainable=False
```

7. Add a new layer and check the summary:

```
classifier.add(Dense(1,activation='sigmoid'))
classifier.summary()
```

The following figure shows the output of the preceding code:

fc1 (Dense)	(None, 4096)	102764544
fc2 (Dense)	(None, 4096)	16781312
dense_1 (Dense)	(None, 1)	4097

```
=================================================================
Total params: 134,264,641
Trainable params: 4,097
Non-trainable params: 134,260,544
```

Figure 8.21: Rechecking the summary after adding the new layer

Now, the last layer is the newly created user-defined layer.

8. Compile the network:

```
classifier.compile(optimizer='adam',loss='binary_
crossentropy',metrics=['accuracy'])
```

> **Note**
>
> Unlike in *Chapter 7, Computer Vision with Convolutional Neural Networks*, where the image size was 64x64, VGG16 needs an image size of 224x224.

9. Process the images and fit the ANN as done in *Chapter 7, Computer Vision with Convolutional Neural Networks*:

```
from keras.preprocessing.image import ImageDataGenerator

generate_train_data = ImageDataGenerator(rescale = 1./255,
                                  shear_range = 0.2,
                                  zoom_range = 0.2,
                                  horizontal_flip = True)

generate_test_data = ImageDataGenerator(rescale =1./255)

training_dataset = generate_train_data.flow_from_directory('dataset/
training_set',
                                          target_size = (224, 224),
```

```
                                                 batch_size = 32,
                                                 class_mode = 'binary')


test_datasetset = generate_test_data.flow_from_directory('dataset/test_
set',
                                              target_size = (224, 224),
                                              batch_size = 32,
                                              class_mode = 'binary')


classifier.fit_generator(training_dataset,
                         steps_per_epoch = 100,
                         epochs = 10,
                         validation_data = test_datasetset,
                         validation_steps = 30)
```

There are 100 training images, so **steps_per_epoch** =**100**, and 30 test images, so **validation_steps=30**.

```
100/100 [==============================] - 2083s 21s/step - loss: 0.5513 - acc: 0.7112 - val_loss: 0.3352 - val_acc: 0.8539
```

Figure 8.22: Fitting the model for 100 train models and 30 test images

10. Predict the new image (the code is same as in *Chapter 7, Computer Vision with Convolutional Neural Networks*):

```
import numpy as np
from keras.preprocessing import image
new_image = image.load_img('../Data/Prediction/test_image_1.jpg', target_
size = (224, 224))
new_image = image.img_to_array(new_image)
new_image = np.expand_dims(new_image, axis = 0)
result = classifier.predict(new_image)
training_set.class_indices
if result[0][0] == 1:
    prediction = 'It is a Dog'
else:
    prediction = 'It is a Cat'

print(prediction)
```

The following figure shows the output of the preceding code:

```
It is a Cat
```

Figure 8.23: Final image predicted

So, we can see that the algorithm has done the correct image classification by identifying the image of the cat. We just used a pre-build VGG16 model for image classification by tweaking its layers and molding it as per our requirement. This is a very powerful technique for image classification.

Exercise 26: Image Classification with ResNet

Finally, before closing this chapter, let's work on an exercise with the ResNet40 network. Let's use a beach image and try to predict it through the network:

1. Import the libraries:

    ```
    import numpy as np
    from keras.applications.resnet50 import ResNet50
    from keras.preprocessing import image
    from keras.applications.resnet50 import preprocess_input
    ```

2. Initiate the model:

    ```
    classifier=ResNet50()
    print(classifier.summary())
    ```

    The following figure shows the output of the preceding code:

```
activation_49 (Activation)      (None, 7, 7, 2048)    0          add_16[0][0]
_____
avg_pool (GlobalAveragePooling2 (None, 2048)          0          activation_49[0][0]
_____
fc1000 (Dense)                  (None, 1000)          2049000    avg_pool[0][0]
=========================================================================================
Total params: 25,636,712
Trainable params: 25,583,592
Non-trainable params: 53,120
_____
None
```

Figure 8.24: Shows a summary of the model

3. Load the image. `'../Data/Prediction/test_image_3.jpg'` is the path of the image on our system. It will be different on your system:

```
new_image= image.load_img('../Data/Prediction/test_image_3.jpg', target_
size=(224, 224))
new_image
```

Figure 8.25: Sample beach image for prediction

Note that the target size should be 224x224. as ResNet50 accepts only **(224,224)**.

4. Change the image to an array by using the **img_to_array** function:

```
transformed_image= image.img_to_array(new_image)
transformed_image.shape
```

5. To process the image further, it has to be in a four-dimensional form for ResNet50. So, we need to expand the dimension of the image as follows:

```
transformed_image=np.expand_dims(transformed_image,axis=0)
transformed_image.shape
```

6. Preprocess the image:

```
transformed_image=preprocess_input(transformed_image)
transformed_image
```

7. Create the predictor variable:

```
y_pred= classifier.predict(transformed_image)
y_pred
```

8. Check the shape of the image. It should be of the **(1,1000)** shape:

```
y_pred.shape
```

The following figure shows the output of the preceding code:

$$(1, 1000)$$

Figure 8.26: Expected image shape

9. Select the top five probabilities of what our image is:

```
from keras.applications.vgg16 import decode_predictions
decode_predictions(y_pred,top=5)
```

The following figure shows the output of the preceding code:

```
[[('n09428293', 'seashore', 0.5665935),
  ('n09421951', 'sandbar', 0.25813007),
  ('n09332890', 'lakeside', 0.028795514),
  ('n01665541', 'leatherback_turtle', 0.022180557),
  ('n09288635', 'geyser', 0.015906854)]]
```

Figure 8.27: Top five probabilities of what our image is

The first column of the array is an internal code number, the second is the label, and the third is the probability of the image being the label.

10. Make the predictions in a human-readable form. We extract the most probable label from the output as follows:

```
label = decode_predictions(y_pred)
# Most likely result is retrieved, for example highest probability
decoded_label = label[0][0]
# The classification is printed
print('%s (%.2f%%)' % (decoded_label[1], decoded_label[2]*100 ))
```

The following figure shows the output of the preceding code:

seashore (56.66%)

Figure 8.28: Final predicted image using ResNet

So, the model clearly shows, with a probability of 57%, that the picture is that of a seashore. Note that a seashore does not have specific features, such as edges, as in cats and dog faces. Still, our algorithm successfully classified the image as seashore. This is the power of pre-trained models, and Keras gives us so much flexibility to use and tweak these models.

Activity 16: Image Classification with ResNet

Now, let's work on an activity that uses another pre-trained network, known as ResNet. We will use the same image, but this time we can use it with the **ResNet** model.

We have an image of an elephant at this path: **../Data/Prediction/test_image_2**. We will use the ResNet50 network to predict the image. To implement the activity, follow these steps:

1. Import the required libraries.
2. Initiate the **ResNet** model.
3. Load the image that needs to be classified.
4. Pre-process the image by applying appropriate transformations.
5. Create a predictor variable to predict the image.
6. Label the image and classify it.

> **Note**
>
> The solution for this activity can be found on page 369.

Summary

In this chapter, we learned the concept of transfer learning and how is it related to pre-trained networks, and we learned how to use a pre-trained deep learning network. We also learned how to use techniques such as feature extraction and fine-tuning for better use of image classification tasks. We used both the VGG16 and ResNet50 networks. First, we learned how to use an existing model and classify images, and then we learned the powerful technique of tweaking existing models and making it work according to our dataset. This technique for building our own ANN over an existing CNN is one of the most powerful techniques used in the industry.

In the next chapter, we will learn about sequential modeling and sequential memory by looking at some real-life cases with Google Assistant. Further to this, we will learn how sequential modeling is related to **Recurrent Neural Networks** (**RNN**). We will learn about the vanishing gradient problem in detail, and how using an LSTM is better than a simple RNN to overcome the vanishing gradient problem. We will apply the learning to time series problems by predicting stock trends that come out as fairly accurate.

Sequential Modeling with Recurrent Neural Networks

Learning Objectives

By the end of this chapter, you will be able to:

- Explain sequential memory and sequential modeling
- Explain Recurrent Neural Networks (RNNs)
- Describe the vanishing gradient problem
- Implement Long Short-Term Memory (LSTM) architectures
- Apply RNNs on a stock market dataset

In this chapter, we will learn about sequential modeling with RNNs using the stock price data of Apple and Microsoft. We will understand the vanishing gradient problem and, finally, we will implement the concept of LSTM.

Introduction

Neural networks are the building blocks of all deep learning models. In traditional neural networks, all the inputs and outputs are independent. However, there are instances where a particular output is dependent on the previous output of the system. Consider the stock price of a company as an example – the output at the end of any given day is related to the output of the previous day. Similarly, in **Natural Language Processing** (**NLP**), the final words in a sentence are dependent on the previous words in the sentence. A special type of neural network, called a **Recurrent Neural Network** (**RNN**), is used to solve these types of problems where the network needs to remember previous outputs. This chapter introduces and explores the concepts and applications of RNNs. It also explains how RNNs are different from standard feedforward neural networks. You will also gain an understanding of what the vanishing gradient problem is and a **Long-Short-Term-Memory** (**LSTM**) network. This chapter also introduces you to sequential data and its processing. We will be working with share market data for stock price forecasting to learn all about these concepts.

Sequential Memory and Sequential Modeling

If we analyze the stock price of Apple for the past five months, as shown in Figure 9.1, we can see that there is a trend. To predict or forecast future stock prices, we need to gain an understanding of this trend and then do our mathematical computations while keeping this trend in mind:

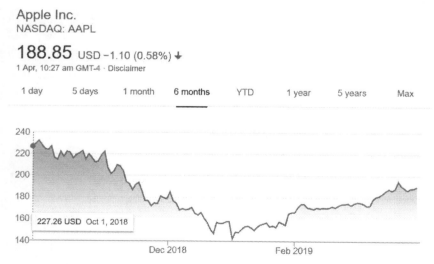

Figure 9.1: Apple's stock price over the last five months

This trend is deeply related to sequential memory and sequential modeling. If you have a model that can remember the previous outputs and then predict the next output based on the previous outputs, we say that the model has sequential memory.

The modeling that is done to process this sequential memory is known as **sequential modeling**. This is not only true for stock market data, but it is also true in NLP applications; we will look at one such example later, when we study RNNs.

Recurrent Neural Networks (RNNs)

RNNs are a class of neural networks that are built on the concept of sequential memory. Unlike in traditional neural networks, an RNN predicts the results in sequential data. Currently, an RNN is the most robust and powerful technique available for processing sequential data.

If you have access to a smartphone that has Google Assistant, try opening it and asking the question: "When was the United Nations formed?". The answer is displayed in the following screenshot:

Figure 9.2: Google Assistant's output

Now ask a second question, "Why was it formed?", as follows:

Figure 9.3: Google Assistant's contextual output

Now ask a third question, "Where are its headquarters?", and you should get the following answer:

Figure 9.4: Google Assistant's output

One interesting thing to note here is that we only mentioned "United Nations" in the first question. In the second and third question, we simply asked the assistant *why it was formed* and *where the headquarters were*, respectively. Google Assistant understood that, since the previous question was about the United Nations, the next question was also in the context of the United Nations, and, similarly, the third question was in the context of the United Nations. This is not a simple thing for a machine. The machine was able to show the expected result because it had processed data in the form of a sequence. The machine understands that the current question is related to the previous question and so, essentially, it remembers the previous question.

Let's consider another simple example; say that we want to predict the next number in the following sequence: 7, 8, 9, and ?. We want the next output to be 9 + 1. Alternatively, if we provide the sequence, 3, 6, 9, and ?, we would like to get 9 + 3 as the output. While in both cases, the last number is 9, the prediction outcome should be different (that is, when we take into account the contextual information of the previous values and not only the last value). The key here is to remember the contextual information that is obtained from the previous values.

On a high level, such networks that can remember previous states are referred to as recurrent networks. To completely understand **RNNs,** let's revisit the traditional neural networks that are also known as **feedforward neural networks**. This is a neural network in which the connections of the neural network do not form cycles, that is, the data only flows in one direction:

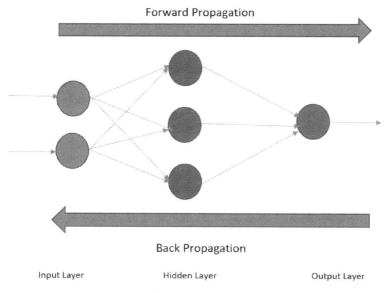

Figure 9.5: A feedforward neural network

In a feedforward neural network, the input layer gets the data and passes it to a hidden layer (with weights). Later, the data from the hidden layer is passed to the output layer. Based on the thresholds, the data is backpropagated, but there is no cyclical flow of data in the hidden layers.

In an RNN, the hidden layer of the network allows the cycle of data and information. As shown in the following figure, the architecture is similar to a feedforward neural network; however, here, the data and information also flows in cycles:

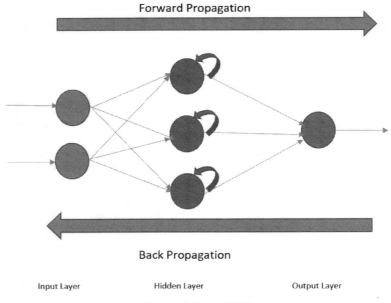

Figure 9.6: An RNN

Here, the defining property of the RNN is that the hidden layer not only gives the output but it also feeds back the information of the output into itself. Before taking a deep dive into RNNs, let's understand why we need RNNs and why Convolutional Neural Networks (CNNs) or normal Artificial Neural Networks (ANNs) fall short when it comes to processing sequential data. Suppose that we are using a CNN to identify images; first, we input an image of a dog and the CNN will label the image as "dog." Then, we input an image of a mango, and the CNN will label the image as "mango." Let's input the image of the dog at time, t, as follows:

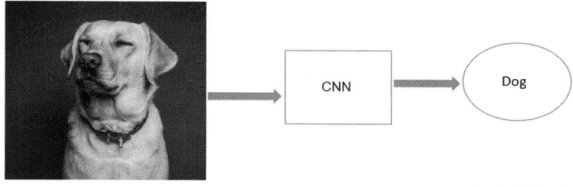

Input image at time t · output at time t

Figure 9.7: An image of a dog with a CNN

Now let's input the image of the mango at time, $t + 1$, as follows:

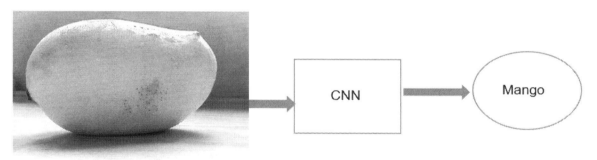

Input Image at time t+1 · Output at time t+1

Figure 9.8: An image of a mango with a CNN

Here, you can clearly see that the output at time, t, for the dog image and the output at time, $t + 1$, for the mango image are totally independent of each other. Therefore, we don't need our algorithms to remember previous instances of the output. However, as mentioned in the Google Assistant example where we asked *when the United Nations was formed* and *why it was formed*, the output of the previous instance has to be remembered by the algorithm in order to process the sequential data. CNNs or ANNs are not able to do this, so we need to use RNNs instead.

In an RNN, we can have multiple outputs over multiple instances of time. The following figure shows a pictorial representation of an RNN. It represents the state of the network from time, $t - 1$, to time, $t + n$:

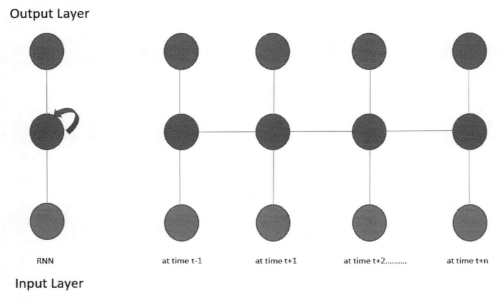

Figure 9.9: An unfolded RNN at various timestamps

The Vanishing Gradient Problem

If someone asks you "What did you have for dinner last night?", it is pretty easy to remember and correctly answer them. Now, if someone asks you "What did you have for dinner over the past 30 days?", then you might be able to remember the menu of the past three or four days, but then the menu for the days before that will be a bit difficult to remember. This ability to recall information from the past is the basis of the vanishing gradient problem, which we will be studying here. Put simply, the vanishing gradient problem refers to information that is lost or has decayed over a period of time.

The following figure represents the state of the RNN at different instances of time, t. The top dots (in red) represent the output layer, the middle dots (in blue) represent the hidden layer, and the bottom dots (in green) represent the input layer:

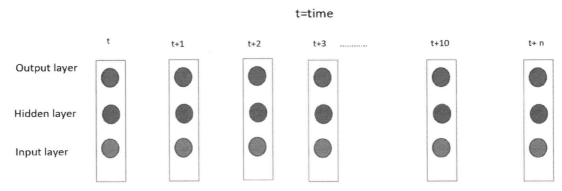

Figure: 9.10: Information decaying over time

If you are at t + 10, it will be difficult for you to remember what dinner menu you had at time, t (which is 10 days prior to the current day). Additionally, if you are at t + 100, it is likely to be impossible for you to remember your dinner menu prior to 100 days, assuming that you make dinner randomly and that there is no pattern to it. In the context of machine learning, the vanishing gradient problem is a difficulty that is found when training ANNs using gradient-based learning methods and backpropagation. We can recall how a neural network works, as follows:

1. We initialize the network with random weights and bias values.

2. We get a predicted output; this output is compared with the actual output and the difference is known as the cost.

3. The training process utilizes a gradient, which measures the rate at which the cost changes with respect to the weights or biases.

4. Then, we try to lower the cost by adjusting the weights and biases repeatedly throughout the training process, until the lowest possible value is obtained.

For example, if you place a ball on a steep floor, then the ball will roll down quickly, but if you place the ball on a flat surface, it will roll slowly. Similarly, in a deep neural network, the model learns quickly when the gradient is large. However, if the gradient is small, then the model's learning rate becomes very low. Remember that, at any point, the gradient is the product of all the gradients up to that point (that is, it follows the calculus chain rule). Additionally, the gradient is usually a small number between 0 and 1 and the product of two numbers between 0 and 1 gives you an even smaller number. The deeper your network is then the smaller the gradient is in the initial layers of the network. In some cases, it reaches a point that is so small that no training happens in that network – this is the vanishing gradient problem. The following figure shows the gradients following the calculus chain rule:

$$\frac{\partial C}{\partial b_1} = \sigma'(z_1) \times w_2 \times \sigma'(z_2) \times w_3 \times \sigma'(z_3) \times w_4 \times \sigma'(z_4) \times \frac{\partial C}{\partial a_4}$$

Figure 9.11: The vanishing gradient with cost, C, and the calculus chain rule

Referring to Figure 9.10, suppose that we are at the $t + 10$ instance and we get an output that will be backpropagated to t, which is 10 steps away. Now when the weight is updated, there will be 10 gradients (which are themselves very small), and when they multiply by each other the number becomes so small that it is almost negligible. This is known as the vanishing gradient.

A Brief Explanation of the Exploding Gradient Problem

If, instead of the weights being small, the weights are greater than one, then the subsequent multiplication will increase the gradient exponentially – this is known as the exploding gradient. The exploding gradient is simply the opposite of the vanishing gradient. As in the case of the vanishing gradient, the values become too small, while in the case of the exploding gradient, the values become very large and, as a result, the network suffers heavily and is unable to predict anything. We don't get the exploding gradient problem as frequently as vanishing gradients, but it is good to have a brief understanding of exploding gradients.

Long Short-Term Memory (LSTM)

LSTMs are RNNs whose main objective is to overcome the shortcomings of the vanishing gradient and exploding gradient problem. The architecture is built such that they remember data and information for a long period of time.

LSTMs were designed to overcome the limitation of the vanishing and exploding gradient problems. LSTM networks are a special kind of RNN, which are capable of learning long-term dependencies. They are designed to avoid the long-term dependency problem; being able to remember information for long intervals of time is how they are wired. The following diagram displays a standard recurrent network where the repeating module has a **tanh** activation function. This is a simple RNN; in this architecture, we often have to face the vanishing gradient problem:

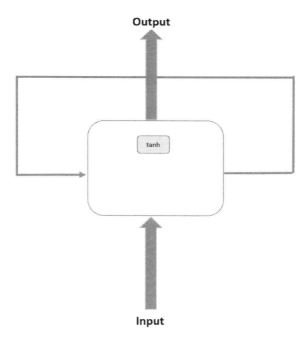

Figure 9.12: A simple RNN model

LSTM architecture is similar to simple RNNs but their repeating module has different components, as shown in the following diagram:

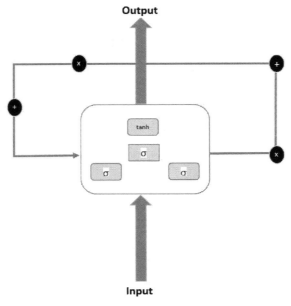

Figure 9.13: The LSTM model architecture

In addition to a simple RNN, an LSTM consists of the following:

- Sigmoid activation functions (σ)
- Mathematical computational functions (the black circles with + and x)
- Gated cells (or gates):

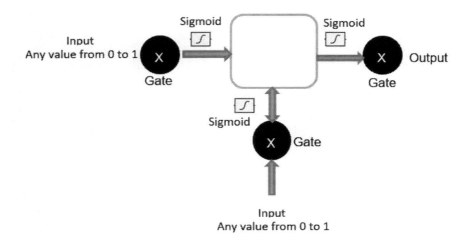

Figure 9.14: An LSTM in detail

The main difference between a simple RNN and LSTM is the presence of gated cells. You can just think of gates as computer memory, where information can be written, read, or stored. The cells in the gates make decisions on what to store and when to allow values to be read or written. The gates accept any information from 0 to 1; that is, if it is 0, then the information is blocked; if it is 1, then the all the information flows through; and if the input is between 0 and 1, then only partial information flows.

Besides these input gates, the gradient of a network is dependent on two factors: namely, weight and the activation function. The gates decide which memory needs to be remembered and which memory needs to be forgotten. In this way, the gates are like water valves, that is, the network can select which valve will allow the water to flow and which valve won't allow the water to flow.

The valves are adjusted in such a way that the values of the output will never yield a gradient (vanishing or exploding) problem. For example, if the value becomes too large, then there is a forget gate that will forget the value and no longer consider it for computations. Essentially, what a forget gate does is to multiply the information by 0 or 1. If the information needs to be processed further, then the forget gate multiplies the information by 1, and if it needs to be forgotten, then it multiplies the information by 0. Each gate is assisted with a sigmoid function that squashes the information between 0 and 1. In order for us to gain a better understanding of this, let's take a look at some activities and exercises.

> **Note**
>
> All the activities in this chapter will be developed in the Jupyter Notebook; you can download the GitHub repository with all the prepared templates at https://github.com/TrainingByPackt/Applied-Deep-Learning-with-Keras/tree/master/Lesson09.

Exercise 27: Predict the Trend of Apple's Stock Price Using an LSTM with 50 Units (Neurons)

We will examine the stock price of Apple over a period of 5 years; that is, from January 1, 2014 to December 31, 2018. In doing so, we will try to predict and forecast the company's future trend for January 2019 using RNNs. We have the actual values for January 2019, so we will be able to later compare our predictions with the actual values:

1. Import the required libraries:

```
import numpy as np
import matplotlib.pyplot as plt
import pandas as pd
```

2. Import the dataset:

```
dataset_training = pd.read_csv('AAPL_train.csv')
dataset_training.head()
```

The following figure shows the output of the preceding code:

	Date	Open	High	Low	Close	Adj Close	Volume
0	2013-12-31	79.167145	80.182854	79.142860	80.145714	67.919533	55771100
1	2014-01-02	79.382858	79.575714	78.860001	79.018570	66.964325	58671200
2	2014-01-03	78.980003	79.099998	77.204285	77.282860	65.493416	98116900
3	2014-01-06	76.778572	78.114288	76.228569	77.704285	65.850533	103152700
4	2014-01-07	77.760002	77.994286	76.845711	77.148575	65.379593	79302300

Figure 9.15: The first five rows of the AAPL_Training dataset

3. We are going to make our prediction using the **Open** stock price; therefore, we will extract the **Open** stock price column as follows:

```
training_data = dataset_training.iloc[:, 1:2].values
training_data
```

The following figure shows the output of the preceding code:

```
array([[0.0526565 ],
       [0.05400437],
       [0.05148716],
       ...,
       [0.48462887],
       [0.53174205],
       [0.54211448]])
```

Figure 9.16: The data of the Open stock price column

4. Then, perform feature scaling by normalizing the data:

```
from sklearn.preprocessing import MinMaxScaler
sc = MinMaxScaler(feature_range = (0, 1))
training_data_scaled = sc.fit_transform(training_data)
training_data_scaled
```

The following figure shows the output of the preceding code:

```
array([[0.0526565 ],
       [0.05400437],
       [0.05148716],
       ...,
       [0.48462887],
       [0.53174205],
       [0.54211448]])
```

Figure 9.17: Feature scaling by normalizing the data

5. Create the data to get 60 timestamps from the current instance. We chose 60 here as it will give us a sufficient number of previous instances in order to understand the trend; technically, this can be any number, but 60 is the optimal value. Additionally, the upper bound value here is **1258**, which is the index or count of rows (or records) in the training set:

```
X_train = []
y_train = []
for i in range(60, 1258):
    X_train.append(training_data_scaled[i-60:i, 0])
    y_train.append(training_data_scaled[i, 0])
X_train, y_train = np.array(X_train), np.array(y_train)
```

6. Next, reshape the data as follows:

```
X_train = np.reshape(X_train, (X_train.shape[0], X_train.shape[1], 1))
X_train
```

The following figure shows the output of the preceding code:

```
array([[[0.0526565 ],
        [0.05400437],
        [0.05148716],
        ...,
        [0.0413468 ],
        [0.04582785],
        [0.04002572]],

       [[0.05400437],
        [0.05148716],
        [0.03773165],
```

Figure 9.18: The data of a few timestamps from the current instance

7. Import the following libraries to build the RNN:

```
from keras.models import Sequential
from keras.layers import Dense
from keras.layers import LSTM
from keras.layers import Dropout
```

8. Initiate the sequential model, as follows:

```
model = Sequential()
```

9. Build the ANN architecture, as follows:

```
model.add(LSTM(units = 50, return_sequences = True, input_shape = (X_
train.shape[1], 1)))
# Adding a second LSTM layer and some Dropout regularisation
model.add(LSTM(units = 50, return_sequences = True))
# Adding a third LSTM layer and some Dropout regularisation
model.add(LSTM(units = 50, return_sequences = True))
# Adding a fourth LSTM layer and some Dropout regularisation
model.add(LSTM(units = 50))
# Adding the output layer
model.add(Dense(units = 1))
```

10. Compile the network, as follows:

```
# Compiling the RNN
model.compile(optimizer = 'adam', loss = 'mean_squared_error')

# Fitting the RNN to the Training set
model.fit(X_train, y_train, epochs = 100, batch_size = 32)
```

11. Load and process the test data (which is treated as actual data here):

```
dataset_testing = pd.read_csv("AAPL_test.csv")
actual_stock_price = dataset_testing.iloc[:, 1:2].values
actual_stock_price
```

The following figure shows the output of the preceding code:

```
array([[158.529999],
       [154.889999],
       [143.979996],
       [144.529999],
       [148.699997],
       [149.559998],
       [151.289993],
       [152.5     ],
       [152.880005],
       [150.850006],
       [150.270004],
       [153.080002],
       [154.199997],
       [157.5     ],
       [156.410004],
       [154.149994],
       [154.110001],
       [155.479996],
       [155.789993],
       [156.25    ],
       [163.25    ]])
```

Figure 9.19: The actual processed data

12. Concatenate the data, as we will need 60 previous instances in order to get the stock price for each day; therefore, we will need both training and testing data:

```
total_data = pd.concat((dataset_training['Open'], dataset_
testing['Open']), axis = 0)
```

13. Reshape and scale the input to prepare the test data. Note that we are predicting the January monthly trend, which has 21 financial days, so in order to prepare the test set we take the lower bound value as 60, and the upper bound value as 81; this ensures that the difference of 21 is maintained:

```
inputs = total_data[len(total_data) - len(dataset_testing) - 60:].values
inputs = inputs.reshape(-1,1)
inputs = sc.transform(inputs)
X_test = []
for i in range(60, 81):
    X_test.append(inputs[i-60:i, 0])
X_test = np.array(X_test)
X_test = np.reshape(X_test, (X_test.shape[0], X_test.shape[1], 1))
```

```
predicted_stock_price = model.predict(X_test)
predicted_stock_price = sc.inverse_transform(predicted_stock_price)
```

14. Visualize the results as follows:

```
# Visualising the results
plt.plot(actual_stock_price, color = 'green', label = 'Real Apple Stock
Price',ls='--')
plt.plot(predicted_stock_price, color = 'red', label = 'Predicted Apple
Stock Price',ls='-')
plt.title('Predicted Stock Price')
plt.xlabel('Time in days')
plt.ylabel('Real Stock Price')
plt.legend()
plt.show()
```

Please note that your results may differ slightly to the actual stock price of Apple.

Expected output:

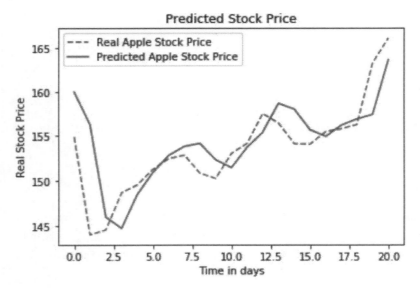

Figure 9.20: The real versus predicted stock price

This concludes *Exercise 27, Predict the Trend of Apple's Stock Price Using an LSTM with 50 Units (Neurons)*, where we have predicted Apple's stock trends with the help of an LSTM. As you can see in the preceding figure, the trend has been fairly captured.

Activity 17: Predict the Trend of Microsoft's Stock Price Using an LSTM with 50 Units (Neurons)

In this activity, we will examine the stock price of Microsoft for the last 5 years; that is, from January 1, 2014 to December 31, 2018. In doing so, we will try to predict and forecast the company's future trend for January 2019 using an RNN and LSTM. We have the actual values for January 2019, so we can later compare our predictions to the actual values:

1. Import the required libraries.

2. From the full dataset, extract the **Open** column as the predictions will be made on the open stock value. Download the dataset from GitHub repository; you can find the dataset at https://github.com/TrainingByPackt/Applied-Deep-Learning-with-Keras/tree/master/Lesson09.

3. Normalize the data between 0 and 1.

4. Then, create timestamps; the values of each day in January 2019 will be predicted by the previous 60 days. So, if January 1 is predicted by using the value from the nth day up to December 31, then January 2 will be predicted by using the $n + 1$th day and January 1, and so on.

5. Reshape the data into three dimensions as the network needs data in three dimensions.

6. Build an LSTM in Keras using 50 units (here, units refer to neurons). The first step should provide the input shape. Note that the final LSTM layer always adds **return_sequences=True**.

7. Process and prepare the test data that is the actual data for January 2019.

8. Combine and process the training and test data.

9. Visualize the results.

> **Note**
>
> The solution for this activity can be found on page 372.

Now let's try and improve the performance by tweaking our LSTM. There is no gold standard on how to build an LSTM; however, the following permutation combinations can be tried in order to improve the performance:

1. Build an LSTM with moderate units such as 50.

2. Build an LSTM with over 100 units.

3. Use more data; that is, instead of 5 years, take data from 10 years.

4. Apply regularization using 100 units.

5. Apply regularization using 50 units.

6. Apply regularization using more data and 50 units.

This list can have a number of combinations; whichever combination offers the best results can be considered a good algorithm for that particular dataset.

Exercise 28: Predicting the Trend of Apple's Stock Price Using an LSTM with 100 units

We will examine the stock price of Apple over the last 5 years, from January 1, 2014 to December 31, 2018. In doing so, we will try to predict and forecast the company's future trend for January 2019 using RNNs. We have the actual values for January 2019, so we will compare our predictions with the actual values. This is the same task as the first exercise, but now we're using 100 units instead. Make sure that you compare the output with *Exercise 27, Predict the Trend of Apple's Stock Price Using an LSTM with 50 Units (Neurons)*:

1. Import the required libraries:

   ```
   import numpy as np
   import matplotlib.pyplot as plt
   import pandas as pd
   ```

2. Import the dataset:

   ```
   dataset_training = pd.read_csv('AAPL_train.csv')
   dataset_training.head()
   ```

3. We are going to make the prediction using the **Open** stock price, so we will extract the **Open** stock price column as follows:

   ```
   training_data = dataset_training.iloc[:, 1:2].values
   training_data
   ```

4. Then, perform feature scaling by normalizing the data:

```
from sklearn.preprocessing import MinMaxScaler
sc = MinMaxScaler(feature_range = (0, 1))

training_data_scaled = sc.fit_transform(training_data)
training_data_scaled
```

5. Create the data to get 60 timestamps from the current instance:

```
X_train = []
y_train = []
for i in range(60, 1258):
    X_train.append(training_data_scaled[i-60:i, 0])
    y_train.append(training_data_scaled[i, 0])
X_train, y_train = np.array(X_train), np.array(y_train)
```

6. Reshape the data, as follows:

```
X_train = np.reshape(X_train, (X_train.shape[0], X_train.shape[1], 1))
```

7. Import the following libraries to build the RNN:

```
from keras.models import Sequential
from keras.layers import Dense
from keras.layers import LSTM
from keras.layers import Dropout
```

8. Initiate the sequential model, as follows:

```
model = Sequential()
```

9. Build the ANN architecture, as follows:

```
model.add(LSTM(units = 100, return_sequences = True, input_shape = (X_
train.shape[1], 1)))
# Adding a second LSTM layer and some Dropout regularisation
model.add(LSTM(units = 100, return_sequences = True))
# Adding a third LSTM layer and some Dropout regularisation
model.add(LSTM(units = 100, return_sequences = True))
# Adding a fourth LSTM layer and some Dropout regularisation
model.add(LSTM(units = 100))
# Adding the output layer
model.add(Dense(units = 1))
```

10. Compile the network as follows:

```
# Compiling the RNN
model.compile(optimizer = 'adam', loss = 'mean_squared_error')

# Fitting the RNN to the Training set
model.fit(X_train, y_train, epochs = 100, batch_size = 32)
```

11. Load and process the test data (which is treated as the actual data here):

```
dataset_testing = pd.read_csv("AAPL_test.csv")
actual_stock_price = dataset_testing.iloc[:, 1:2].values
actual_stock_price
```

12. Concatenate the data as we will need 60 previous instances to get the stock price of each day; therefore, we will need both the training and testing data:

```
total_data = pd.concat((dataset_training['Open'], dataset_
testing['Open']), axis = 0)
```

13. Reshape and scale the data in the input:

```
inputs = total_data[len(total_data) - len(dataset_testing) - 60:].values
inputs = inputs.reshape(-1,1)
inputs = sc.transform(inputs)
X_test = []
for i in range(60, 81):
    X_test.append(inputs[i-60:i, 0])
X_test = np.array(X_test)
X_test = np.reshape(X_test, (X_test.shape[0], X_test.shape[1], 1))
predicted_stock_price = model.predict(X_test)
predicted_stock_price = sc.inverse_transform(predicted_stock_price)
```

14. Visualize the results as follows:

```
# Visualising the results
plt.plot(actual_stock_price, color = 'green', label = 'Real Apple Stock
Price',ls='--')
plt.plot(predicted_stock_price, color = 'red', label = 'Predicted Apple
Stock Price',ls='-')
plt.title('Predicted Stock Price')
plt.xlabel('Time in days')
plt.ylabel('Real Stock Price')
plt.legend()
plt.show()
```

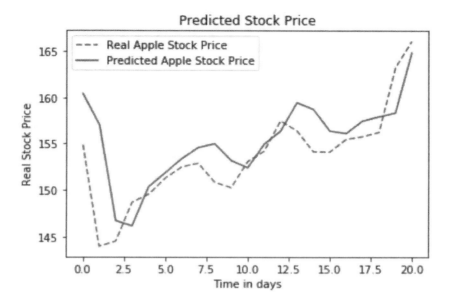

Figure 9.21: Real versus predicted stock price

Now if we compare the LSTM of *Exercise 27, Predict the Trend of Apple's Stock Price Using an LSTM with 50 Units (Neurons)*, which had 50 neurons (units), with this LSTM that uses 100 units, we can see that, unlike in the case of the Microsoft stock price, the Apple stock trend is better captured by using an LSTM with 100 units:

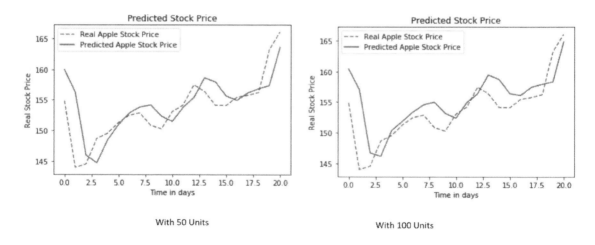

Figure 9.22: Comparing the output with the LSTM of Exercise 27

Thus, we can clearly see that an LSTM with 100 units predicts a more accurate trend than an LSTM with 50 units. Do keep in mind that an LSTM with 100 units will need more computational time but is giving better results in this scenario. As well as modifying our model by adding more units, we can also add regularization. The following activity will test whether adding regularization can make our Microsoft model more accurate.

Activity 18: Predicting Microsoft's Stock Price with Added Regularization

We will examine the stock price of Microsoft over the last 5 years, from January 1, 2014 to December 31, 2018. In doing so, we will try to predict and forecast the company's future trend for January 2019 using RNNs and an LSTM. We have the actual values for January 2019, so we will be able to compare our predictions with the actual values. We initially predicted the trend of Microsoft's stock price using an LSTM with 50 units (or neurons). Here, we will also add dropout regularization and compare the results with Activity 17, *Predict the Trend of Microsoft's Stock Price Using an LSTM with 50 Units (Neurons)*:

1. Import the required libraries.

2. From the full dataset, extract the **Open** column as the predictions will be made on the open stock value. You can download the dataset from the GitHub repository at https://github.com/TrainingByPackt/Applied-Deep-Learning-with-Keras/tree/master/Lesson09.

3. Normalize the data between 0 and 1.

4. Create timestamps; the values of each day in January 2019 will be predicted by the previous 60 days. So, if January 1 is predicted by using the value from the nth day up to December 31, then January 2 will be predicted by using the n + th day and January 1, and so on.

5. Reshape the data into three dimensions as the network needs the data in three dimensions.

6. Build an LSTM in Keras with 50 units (here, units refer to neurons). The first step should provide the input shape. Note that the the final LSTM layer always adds `return_sequences=True`.

7. Add a dropout regularization of 20%.

8. Process and prepare the test data, which is the actual data for January 2019.

9. Combine and process train and test data.

10. Finally, visualize the results.

> **Note**
>
> The solution for this activity can be found on page 376.

Activity 19: Predicting the Trend of Microsoft's Stock Price Using an LSTM with an Increasing Number of LSTM Neurons (100 Units)

We will examine the stock price of Microsoft over the last 5 years, from January 1, 2014 to December 31, 2018. In doing so, we will try to predict and forecast the company's future trend for January 2019 using RNNs. We have the actual values for January 2019, so we will be able to compare our predictions with the actual values. You can also compare the output difference with *Activity 17, Predict the Trend of Microsoft's Stock Price Using an LSTM with 50 Units (Neurons)*:

1. Import the required libraries.

2. From the full dataset, extract the **Open** column as the predictions will be made on the **Open** stock value.

3. Normalize the data between 0 and 1,

4. Create timestamps; the values of each day in January 2019 will be predicted by the previous 60 days. So, if January 1 is predicted by using the value from the nth day up to December 31, then January 2 will be predicted by using the $n + 1$ th day and January 1, and so on.

5. Reshape the data into three dimensions as the network needs data in three dimensions.

6. Build an LSTM in Keras with 50 units (here, units refer to neurons). The first step should provide the input shape. Note that the final LSTM layer always adds **return_sequences=True**.

7. Process and prepare the test data, which is the actual data for January 2019.

8. Combine and process the training and test data.

9. Visualize the results.

> **Note**
>
> The solution for this activity can be found on page 381.

Summary

In this chapter, we learned about sequential modeling and sequential memory by examining some real-life cases with Google Assistant. We further learned how sequential modeling is related to RNNs. We also learned how RNNs are different from traditional feedforward networks. We learned about the vanishing gradient problem in detail, and learned how using an LSTM is better than a simple RNN to overcome the vanishing gradient problem. We applied the learning to time series problems by predicting stock trends.

In this book, we learned the basics of machine learning and Python, while also gaining an in-depth understanding of applying Keras to develop efficient deep learning solutions. We understood the difference between machine and deep learning. We learned how to build a logistic regression model, first with scikit-learn, and then with Keras. We further explored Keras and its different models by creating prediction models for various real-world scenarios, such as disease prediction. Then, we learned how to evaluate, optimize, and improve models to achieve maximum information. We evaluated models by cross-validating them using Keras Wrapper and scikit-learn. We also learned how to apply L1, L2, and dropout regularization techniques to improve the accuracy of models. To maintain accuracy, we applied techniques such as null accuracy, precision, and the AUC-ROC score to fine-tune our model. We ended the book by creating various CNN and RNN networks using a real-world stock price dataset.

Appendix

About

This section is included to assist you to perform the activities in the book.
It includes detailed steps that are to be performed by you to achieve the objectives of the
activities.

Chapter 1: Introduction to Machine Learning with Keras

Activity 1: Adding Regularization to the Model

Solution:

1. Load the feature data from **Exercise 1** and the target data from the second activity. The feature data from the second activity can also be used:

```
import pandas as pd
feats = pd.read_csv('data/bank_data_feats_e3.csv', index_col=0)
target = pd.read_csv('data/bank_data_target_e2.csv', index_col=0)
```

2. We will again create a test and train dataset. We will train the data using the training dataset. This time, however, we will use part of the training dataset for validation in order to choose the most appropriate hyperparameter.

   We will again use **test_size = 0.2**, which means that 20% of the data will be reserved for testing. The size of our validation set will be determined by how many validation folds we have. If we do 10-fold cross-validation, this equates to reserving 10% of the training dataset to validate our model on. Each fold will use a different 10% of the training dataset, and the average error across all folds is used to compare models with different hyperparameters. Assign a random value to the **random_state** variable:

```
from sklearn.model_selection import train_test_split
test_size = 0.2
random_state = 13
X_train, X_test, y_train, y_test = train_test_split(feats, target, test_size=test_size, random_state=random_state)
```

3. We can check to see the dimensions of the DataFrames:

```
print(f'Shape of X_train: {X_train.shape}')
print(f'Shape of y_train: {y_train.shape}')
print(f'Shape of X_test: {X_test.shape}')
print(f'Shape of y_test: {y_test.shape}')
```

   The following figure shows the output of the preceding code:

```
Shape of X_train: (3616, 32)
Shape of y_train: (3616, 1)
Shape of X_test: (905, 32)
Shape of y_test: (905, 1)
```

Figure 1.42: Output of the print command indicating the shapes of the DataFrames

4. Next, we will instantiate the models. We will try two types of regularization parameters, **l1** and **l2**, with 10-fold cross-validation. We will iterate our regularization parameter from 1x10^-2 to 1x10^6 equally in logarithmic space to observe how the parameters affect the results:

```
import numpy as np
from sklearn.linear_model import LogisticRegressionCV
Cs = np.logspace(-2, 6, 9)
model_l1 = LogisticRegressionCV(Cs=Cs, penalty='l1', cv=10,
solver='liblinear', random_state=42)
model_l2 = LogisticRegressionCV(Cs=Cs, penalty='l2', cv=10, random_
state=42)
```

> **Note**
>
> For a logistic regression model with the **l1** regularization parameter, only the **liblinear** solver can be used.

5. Next, we fit the models to the training data:

```
model_l1.fit(X_train, y_train['y'])
model_l2.fit(X_train, y_train['y'])
```

The following figure shows the output of the preceding code:

```
LogisticRegressionCV(Cs=array([1.e-02, 1.e-01, 1.e+00, 1.e+01, 1.e+02, 1.e+03, 1.e+04, 1.e+05,
       1.e+06]),
          class_weight=None, cv=10, dual=False, fit_intercept=True,
          intercept_scaling=1.0, max_iter=100, multi_class='ovr',
          n_jobs=1, penalty='l2', random_state=42, refit=True,
          scoring=None, solver='lbfgs', tol=0.0001, verbose=0)
```

Figure 1.43: Output of the fit command indicating all of the model training parameters

6. We can see what the value of the regularization parameter was for the two different models. The regularization parameter is chosen according to which produced a model with the lowest error:

```
print(f'Best hyperparameter for l1 regularization model: {model_l1.C_
[0]}')
print(f'Best hyperparameter for l2 regularization model: {model_l2.C_
[0]}')
```

The following figure shows the output of the preceding code:

```
Best hyperparameter for l1 regularization model: 1.0
Best hyperparameter for l2 regularization model: 10000.0
```

Figure 1.44: The values for the regularization parameters for the models

> **Note**
>
> The **C_** attribute is only available once the model has been trained because it is set once the best parameter from the cross-validation process has been determined.

7. To evaluate the performance of the models, we will make predictions on the test set, which we'll compare against the true values:

```
y_pred_l1 = model_l1.predict(X_test)
y_pred_l2 = model_l2.predict(X_test)
```

8. To compare these models, we have to calculate the evaluation metrics. First, we will look at the accuracy of the model:

```
from sklearn import metrics
accuracy_l1 = metrics.accuracy_score(y_pred=y_pred_l1, y_true=y_test)
accuracy_l2 = metrics.accuracy_score(y_pred=y_pred_l2, y_true=y_test)
```

The following figure shows the output of the preceding code:

```
Accuracy of the model with l1 regularization is 90.0552%
Accuracy of the model with l2 regularization is 89.6133%
```

Figure 1.45: The accuracy for the models with regularization

9. We can also look at the other evaluation metrics:

```
precision_l1, recall_l1, fscore_l1, _ = metrics.precision_recall_fscore_
support(y_pred=y_pred_l1, y_true=y_test, average='binary')
precision_l2, recall_l2, fscore_l2, _ = metrics.precision_recall_fscore_
support(y_pred=y_pred_l2, y_true=y_test, average='binary')
```

The following figure shows the output of the preceding code:

```
l1
Precision: 0.6200
Recall: 0.3039
fscore: 0.4079


l2
Precision: 0.5741
Recall: 0.3039
fscore: 0.3974
```

Figure 1.46: The model evaluation metrics for models with l1 and l2 regularization parameters

10. The values of the coefficients can also be observed once the model has been trained:

```
coef_list = [f'{feature}: {coef}' for coef, feature in sorted(zip(model_
l1.coef_[0], X_train.columns.values.tolist()))]
for item in coef_list:
    print(item)
```

Note

The **coef_** attribute is only available once the model has been trained, because it is set once the best parameter from the cross-validation process has been determined.

The following figure shows the output of the preceding code:

```
is_loan: -0.8474572703740183
is_housing: -0.579000838262856
is_married: -0.44532254073443145
job_blue-collar: -0.39555311928947184
is_single: -0.17325311462431392
job_unemployed: -0.13411430783658618
job_entrepreneur: -0.10034667623333418
job_services: -0.09134387963624574
campaign: -0.06871503998769422
month: -0.03574802854504004
education_primary: -0.022463329457676342
job_technician: -0.01712422471985195
poutcome_failure: -0.011295531879278774
day: -0.0016886947998909876
education_secondary: 0.0
job_housemaid: 0.0
job_self-employed: 0.0
balance: 5.440788435851004e-06
age: 0.0008144244598940912
duration: 0.00404791638136143 84
previous: 0.005406556796155721
job_management: 0.08746056447020656
education_tertiary: 0.1798507542548706
job_admin.: 0.2119734305727548
was_contacted: 0.29490708422824413
job_student: 0.3480117206677412
poutcome_other: 0.36111119058043945
is_default: 0.3973330185343257
job_retired: 0.5771288331964628
contact_telephone: 0.9444897771683772
contact_cellular: 0.9876468935014132
poutcome_success: 2.369762857417464
```

Figure 1.47: The feature column names and the value of their respective coefficients for the model with l1 regularization

11. The same can be done for the model with an l2 regularization parameter type:

```
coef_list = [f'{feature}: {coef}' for coef, feature in sorted(zip(model_
l2.coef_[0], X_train.columns.values.tolist()))]
for item in coef_list:
    print(item)
```

The following figure shows the output of the preceding code:

```
is_loan: -0.8592515340378091
is_housing: -0.783712827881942
is_married: -0.6802996037641615
job_blue-collar: -0.6674261705865218
is_single: -0.582392797301293
poutcome_failure: -0.5677507629528401
education_secondary: -0.3756656029891896
education_primary: -0.36202533069981596
job_services: -0.3316987241936029
job_unemployed: -0.2512969583482374
education_tertiary: -0.23302637795008607
job_technician: -0.21689248966705305
job_entrepreneur: -0.2124795198493926
job_self-employed: -0.14491995346272177
job_management: -0.08029606833746696
poutcome_other: -0.07864819382375875
job_housemaid: -0.06967734838862087
campaign: -0.06418014227332157
month: -0.05284668153426122
age: -0.01622307108912448
previous: -0.007416369164753172
day: -0.006863251036111899
balance: 4.993642276208674e-06
duration: 0.0039712760293409890
job_student: 0.03841132313343416
job_admin.: 0.04764211881775322
is_default: 0.13966157592044678
contact_telephone: 0.5157083264605774
job_retired: 0.6503402354121294
contact_cellular: 0.6641999591338158
was_contacted: 0.9830126636373128
poutcome_success: 1.6294116205177398
```

Figure 1.48: The feature column names and the value of their respective coefficients for the model with l2 regularization

This activity has taught us how to use regularization in conjunction with cross-validation to appropriately score a model. We have learned how to better fit a model to data using regularization and cross-validation. Regularization is an important technique to use to ensure that models don't overfit the training data. Models trained with regularization will perform better on new data, which is the generally the goal of machine learning models – to predict a target, given new observations of the input data. Choosing the optimal regularization parameter may require iterating over a number of different choices. Cross-validation is a technique that's used to determine which set of regularization parameters fit the data best. Cross-validation will train multiple models with different values for the regularization parameters on different cuts of the data. This technique ensures the best set of regularization parameters are chosen, without adding bias and minimizing variance.

Chapter 2: Machine Learning versus Deep Learning

Activity 2: Creating a Logistic Regression Model Using Keras

Solution:

1. Open a Jupyter Notebook from the start menu to implement this activity. Load in the bank dataset from the previous chapter. This should be somewhat preprocessed, we will use the pandas library for the data loading, so import the **pandas** library:

    ```
    import pandas as pd
    feats = pd.read_csv('bank_data_feats.csv')
    target = pd.read_csv('bank_data_target.csv')
    ```

2. For the purposes of this activity, we will not perform any further preprocessing. As we did in the previous chapter, we will split the dataset into training and testing and leave the testing, until the very end when we evaluate our models:

    ```
    from sklearn.model_selection import train_test_split
    test_size = 0.2
    random_state = 42

    X_train, X_test, y_train, y_test = train_test_split(feats, target, test_size=test_size, random_state=random_state)
    ```

3. We begin creating our model by initializing a model of the **Sequential** class:

    ```
    from keras.models import Sequential
    model = Sequential()
    ```

4. To add a fully connected layer to the model, we will add a layer of the **Dense** class. Here we have to include the number of nodes in the layer. In our case this will be one, since we are performing binary classification and our desired output is zero or one. We also have to specify the input dimensions, which is only done on the first layer of the model and is there to indicate the format of the input data. Here, we pass the number of features:

    ```
    from keras.layers import Dense
    model.add(Dense(1, input_dim=X_train.shape[1]))
    ```

5. On the output of the model, we want to replicate the logistic regression algorithm. We can do this by adding a sigmoid activation function on the output of the previous layer:

```
from keras.layers import Activation
model.add(Activation('sigmoid'))
```

6. Once we have all the model components in the correct order, we must compile the model so that all the learning processes are configured. We will use the **adam** optimizer, a **binary_crossentropy** for the loss, and also track the accuracy of the model by passing the parameter into the metrics argument:

```
model.compile(optimizer='adam', loss='binary_crossentropy',
metrics=['accuracy'])
```

We can print the model summary to verify the model is as we expect:

```
print(model.summary())
```

The following figure shows the output of the preceding code:

```
Layer (type)                      Output Shape                    Param #
===================================================================
dense_1 (Dense)                   (None, 1)                       34

activation_1 (Activation)         (None, 1)                       0
===================================================================
Total params: 34
Trainable params: 34
Non-trainable params: 0


None
```

Figure 2.44: A summary of the model

7. Next, we can fit the model using the **fit** method of the model class. Here, we provide the training data, as well as the number of epochs and how much data to use for validation after each epoch:

```
history = model.fit(X_train, y_train['y'], epochs=10, validation_split=0.2)
```

The following shows the output of the preceding code:

```
Train on 2892 samples, validate on 724 samples
Epoch 1/10
2892/2892 [==============================] - 0s 100us/step - loss: 5.0673 - acc: 0.6653 - val_loss: 2.6053 - val_acc:
0.8343
Epoch 2/10
2892/2892 [==============================] - 0s 82us/step - loss: 2.4830 - acc: 0.8430 - val_loss: 2.4896 - val_acc:
0.8384
Epoch 3/10
2892/2892 [==============================] - 0s 75us/step - loss: 2.4045 - acc: 0.8485 - val_loss: 2.2396 - val_acc:
0.8550
Epoch 4/10
2892/2892 [==============================] - 0s 80us/step - loss: 2.3272 - acc: 0.8541 - val_loss: 2.1492 - val_acc:
0.8633
Epoch 5/10
2892/2892 [==============================] - 0s 74us/step - loss: 2.2786 - acc: 0.8568 - val_loss: 1.9480 - val_acc:
0.8729
Epoch 6/10
2892/2892 [==============================] - 0s 70us/step - loss: 2.1036 - acc: 0.8683 - val_loss: 1.9071 - val_acc:
0.8798
Epoch 7/10
2892/2892 [==============================] - 0s 77us/step - loss: 2.0623 - acc: 0.8703 - val_loss: 1.8837 - val_acc:
0.8826
Epoch 8/10
2892/2892 [==============================] - 0s 80us/step - loss: 2.0263 - acc: 0.8724 - val_loss: 1.8084 - val_acc:
0.8867
Epoch 9/10
2892/2892 [==============================] - 0s 71us/step - loss: 2.0009 - acc: 0.8748 - val_loss: 1.7881 - val_acc:
0.8881
Epoch 10/10
2892/2892 [==============================] - 0s 73us/step - loss: 1.9877 - acc: 0.8759 - val_loss: 1.7801 - val_acc:
0.8895
```

Figure 2.45: The fit method on the model

8. Since we were tracking the loss and accuracy after each epoch, we can plot the values of each:

```
import matplotlib.pyplot as plt
%matplotlib inline

# Plot training and validation accuracy values
plt.plot(history.history['acc'])
plt.plot(history.history['val_acc'])
plt.title('Model accuracy')
plt.ylabel('Accuracy')
plt.xlabel('Epoch')
plt.legend(['Train', 'Validation'], loc='upper left')
plt.show()
```

```
# Plot training and validation loss values
plt.plot(history.history['loss'])
plt.plot(history.history['val_loss'])
plt.title('Model loss')
plt.ylabel('Loss')
plt.xlabel('Epoch')
plt.legend(['Train', 'Validation'], loc='upper left')
plt.show()
```

The following plots show the output of the preceding code:

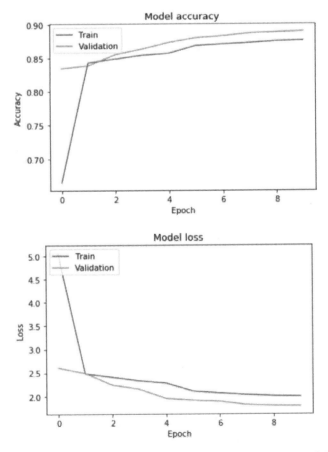

Figure 2.46: The loss and accuracy while fitting the model

9. Finally, we can evaluate our model on the test data we held out from the beginning, which will give an objective evaluation on the performance of the model:

```
test_loss, test_acc = model.evaluate(X_test, y_test['y'])
print(f'The loss on the test set is {test_loss:.4f} and the accuracy is
{test_acc*100:.3f}%')
```

The following image shows the output of the preceding code:

```
905/905 [==============================] - 0s 74us/step
The loss on the test set is 1.8699 and the accuracy is 88.287%
```

Figure 2.47: The model's performance on the test dataset

Chapter 3: Deep Learning with Keras

Activity 3: Building a Single-Layer Neural Network for Performing Binary Classification

Solution

1. Load all the required packages:

```
# import required packages from Keras
from keras.models import Sequential
from keras.layers import Dense, Activation
import numpy


# import required packages for plotting
import matplotlib.pyplot as plt
import matplotlib
%matplotlib inline
import matplotlib.patches as mpatches


# import the simulated dataset and the function for plotting decision
boundary
from utils import load_dataset, plot_decision_boundary
```

2. Set up a seed:

```
# define a seed for random number generator so the result will be
reproducible
seed = 1
```

3. Load the simulated dataset, and **print** the **size** of **X** and **Y** and the number of examples:

```
# load the dataset, print the shapes of input and output and the number of
examples
X, Y = load_dataset()
print("X size = ", X.shape)
print("Y size = ", Y.shape)
print("Number of examples = ", X.shape[0])
```

Expected output:

```
X size =  (400, 2)
Y size =  (400,)
Number of examples =  400
```

Figure 3.18: The size of X and Y and the number of examples

4.   Plot the dataset:

```
# changing the size of the plots
matplotlib.rcParams['figure.figsize'] = (10.0, 8.0)
# plot the dataset
reds = Y == 0
blues = Y == 1
class_1=plt.scatter(X[reds, 0], X[reds, 1], c="red", s=40, edgecolor='k')
class_2=plt.scatter(X[blues, 0], X[blues, 1], c="blue", s=40,
edgecolor='k')
plt.legend((class_1, class_2),('class 1','class 2'))
```

The following figure shows the output of the preceding code:

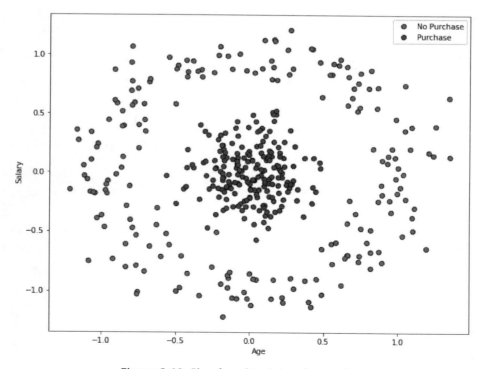

Figure 3.19: Simulated training data points

5. This is the logistic regression model:

```
# Logistic Regression model
numpy.random.seed(seed)
model = Sequential()
model.add(Dense(1, activation='sigmoid', input_dim=2))
model.compile(optimizer='sgd', loss='binary_crossentropy')

# train the model for 100 epoches and batch size 5
model.fit(X, Y, batch_size=5, epochs=100,verbose=1)
# changing the size of the plots
matplotlib.rcParams['figure.figsize'] = (10.0, 8.0)
# Plot the decision boundary
plot_decision_boundary(lambda x: model.predict(x), X, Y)
plt.title("Logistic Regression")
```

Expected Output:

The loss after 100 epochs = 0.6932:

```
Epoch 96/100
400/400 [==============================] - 0s 573us/step - loss: 0.6933
Epoch 97/100
400/400 [==============================] - 0s 573us/step - loss: 0.6933
Epoch 98/100
400/400 [==============================] - 0s 562us/step - loss: 0.6932
Epoch 99/100
400/400 [==============================] - 0s 570us/step - loss: 0.6933
Epoch 100/100
400/400 [==============================] - 0s 577us/step - loss: 0.6932
```

Figure 3.20: The loss details of the last 5 epochs out of 100 epochs

The following figure shows the output of the preceding code:

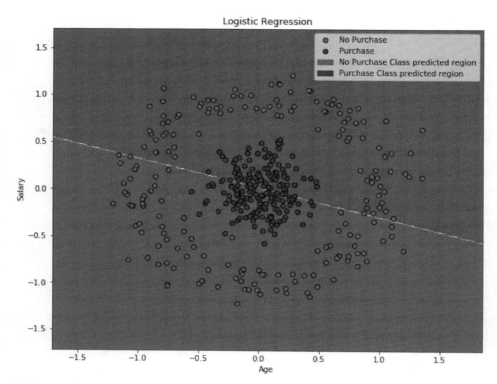

Figure 3.21: The decision boundary of logistic regression model

The linear decision boundary of the logistic regression model is obviously not able to capture the circular decision boundary between the two classes.

6. This is the neural network, with one hidden layer with three nodes:

```
# Neural network with hidden layer size = 3
numpy.random.seed(seed)
model = Sequential()
model.add(Dense(3, activation='relu', input_dim=2))
model.add(Dense(1, activation='sigmoid'))
model.compile(optimizer='sgd', loss='binary_crossentropy')
# train the model for 200 epochs and batch size 5
model.fit(X, Y, batch_size=5, epochs=200, verbose=1)
```

```
# changing the size of the plots
matplotlib.rcParams['figure.figsize'] = (10.0, 8.0)
# Plot the decision boundary
plot_decision_boundary(lambda x: model.predict(x), X, Y)
plt.title("Decision Boundary for Neural Network with hidden layer size 3")
```

Expected Output:

The loss after 200 epochs = 0.0856:

```
Epoch 196/200
400/400 [==============================] - 0s 625us/step - loss: 0.0879
Epoch 197/200
400/400 [==============================] - 0s 655us/step - loss: 0.0873
Epoch 198/200
400/400 [==============================] - 0s 630us/step - loss: 0.0867
Epoch 199/200
400/400 [==============================] - 0s 628us/step - loss: 0.0862
Epoch 200/200
400/400 [==============================] - 0s 630us/step - loss: 0.0856
```

Figure 3.22: The loss details of the last 5 epochs out of 200 epochs

The following figure shows the output of the preceding code:

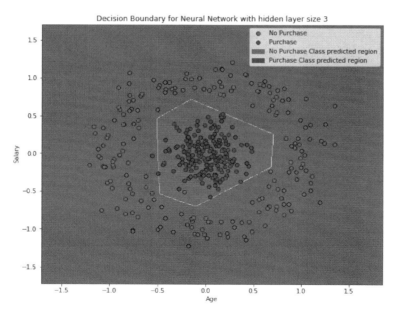

Figure 3.23: The decision boundary for the neural network with a hidden layer
size of 3 and a ReLU activation function

Having three processing units, instead of one, dramatically improved the capability of the model in capturing the non-linear boundary between the two classes. Notice that the loss value is decreased drastically in comparison to the previous step.

7. This is the neural network with one hidden layer and six nodes:

```
# Neural network with hidden layer size = 6
numpy.random.seed(seed)
model = Sequential()
model.add(Dense(6, activation='relu', input_dim=2))
model.add(Dense(1, activation='sigmoid'))
model.compile(optimizer='sgd', loss='binary_crossentropy')
# train the model for 400 epoches
model.fit(X, Y, batch_size=5, epochs=400, verbose=1)

# changing the size of the plots
matplotlib.rcParams['figure.figsize'] = (10.0, 8.0)
# Plot the decision boundary
plot_decision_boundary(lambda x: model.predict(x), X, Y)
plt.title("Decision Boundary for Neural Network with hidden layer size 6")
```

Expected Output:

The loss after 400 epochs = 0.0274:

```
Epoch 396/400
400/400 [==============================] - 0s 655us/step - loss: 0.0277
Epoch 397/400
400/400 [==============================] - 0s 630us/step - loss: 0.0276
Epoch 398/400
400/400 [==============================] - 0s 625us/step - loss: 0.0276
Epoch 399/400
400/400 [==============================] - 0s 638us/step - loss: 0.0275
Epoch 400/400
400/400 [==============================] - 0s 642us/step - loss: 0.0274
```

Figure 3.24: The loss details of the last 5 epochs out of 400 epochs

The following figure shows the output of the preceding code:

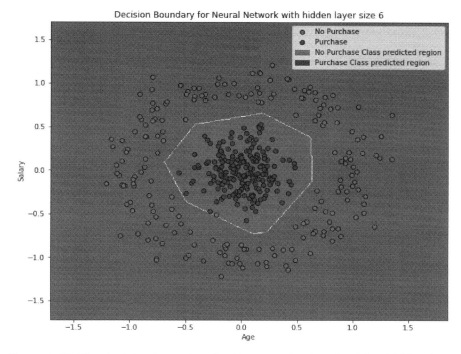

Figure 3.25: The decision boundary for the neural network with a hidden layer
size of 6 and the ReLU activation function

By doubling the number of units in the hidden layer, the decision boundary of the
model gets closer to a true circular shape, and the loss value is decreased even
more in comparison to the previous step.

8. This is the neural network with one hidden layer with three nodes and the **'tanh'**
activation function:

```
# Neural network with hidden layer size = 3 with tanh activation function
numpy.random.seed(seed)
model = Sequential()
model.add(Dense(3, activation='tanh', input_dim=2))
model.add(Dense(1, activation='sigmoid'))
model.compile(optimizer='sgd', loss='binary_crossentropy')

# train the model for 200 epoches and batch size 5
model.fit(X, Y, batch_size=5, epochs=200, verbose=1)
```

```
# changing the size of the plots
matplotlib.rcParams['figure.figsize'] = (10.0, 8.0)
# Plot the decision boundary
plot_decision_boundary(lambda x: model.predict(x), X, Y)
plt.title("Decision Boundary for Neural Network with hidden layer size 3")
```

Expected Output:

The loss after 200 epochs = 0.1544:

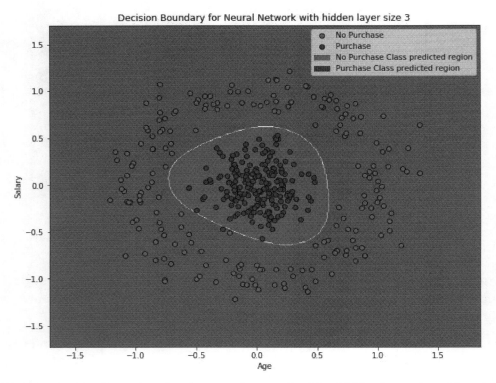

Figure 3.26: The decision boundary for the neural network with a hidden layer size of 3 and the tanh activation function

Using the 'tanh' activation function has got rid of the sharp edges in the decision boundary. In other words, it has made the decision boundary smoother. However, the model is not performing better, since we see an increase in the loss value. We mentioned before that learning parameters for 'tanh' are slower than they are for 'relu'. Therefore, with a fixed number of epochs, the 'tanh' activation function is performing worse.

9. This is the neural network with one hidden layer with five nodes and **'tanh'** activation:

```
# Neural network with hidden layer size = 6 with tanh activation function
numpy.random.seed(seed)
model = Sequential()
model.add(Dense(6, activation='tanh', input_dim=2))
model.add(Dense(1, activation='sigmoid'))
model.compile(optimizer='sgd', loss='binary_crossentropy')

# train the model for 400 epoches
model.fit(X, Y, batch_size=5, epochs=400, verbose=1)

# changing the size of the plots
matplotlib.rcParams['figure.figsize'] = (10.0, 8.0)
# Plot the decision boundary
plot_decision_boundary(lambda x: model.predict(x), X, Y)
plt.title("Decision Boundary for Neural Network with hidden layer size 6")
```
Expected Output:

The loss after 400 epochs = 0.0457:

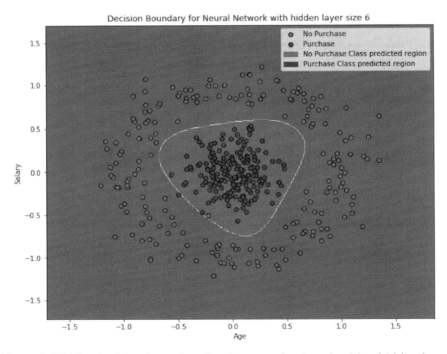

Figure 3.27. The decision boundary for the neural network with a hidden layer
size of 6 and the tanh activation function

Again, using the 'tanh' activation function, instead of 'relu', with a fixed number of epochs has made the performance of the model worse in comparison to step 7. You may want to repeat steps 8 and 9 with larger values of **epochs** and observe how the shape of the decision boundary and the loss value change.

Activity 4: Diabetes Diagnosis with Neural Networks

Solution:

1. Load the dataset:

```
# Load The dataset
import numpy
data = numpy.loadtxt("./data/pima-indians-diabetes.csv", delimiter=",")
X = data[:,0:8]
y = data[:,8]


# Print the sizes of the dataset
print("Number of Examples in the Dataset = ", X.shape[0])
print("Number of Features for each example = ", X.shape[1])
print("Possible Output Classes = ", numpy.unique(y))
```

Expected Output:

```
Number of Examples in the Dataset =  768
Number of Features for each example =  8
Possible Output Classes =  [0. 1.]
```

Figure 3.28: The size of the dataset

2. Split the dataset into the training set and test set:

```
# set up a seed for random number generator so the result will be
reproducible
seed = 1
numpy.random.seed(seed)


# Split the dataset into training set and test set with a 0.7-0.3 ratio
from sklearn.model_selection import train_test_split
X_train, X_test, y_train, y_test = train_test_split(X, y, test_size=0.3,
random_state=0)


# Print the information regarding dataset sizes
print(X_train.shape)
print(y_train.shape)
```

```
print(X_test.shape)
print(y_test.shape)
print ("Number of examples in training set = ", X_train.shape[0])
print ("Number of examples in test set = ", X_test.shape[0])])
```

Expected Output:

```
(537, 8)
(537,)
(231, 8)
(231,)
Number of examples in training set =  537
Number of examples in test set =  231
```

Figure 3.29: The size of the dataset after splitting it into training and test sets

3. Implement a deep neural network with 1 hidden layer of size 8:

```
# define a seed for random number generator so the result will be
reproducible
numpy.random.seed(seed)

# define the keras model
from keras.models import Sequential
from keras.layers import Dense
classifier = Sequential()
classifier.add(Dense(units = 8, activation = 'relu'))
classifier.add(Dense(units = 1, activation = 'sigmoid'))
classifier.compile(optimizer = 'adam', loss = 'binary_crossentropy',
metrics = ['accuracy'])

# train the model while storing all loss values
history=classifier.fit(X_train, y_train, batch_size = 5, epochs = 300,
validation_data=(X_test, y_test))
```

4. Plot the training error rate and test error rate for every epoch:

```
# import require packages for plotting
import matplotlib.pyplot as plt
import matplotlib
%matplotlib inline
matplotlib.rcParams['figure.figsize'] = (10.0, 8.0)

# plot training error and test error plots
plt.plot(history.history['loss'])
```

```
plt.plot(history.history['val_loss'])
plt.ylabel('loss')
plt.xlabel('epoch')
plt.legend(['train loss', 'test loss'], loc='upper right')

# print the best accuracy reached on training set and the test set
print("Best Accuracy on training set = ", max(history.history['acc'])*100)
print("Best Accuray on test set = ", max(history.history['val_acc'])*100)
```

Expected Output:

```
Best Accuracy on training set =  79.14339030366148
Best Accuray on test set =  74.45887533617226
```

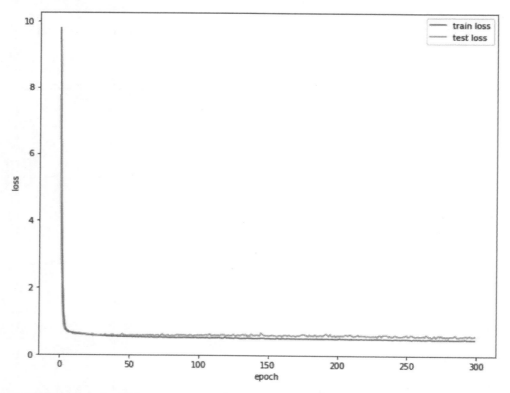

Figure 3.30: A plot of training error rate and test error rate during the training for the model
with 1 hidden layer of size 8

5. Implement a deep neural network with 2 hidden layers of sizes 16 and 8:

```
# set up a seed for random number generator so the result will be
reproducible
numpy.random.seed(seed)

# define the keras model
classifier = Sequential()
classifier.add(Dense(units = 16, activation = 'relu', input_dim = 8))
classifier.add(Dense(units = 8, activation = 'relu'))
classifier.add(Dense(units = 1, activation = 'sigmoid'))
classifier.compile(optimizer = 'adam', loss = 'binary_crossentropy',
metrics = ['accuracy'])

# train the model while storing all loss values
history=classifier.fit(X_train, y_train, batch_size = 5, epochs = 350,
validation_data=(X_test, y_test))
```

6. Plot training and test error plots with two hidden layers of size 16 and 8. Print the best accuracy reached on the training and test sets:

```
# plot training error and test error plots
matplotlib.rcParams['figure.figsize'] = (10.0, 8.0)
plt.plot(history.history['loss'])
plt.plot(history.history['val_loss'])
plt.ylabel('loss')
plt.xlabel('epoch')
plt.legend(['train loss', 'test loss'], loc='upper right')

# print the best accuracy reached on training set and the test set
print("Best Accuracy on training set = ", max(history.history['acc'])*100)
print("Best Accuray on test set = ", max(history.history['val_acc'])*100)
```

Expected Output:

```
Best Accuracy on training set =  82.30912571068805
Best Accuray on test set =  76.62337782321038
```

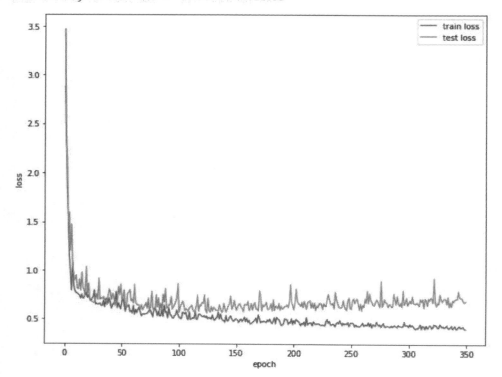

Figure 3.31: A plot of the training error and test error rates during the training
for the model with 2 hidden layers of sizes 16 and 8

7. Implement a deep neural network with 3 hidden layers of sizes 16, 8, and 4:

```
# define a seed for random number generator so the result will be
reproducible
numpy.random.seed(seed)

# define the keras model
classifier = Sequential()
classifier.add(Dense(units = 16, activation = 'relu', input_dim = 8))
classifier.add(Dense(units = 8, activation = 'relu'))
classifier.add(Dense(units = 4, activation = 'relu'))
classifier.add(Dense(units = 1, activation = 'sigmoid'))
classifier.compile(optimizer = 'adam', loss = 'binary_crossentropy',
metrics = ['accuracy'])
```

```
# train the model while storing all loss values
history=classifier.fit(X_train, y_train, batch_size = 5, epochs = 400,
validation_data=(X_test, y_test))
```

8. Plot the training and test error plots with 3 hidden layers of sizes 16, 8, and 4. Print the best accuracy reached on the training and test sets:

```
# plot training error and test error plots
matplotlib.rcParams['figure.figsize'] = (10.0, 8.0)
plt.plot(history.history['loss'])
plt.plot(history.history['val_loss'])
plt.ylabel('loss')
plt.xlabel('epoch')
plt.legend(['train loss', 'test loss'], loc='upper right')

# print the best accuracy reached on training set and the test set
print("Best Accuracy on training set = ", max(history.history['acc'])*100)
print("Best Accuracy on test set = ", max(history.history['val_acc'])*100)
```

Expected Output:

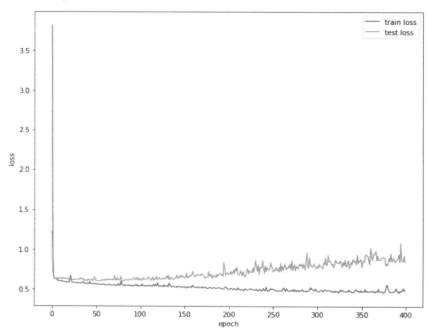

Figure 3.32: A plot of the training error and test error rates during the training for the model with 3 hidden layers of sizes 16, 8, and 4.

Please note that all three models were able to get a better accuracy rate on the training set, and the training error rate kept decreasing when trained for a great number of epochs. However, the test error rate decreased during training to a certain value, and after that, it started increasing, which is indicative of overfitting to the training data. The maximum test accuracy corresponds to the point on the plots where the test loss is at its lowest and is truly representative of how well the model will perform on independent examples later.

Chapter 4: Evaluate Your Model with Cross-Validation with Keras Wrappers

Activity 5: Model Evaluation Using Cross-Validation for a Diabetes Diagnosis Classifier

Solution:

1. Load the dataset and print its properties:

```
# Load the dataset
import numpy
data = numpy.loadtxt("./data/pima-indians-diabetes.csv", delimiter=",")
X = data[:,0:8]
y = data[:,8]

# Print the sizes of the dataset
print("Number of Examples in the Dataset = ", X.shape[0])
print("Number of Features for each example = ", X.shape[1])
print("Possible Output Classes = ", numpy.unique(y))
```

2. Here's the expected output:

```
Number of Examples in the Dataset =  768
Number of Features for each example =  8
Possible Output Classes =  [0. 1.]
```

Figure 4.15: Properties of the pima-indians-diabets.csv dataset

3. Define the function that returns the Keras model:

```
from keras.models import Sequential
from keras.layers import Dense
# Create the function that returns the keras model
def build_model():
    model = Sequential()
    model.add(Dense(16, input_dim=8, activation='relu'))
    model.add(Dense(8, activation='relu'))
    model.add(Dense(1, activation='sigmoid'))
    model.compile(loss='binary_crossentropy', optimizer='adam',
metrics=['accuracy'])
    return model
```

4. Build the Keras wrapper with scikit-learn, define the cross-validation iterator, perform k-fold cross-validation, and store the scores:

```
# import required packages
import numpy
from keras.wrappers.scikit_learn import KerasClassifier
from sklearn.model_selection import StratifiedKFold
from sklearn.model_selection import cross_val_score

# define a seed for random number generator so the result will be
reproducible
seed =1
numpy.random.seed(seed)

# determine the number of folds for k-fold cross-validation, number of
epochs and batch size
n_folds = 5
epochs=300
batch_size=5

# build the scikit-learn interface for the keras model
classifier = KerasClassifier(build_fn=build_model, epochs=epochs, batch_
size=batch_size, verbose=1)
# define the cross-validation iterator
kfold = StratifiedKFold(n_splits=n_folds, shuffle=True, random_state=seed)
# perform the k-fold cross-validation and store the scores in results
results = cross_val_score(classifier, X, y, cv=kfold)
```

5. Print the results:

```
# print accuracy for each fold
for f in range(n_folds):
    print("Test accuracy at fold ", f+1, " = ", results[f])
print("\n")

# print overal cross-validation acuuracy plus the standard deviation of
the accuracies
print("Final Cross-validation Test Accuracy:", results.mean())
print("Standard Deviation of Final Test Accuracy:", results.std())
```

6. Here's the expected output:

```
Test accuracy at fold  1  =  0.7207792333581231
Test accuracy at fold  2  =  0.7077922224030866
Test accuracy at fold  3  =  0.7727272835644808
Test accuracy at fold  4  =  0.7581699461329217
Test accuracy at fold  5  =  0.6535947840003407


Final Cross Validation Test Accuracy: 0.7226126938917905
Standard Deviation of Final Test Accuracy: 0.04186232225632458
```

Figure 4.16: The test accuracy of all five folds, final cross-validation, and the standard deviation of the final test accuracy

Activity 6: Model Selection Using Cross-Validation for the Diabetes Diagnosis Classifier

Solution:

1. Import all the required packages and load the dataset:

```
# import the required packages
from keras.models import Sequential
from keras.layers import Dense
from keras.wrappers.scikit_learn import KerasClassifier
from sklearn.model_selection import StratifiedKFold
from sklearn.model_selection import cross_val_score
import numpy

# Load the dataset
data = numpy.loadtxt("./data/pima-indians-diabetes.csv", delimiter=",")
X = data[:,0:8]
y = data[:,8]
```

2. Define three functions, each returning a different Keras model:

```
# Create the function that returns the keras model 1
def build_model_1(activation='relu', optimizer='adam'):
    # create model 1
    model = Sequential()
    model.add(Dense(4, input_dim=8, activation=activation))
    model.add(Dense(4, activation=activation))
    model.add(Dense(4, activation=activation))
    model.add(Dense(1, activation='sigmoid'))
```

```python
    # Compile model
    model.compile(loss='binary_crossentropy', optimizer=optimizer,
metrics=['accuracy'])
    return model

# Create the function that returns the keras model 2
def build_model_2(activation='relu', optimizer='adam'):
    # create model 2
    model = Sequential()
    model.add(Dense(16, input_dim=8, activation=activation))
    model.add(Dense(8, activation=activation))
    model.add(Dense(1, activation='sigmoid'))
    # Compile model
    model.compile(loss='binary_crossentropy', optimizer=optimizer,
metrics=['accuracy'])
    return model

# Create the function that returns the keras model 3
def build_model_3(activation='relu', optimizer='adam'):
    # create model 3
    model = Sequential()
    model.add(Dense(8, input_dim=8, activation=activation))
    model.add(Dense(8, activation=activation))
    model.add(Dense(1, activation='sigmoid'))
    # Compile model
    model.compile(loss='binary_crossentropy', optimizer=optimizer,
metrics=['accuracy'])
    return model
```

3. Write the code to loop over the 3 models and perform 5-fold cross-validation:

```python
# define a seed for random number generator so the result will be
reproducible
seed = 2
numpy.random.seed(seed)
# determine the number of folds for k-fold cross-validation, number of
epochs and batch size
n_folds = 5
batch_size=5
epochs=300
# define the list to store cross-validation scores
results =[]
# define the possible options for the model
```

```
models = [build_model_1, build_model_2, build_model_3]
# loop over models
for m in range(len(models)):
    # build the scikit-learn interface for the keras model
    classifier = KerasClassifier(build_fn=models[m], epochs=epochs, batch_
size=batch_size, verbose=0)
    # define the cross-validation iterator
    kfold = StratifiedKFold(n_splits=n_folds, shuffle=True, random_
state=seed)
    # perform the k-fold cross-validation and store the scores in result
    result = cross_val_score(classifier, X, y, cv=kfold)
    # add the scores to the results list
    results.append(result)


# Print cross-validation score for each model
for m in range(len(models)):
    print("Model", m+1,"Test Accuracy =", results[m].mean())
```

4. Here's the expected output. Model 3 has the best cross-validation test accuracy, as shown in the following figure:

```
Model 1 Test Accuracy = 0.6966556446623462
Model 2 Test Accuracy = 0.7265087974977386
Model 3 Test Accuracy = 0.7370257314073545
```

Figure 4.17: The test accuracy of all three models

5. Write the code to use **epochs = [250, 300]** and **batches = [5, 10]** values and perform 5-fold cross-validation:

```
# define a seed for random number generator so the result will be
reproducible
numpy.random.seed(seed)
# determine the number of folds for k-fold cross-validation
n_folds = 5
# define possible options for epochs and batch_size
epochs = [250, 300]
batches = [5, 10]
# define the list to store cross-validation scores
results =[]
# loop over all possible pairs of epochs, batch_size
for e in range(len(epochs)):
    for b in range(len(batches)):
```

```
           # build the scikit-learn interface for the keras model
           classifier = KerasClassifier(build_fn=build_model_3,
     epochs=epochs[e], batch_size=batches[b], verbose=0)
           # define the cross-validation iterator
           kfold = StratifiedKFold(n_splits=n_folds, shuffle=True, random_
     state=seed)
           # perform the k-fold cross-validation.
           # store the scores in result
           result = cross_val_score(classifier, X, y, cv=kfold)
           # add the scores to the results list
           results.append(result)

     # Print cross-validation score for each possible pair of epochs, batch_
     size
     c = 0
     for e in range(len(epochs)):
         for b in range(len(batches)):
             print("batch_size =", batches[b],",", epochs =", epochs[e], ", Test
     Accuracy =", results[c].mean())
             c += 1
```

6. Here's the expected output:

```
batch_size = 5 , epochs = 250 , Test Accuracy = 0.6538409411974232
batch_size = 10 , epochs = 250 , Test Accuracy = 0.6539088364283578
batch_size = 5 , epochs = 300 , Test Accuracy = 0.7108904297936095
batch_size = 10 , epochs = 300 , Test Accuracy = 0.7344792467954254
```

Figure 4.18: Cross-validation scores for each pair of epochs and batch_size

7. The **batch_size= 10**, **epochs=300** pair has the best cross-validation test accuracy.

8. Write the code to loop over **optimizers = ['rmsprop', 'adam','sgd']** and **activations = ['relu', 'tanh']** values and perform 5-fold cross-validation:

```
     # define a seed for random number generator so the result will be
     reproducible
     numpy.random.seed(seed)
     # determine the number of folds for k-fold cross-validation, number of
     epochs and batch size
     n_folds = 5
     batch_size=10
     epochs=300
     # define the list to store cross-validation scores
     results =[]
```

```
# define possible options for optimizer and activation
optimizers = ['rmsprop', 'adam','sgd']
activations = ['relu', 'tanh']
# loop over all possible pairs of optimizer, activation
for o in range(len(optimizers)):
    for a in range(len(activations)):
        optimizer = optimizers[o]
        activation = activations[a]
        # build the scikit-learn interface for the keras model
        classifier = KerasClassifier(build_fn=build_model_3, epochs=epochs,
batch_size=batch_size, verbose=0)
        # define the cross-validation iterator
        kfold = StratifiedKFold(n_splits=n_folds, shuffle=True, random_
state=seed)
        # perform the k-fold cross-validation.
        # store the scores in result
        result = cross_val_score(classifier, X, y, cv=kfold)
        # add the scores to the results list
        results.append(result)

# Print cross-validation score for each possible pair of optimizer,
activation
c = 0
for o in range(len(optimizers)):
    for a in range(len(activations)):
        print("activation = ", activations[a],",", optimizer = ",
optimizers[o], ", Test accuracy = ", results[c].mean())
        c += 1
```

9. Here's the expected output:

```
activation =  relu , optimizer =  rmsprop , Test accuracy =  0.7265851785979585
activation =  tanh , optimizer =  rmsprop , Test accuracy =  0.7161191768055708
activation =  relu , optimizer =  adam , Test accuracy =  0.7188099491576996
activation =  tanh , optimizer =  adam , Test accuracy =  0.7319157992535724
activation =  relu , optimizer =  sgd , Test accuracy =  0.7370851354560143
activation =  tanh , optimizer =  sgd , Test accuracy =  0.7266021576516446
```

Figure 4.19: Cross-validation scores for each pair of optimizer and activation functions

10. The `activation='relu'` and `optimizer='sgd'` pair has the best cross-validation test accuracy. Also, the `activation='tanh'` and `optimizer='adam'` pair results in almost the same performance. Therefore, we can choose either pair for the final model.

Activity 7: Model Selection Using Cross-validation on the Boston House Prices Dataset

Solution:

1. Import all the required packages and load the dataset:

    ```
    # import the required packages
    from keras.models import Sequential
    from keras.layers import Dense
    from keras.wrappers.scikit_learn import KerasRegressor
    from sklearn.model_selection import KFold
    from sklearn.model_selection import cross_val_score
    from sklearn.preprocessing import StandardScaler
    from sklearn.pipeline import make_pipeline
    import numpy
    ```

2. Load the dataset and print the input and output size. Also, print the range of the output:

    ```
    # Load the dataset
    from sklearn.datasets import load_boston
    boston = load_boston()
    # Print the sizes of input data and output data
    print("Input data size = ", boston.data.shape)
    print("Output size = ", boston.target.shape)
    # store data examples in X and their corresponding outputs in y
    X = boston.data
    y = boston.target
    # Print the range for output
    print("Output Range = (", min(y), ", ", max(y), ")")
    ```

3. Here's the expected output:

    ```
    Input data size =  (506, 13)
    Output size =  (506,)
    Output Range = ( 5.0 ,  50.0 )
    ```

    Figure 4.20: The input size, output size, and output range of the dataset

4. Define three functions, each returning a different Keras model:

```
# Create the function that returns the keras model 1
def build_model_1(optimizer='adam'):
    # create model 1
    model = Sequential()
    model.add(Dense(10, input_dim=13, activation='relu'))
    model.add(Dense(1))
    # Compile model
    model.compile(loss='mean_squared_error', optimizer=optimizer)
    return model

# Create the function that returns the keras model 2
def build_model_2(optimizer='adam'):
    # create model 2
    model = Sequential()
    model.add(Dense(10, input_dim=13, activation='relu'))
    model.add(Dense(10, activation='relu'))
    model.add(Dense(1))
    # Compile model
    model.compile(loss='mean_squared_error', optimizer=optimizer)
    return model

# Create the function that returns the keras model 3
def build_model_3(optimizer='adam'):
    # create model 3
    model = Sequential()
    model.add(Dense(10, input_dim=13, activation='relu'))
    model.add(Dense(10, activation='relu'))
    model.add(Dense(10, activation='relu'))
    model.add(Dense(1))
    # Compile model
    model.compile(loss='mean_squared_error', optimizer=optimizer)
    return model
```

5. Write the code to loop over the 3 models and perform 5-fold cross-validation:

```
# define a seed for random number generator so the result will be
reproducible
seed = 1
numpy.random.seed(seed)
# determine the number of folds for k-fold cross-validation
n_folds = 5
```

```
# define the list to store cross-validation scores
results =[]
# define the possible options for the model
models = [build_model_1, build_model_2, build_model_3]
# loop over models
for i in range(len(models)):
    # build the scikit-learn interface for the keras model
    regressor = KerasRegressor(build_fn=models[i], epochs=100, batch_
size=5, verbose=0)
    # build the pipeline of transformations so for each fold training set
will be scaled
    # and test set will be scaled accordingly.
    model = make_pipeline(StandardScaler(), regressor)
    # define the cross-validation iterator
    kfold = KFold(n_splits=n_folds, shuffle=True, random_state=seed)
    # perform the k-fold cross-validation.
    # store the scores in result
    result = cross_val_score(model, X, y, cv=kfold)
    # add the scores to the results list
    results.append(result)

# Print cross-validation score for each model
for i in range(len(models)):
    print("Model ", i+1," test error rate = ", abs(results[i].mean()))
```

6. Expected output:

```
Model  1  test error rate =  16.37153442611835
Model  2  test error rate =  11.790108379481824
Model  3  test error rate =  12.730149378118828
```

Figure 4.21: Cross-validation scores for all three models

7. Model 2 (a 2-layer neural network) has the lowest test error rate.

8. Write the code to loop over **epochs = [80, 100]** and **batches = [5, 10]** and perform 5-fold cross-validation:

```
# determine the number of folds for k-fold cross-validation
n_folds = 5
# define the list to store cross-validation scores
results =[]
# define possible options for epochs and batch_size
epochs = [80, 100]
```

```
batches = [5, 10]
# loop over all possible pairs of epochs, batch_size
for i in range(len(epochs)):
    for j in range(len(batches)):
        # build the scikit-learn interface for the keras model
        regressor = KerasRegressor(build_fn=build_model_2,
epochs=epochs[i], batch_size=batches[j], verbose=0)
        # build the pipeline of transformations so for each fold trainind
set will be scaled
        # and test set will be scaled accordingly.
        model = make_pipeline(StandardScaler(), regressor)
        # define the cross-validation iterator
        kfold = KFold(n_splits=n_folds, shuffle=True, random_state=seed)
        # perform the k-fold cross-validation.
        # store the scores in result
        result = cross_val_score(model, X, y, cv=kfold)
        # add the scores to the results list
        results.append(result)

# Print cross-validation score for each possible pair of epochs, batch_
size
c = 0
for i in range(len(epochs)):
    for j in range(len(batches)):
        print("batch_size = ", batches[j],", epochs = ", epochs[i], ",
Test error rate = ", abs(results[c].mean()))
        c += 1
```

9. Here's the expected output:

```
batch_size =    5 , epochs =   80 , Test error rate =   12.594723399326138
batch_size =   10 , epochs =   80 , Test error rate =   14.177633668686251
batch_size =    5 , epochs =  100 , Test error rate =   11.910661792893794
batch_size =   10 , epochs =  100 , Test error rate =   13.96304562220889
```

Figure 4.22: 5-fold cross-validation scores for each pair of epochs and batch_size

10. The pair of **batch_size=5** and **epochs=100** has the lowest test error rate.

11. Write the code to loop over **optimizers = ['rmsprop', 'sgd', 'adam']** and perform 5-fold cross-validation:

```
# determine the number of folds for k-fold cross-validation
n_folds = 5
# define the list to store cross-validation scores
results =[]
# define the possible options for the optimizer
optimizers = ['adam', 'sgd', 'rmsprop']
# loop over optimizers
for i in range(len(optimizers)):
    optimizer=optimizers[i]
    # build the scikit-learn interface for the keras model
    regressor = KerasRegressor(build_fn=build_model_2, epochs=80, batch_size=5, verbose=0)
    # build the pipeline of transformations so for each fold trainind set will be scaled
    # and test set will be scaled accordingly.
    model = make_pipeline(StandardScaler(), regressor)
    # define the cross-validation iterator
    kfold = KFold(n_splits=n_folds, shuffle=True, random_state=seed)
    # perform the k-fold cross-validation.
    # store the scores in result
    result = cross_val_score(model, X, y, cv=kfold)
    # add the scores to the results list
    results.append(result)
# Print cross-validation score for each optimizer
for i in range(len(optimizers)):
    print("optimizer=", optimizers[i]," test error rate = ",
abs(results[i].mean()))
```

12. Here's the expected output:

```
optimizer= adam   test error rate =   12.594723399326138
optimizer= sgd   test error rate =   13.703539213191604
optimizer= rmsprop   test error rate =   12.510377227410695
```

Figure 4.23: Cross-validation scores for each optimizer (adam, sgd, and rmsprop)

13. **optimizer='rmsprop'** has the lowest test error rate. Also, **optimizer='adam'** results in almost as good performance. Therefore, we can say that the **'rmsprop'** and **'adam'** optimizers outperform **'sgd'** for this particular problem and this particular model.

Chapter 5: Improving Model Accuracy

Activity 8: Weight Regularization on a Diabetes Diagnosis Classifier

Solution:

1. Load the dataset and split the dataset into a training set and a test set:

```
# Load The dataset
import numpy
data = numpy.loadtxt("./data/pima-indians-diabetes.csv", delimiter=",")
X = data[:,0:8]
y = data[:,8]

# Split the dataset into training set and test set with a 0.7-0.3 ratio
from sklearn.model_selection import train_test_split
X_train, X_test, y_train, y_test = train_test_split(X, y, test_size=0.3,
random_state=0)
```

2. Define a Keras model with two hidden layers of size eight to perform the classification. Train the model and plot the trends in training error and test error:

```
# define a seed for random number generator so the result will be
reproducible
import numpy
seed = 1
numpy.random.seed(seed)

# define the keras model
from keras.models import Sequential
from keras.layers import Dense
model = Sequential()
model.add(Dense(8, input_dim=8, activation='relu'))
model.add(Dense(8, activation='relu'))
model.add(Dense(1, activation='sigmoid'))
model.compile(loss='binary_crossentropy', optimizer='sgd',
metrics=['accuracy'])
# train the model using training set while evaluationg on test set
history=model.fit(X_train, y_train, batch_size = 10, epochs = 300,
validation_data=(X_test, y_test), verbose=0)
```

3. Import the required packages:

```
import matplotlib.pyplot as plt
import matplotlib
%matplotlib inline
```

4. Plot the training error and test error:

```
matplotlib.rcParams['figure.figsize'] = (10.0, 8.0)
plt.plot(history.history['loss'])
plt.plot(history.history['val_loss'])
plt.ylim(0,1)
plt.ylabel('loss')
plt.xlabel('epoch')
plt.legend(['train loss', 'test loss'], loc='upper right')

# print the best accuracy reached on the test set
print("Best Accuray on Test Set =", max(history.history['val_acc']))
```

Expected output:

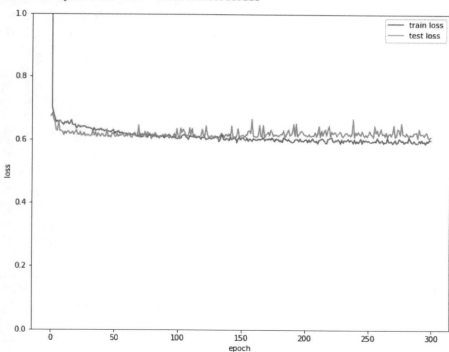

Figure 5.12: A plot of the training error and test error during training for the model without regularization

The test error decreases to a certain amount and then starts increasing, while training error keeps decreasing slowly. This is indicative of the model overfitting the training examples.

5. Add L2 regularizers with **lambda=0.01** to the hidden layers of your model and repeat step 4 to plot the training error and test error:

```
# set up a seed for random number generator so the result will be
reproducible
numpy.random.seed(seed)

# define the keras model with l2 regularization with lambda = 0.01
from keras.regularizers import l2
model = Sequential()
model.add(Dense(8, input_dim=8, activation='relu', kernel_
regularizer=l2(0.01)))
model.add(Dense(8, activation='relu', kernel_regularizer=l2(0.01)))
model.add(Dense(1, activation='sigmoid'))
model.compile(loss='binary_crossentropy', optimizer='sgd',
metrics=['accuracy'])

# train the model using training set while evaluating on test set
history=model.fit(X_train, y_train, batch_size = 10, epochs = 300,
validation_data=(X_test, y_test), verbose=0)
```

Expected output:

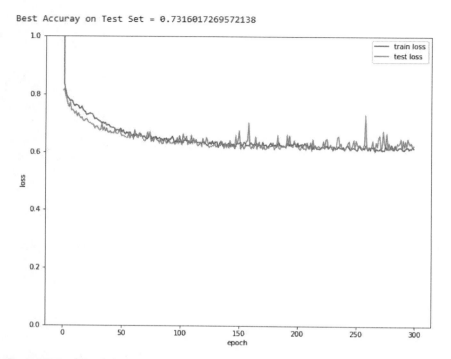

Figure 5.13: A plot of the training error and test error during training for the model with L2 weight regularization (lambda=0.01)

It can be seen from Figure 5.13 that the test error **almost** plateaus after being decreased to a certain amount. The gap between the training error and the test error at the end of training process is smaller, which is indicative of reduced **overfitting** of the model to the training examples.

6. Repeat the previous step, this time with `lambda=0.1`. Repeat step 4 to plot the training error and test error:

```
set up a seed for random number generator so the result will be
reproducible
numpy.random.seed(seed)

# define the keras model with l2 regularization with lambda = 0.1
from keras.regularizers import l2
model = Sequential()
model.add(Dense(8, input_dim=8, activation='relu', kernel_
regularizer=l2(0.1)))
model.add(Dense(8, activation='relu', kernel_regularizer=l2(0.1)))
model.add(Dense(1, activation='sigmoid'))
```

```
model.compile(loss='binary_crossentropy', optimizer='sgd',
metrics=['accuracy'])

# train the model using training set while evaluationg on test set
history=model.fit(X_train, y_train, batch_size = 10, epochs = 300,
validation_data=(X_test, y_test), verbose=0)
```

7. Expected output:

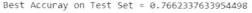

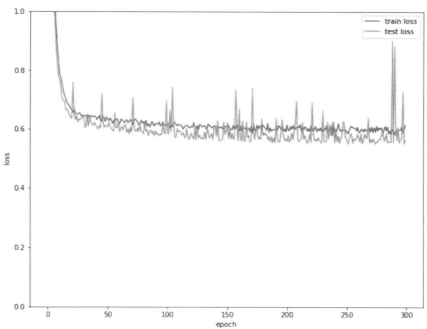

Figure 5.14: A plot of the training error and test error during training for the model with L2 weight regularization (lambda=0.1)

The test error does not increase after being decreased to a certain amount, which is indicative of the model not overfitting to the training examples. Here, the test error is lower than the previous step, but the test error shows more intense fluctuations.

8. Repeat the previous step, this time with **lambda=0.5**. Repeat step 4 to plot the training error and test error:

```
# set up a seed for random number generator so the result will be
reproducible
numpy.random.seed(seed)
```

```
# define the keras model with l2 regularization with lambda = 0.5
from keras.regularizers import l2
model = Sequential()
model.add(Dense(8, input_dim=8, activation='relu', kernel_
regularizer=l2(0.5)))
model.add(Dense(8, activation='relu', kernel_regularizer=l2(0.5)))
model.add(Dense(1, activation='sigmoid'))
model.compile(loss='binary_crossentropy', optimizer='sgd',
metrics=['accuracy'])

# train the model using training set while evaluationg on test set
history=model.fit(X_train, y_train, batch_size = 10, epochs = 300,
validation_data=(X_test, y_test), verbose=0)
```

Expected output:

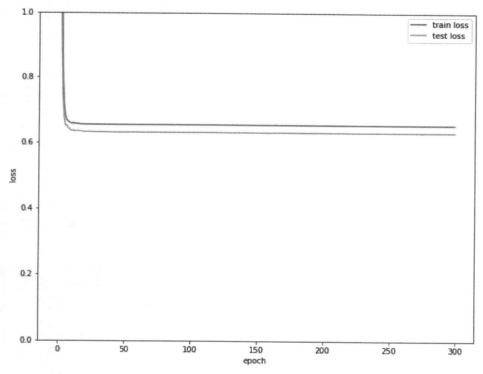

Figure 5.15: A plot of the training error and test error during training for the model with L2 weight regularization (lambda=0.5)

Again, the test error does not increase after being decreased to a certain amount, which is indicative of the model not overfitting to the training examples. Here, the test error is higher than the previous step, but there are no fluctuations in the test error. It seems that L2 weight regularization with **lambda=0.1** achieves the lowest test error while preventing model from overfitting.

9. Add L1 regularizers with **lambda=0.01** to the hidden layers of your model and repeat step 4 to plot the training error and test error:

```
# set up a seed for random number generator so the result will be
reproducible
numpy.random.seed(seed)

# define the keras model with l1 regularization with lambda = 0.01
from keras.regularizers import l1
model = Sequential()
model.add(Dense(8, input_dim=8, activation='relu', kernel_
regularizer=l1(0.01)))
model.add(Dense(8, activation='relu', kernel_regularizer=l1(0.01)))
model.add(Dense(1, activation='sigmoid'))
model.compile(loss='binary_crossentropy', optimizer='sgd',
metrics=['accuracy'])

# train the model using training set while evaluationg on test set
history=model.fit(X_train, y_train, batch_size = 10, epochs = 300,
validation_data=(X_test, y_test), verbose=0)
```

Expected output:

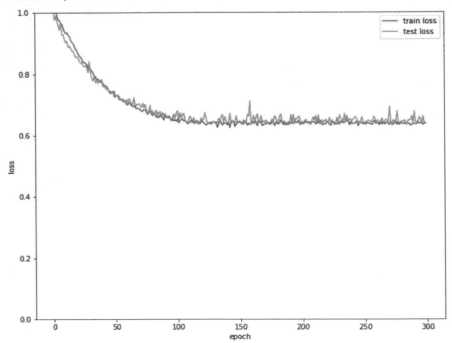

Best Accuray on Test Set = 0.735930733608477

Figure 5.16: A plot of the training error and test error during training for the model with L1 weight regularization (lambda=0.01)

10. Add L1 regularizers with **lambda=0.1** to the hidden layers of your model and repeat step 4 to plot the training error and test error:

```
# set up a seed for random number generator so the result will be
reproducible
numpy.random.seed(seed)

# define the keras model with l1 regularization with lambda = 0.1
from keras.regularizers import l1
model = Sequential()
model.add(Dense(8, input_dim=8, activation='relu', kernel_
regularizer=l1(0.1)))
model.add(Dense(8, activation='relu', kernel_regularizer=l1(0.1)))
model.add(Dense(1, activation='sigmoid'))
model.compile(loss='binary_crossentropy', optimizer='sgd',
metrics=['accuracy'])

# train the model using training set while evaluationg on test set
```

```
history=model.fit(X_train, y_train, batch_size = 10, epochs = 300,
validation_data=(X_test, y_test), verbose=0)
```

Expected output:

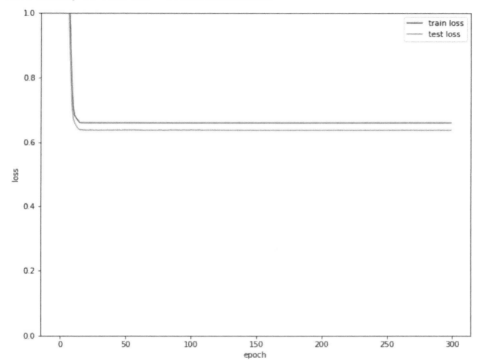

Figure 5.17: The plot of the training error and test error during training for the model
with L1 weight regularization (lambda=0.1)

It seems that L1 weight regularization with **lambda=0.01** achieves a better test error
while preventing the model from overfitting.

11. Add L1 and L2 regularizers with L1 **lambda=0.01** and the L2 **lambda = 0.1** to the
hidden layers of your model and repeat step 4 to plot the training error and test
error:

```
# set up a seed for random number generator so the result will be
reproducible
numpy.random.seed(seed)

# define the keras model with l1_l2 regularization with l1_ambda = 0.01 and
l2_ambda = 0.1
from keras.regularizers import l1_l2
```

```
model = Sequential()
model.add(Dense(8, input_dim=8, activation='relu', kernel_regularizer=l1_
l2(l1=0.01, l2=0.1)))
model.add(Dense(8, activation='relu', kernel_regularizer=l1_l2(l1=0.01,
l2=0.1)))
model.add(Dense(1, activation='sigmoid'))
model.compile(loss='binary_crossentropy', optimizer='sgd',
metrics=['accuracy'])

# train the model using training set while evaluationg on test set
history=model.fit(X_train, y_train, batch_size = 10, epochs = 300,
validation_data=(X_test, y_test), verbose=0)
```

Expected output:

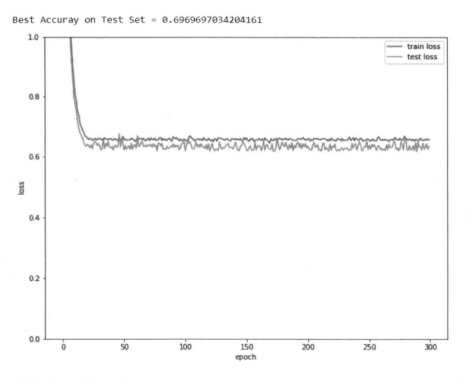

Figure 5.18: A plot of the training error and test error during training for the model with L1 lambda equal to 0.01 and l2 lambda equal to 0.1

While L1 and L2 regularization are successful in preventing the model from overfitting, it seems that by applying either L1 regularization or L2 regularization, we were able to get a lower test error.

Activity 9: Dropout Regularization on Boston House Prices Dataset

Solution:

1. Load the dataset, split the dataset into a training set and test set, and scale the input data:

```
# Load the dataset
from sklearn.datasets import load_boston
boston = load_boston()

# store data examples in X and their corresponding outputs in y
X = boston.data
y = boston.target

# Split the dataset into training set and test set with a 0.7-0.3 ratio
from sklearn.model_selection import train_test_split
X_train, X_test, y_train, y_test = train_test_split(X, y, test_size=0.3,
random_state=0)

# Preprocessing
# scale the input features in the training set to have mean equal 0 and
variance equal to 1
from sklearn.preprocessing import StandardScaler
scaler = StandardScaler()
X_train = scaler.fit_transform(X_train)
X_test = scaler.transform(X_test)
```

2. Define a Keras model with 2 hidden layers of size 10 and train the model:

```
# define a seed for random number generator so the result will be
reproducible
import numpy
seed = 1
numpy.random.seed(seed)
```

```
from keras.models import Sequential
from keras.layers import Dense
# create model
model = Sequential()
model.add(Dense(10, input_dim=13, activation='relu'))
model.add(Dense(10, activation='relu'))
model.add(Dense(1))
# Compile model
model.compile(loss='mean_squared_error', optimizer='rmsprop')
# train the model using training set while evaluating on test set
history=model.fit(X_train, y_train, batch_size = 5, epochs = 150,
validation_data=(X_test, y_test), verbose=0)
```

3. Import the required packages for plotting:

```
import matplotlib.pyplot as plt
import matplotlib
%matplotlib inline
```

4. Plot the trends in the training error and test error. Print the best accuracy reached on the test set:

```
matplotlib.rcParams['figure.figsize'] = (10.0, 8.0)
# plot training error and test error plots
plt.plot(history.history['loss'])
plt.plot(history.history['val_loss'])
plt.ylim((0, 100))
plt.ylabel('loss')
plt.xlabel('epoch')
plt.legend(['train loss', 'test loss'], loc='upper right')

# print the best accuracy reached on the test set
print("Lowest error on training set = ", min(history.history['loss']))
print("Lowest error on test set = ", min(history.history['val_loss']))
```

Expected output:

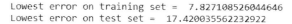

```
Lowest error on training set =  7.827108526044646
Lowest error on test set =  17.420035562232922
```

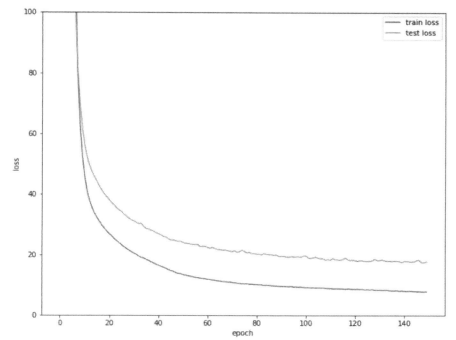

Figure 5.19: A plot of the training error and test error during training for the model without regularization

In the training error and test error values, there is a large gap between the training error and test error, which is indicative of overfitting.

5. Add dropout regularization with **rate=0.2** to the first hidden layer of your model. Repeat step 4 to plot the trends in the training and test errors and print the best accuracy reached on the test set:

```
# define a seed for random number generator so the result will be
reproducible
numpy.random.seed(seed)

from keras.layers import Dropout
# create model
model = Sequential()
model.add(Dense(10, input_dim=13, activation='relu'))
model.add(Dropout(0.2))
model.add(Dense(10, activation='relu'))
model.add(Dense(1))
```

```
# Compile model
model.compile(loss='mean_squared_error', optimizer='rmsprop')
# train the model using training set while evaluationg on test set
history=model.fit(X_train, y_train, batch_size = 5, epochs = 200,
validation_data=(X_test, y_test), verbose=0)

matplotlib.rcParams['figure.figsize'] = (10.0, 8.0)
```

Expected output:

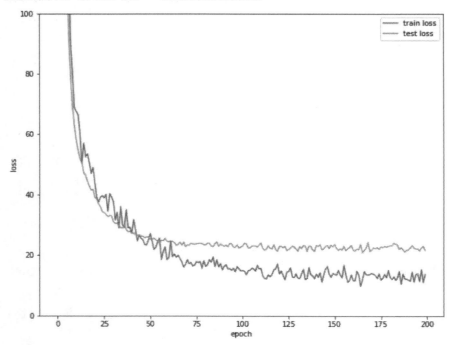

Figure 5.20: A plot of the training error and test error during training for the model with dropout regularization (rate=0.2) in the first layer

There is still a large gap between the training error and the test error, which is indicative of overfitting. Therefore, the dropout (rate=0.2) on the first layer did not help with overfitting. Please note that randomly removing nodes from the network causes the loss values to fluctuate in every iteration. This explains the noise in the plot.

6. Repeat the previous step, this time adding dropout regularization with rate=0.2 to both hidden layers of your model. Repeat step 4 to plot the trends in the training and test errors and print the best accuracy reached on the test set:

```
# define a seed for random number generator so the result will be
reproducible
numpy.random.seed(seed)

# create model
model = Sequential()
model.add(Dense(10, input_dim=13, activation='relu'))
model.add(Dropout(0.2))
model.add(Dense(10, activation='relu'))
model.add(Dropout(0.2))
model.add(Dense(1))
# Compile model
model.compile(loss='mean_squared_error', optimizer='rmsprop')
# train the model using training set while evaluating on test set
history=model.fit(X_train, y_train, batch_size = 5, epochs = 200,
validation_data=(X_test, y_test), verbose=0)

matplotlib.rcParams['figure.figsize'] = (10.0, 8.0)
```

Expected output:

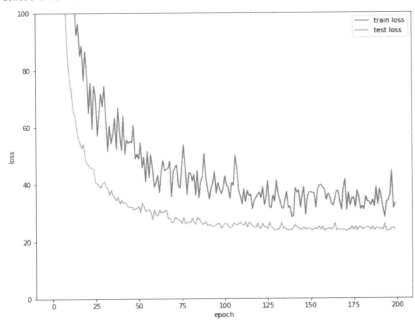

Figure 5.21: A plot of the training error and test error during training for the model
with dropout regularization (rate=0.2) in both layers

The gap between the training error and test error seems to be reducing; however, both the training error and test error are higher in comparison to the model with no regularization.

7. Repeat the previous step, this time with rate=0.1, and train the model. Repeat step 4 to plot the trends in the training and test errors, and print the best accuracy reached on the test set:

```
# define a seed for random number generator so the result will be
reproducible
numpy.random.seed(seed)

# create model
model = Sequential()
model.add(Dense(10, input_dim=13, activation='relu'))
model.add(Dropout(0.1))
model.add(Dense(10, activation='relu'))
model.add(Dropout(0.1))
model.add(Dense(1))
# Compile model
model.compile(loss='mean_squared_error', optimizer='rmsprop')
# train the model using training set while evaluationg on test set
history=model.fit(X_train, y_train, batch_size = 5, epochs = 200,
validation_data=(X_test, y_test), verbose=0)

matplotlib.rcParams['figure.figsize'] = (10.0, 8.0)
```

Expected output:

```
Lowest error on training set =  17.283494630775884
Lowest error on test set =  17.221214021507063
```

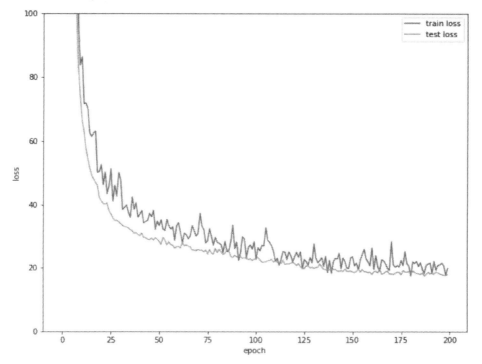

Figure 5.22: A plot of training errors and test errors during training for the model with dropout regularization (rate=0.1) in both layers

The gap between training error and test error is dramatically decreased. This indicates that dropout regularization here succeeds in preventing the model from overfitting. Also, the error values are comparable to the original model with no regularization. This means that reducing overfitting was not achieved at the cost of a dramatic increase in the error rate.

Activity 10: Hyperparameter Tuning on the Diabetes Diagnosis Classifier

Solution:

1. Load the dataset and import the libraries:

```
# Load The dataset
import numpy
data = numpy.loadtxt("./data/pima-indians-diabetes.csv", delimiter=",")
X = data[:,0:8]
y = data[:,8]
```

2. Define a function that returns a Keras model with 2 hidden layers of size 8, and apply L2 weight regularization on each hidden layer:

```
# Create the function that returns the keras model
from keras.models import Sequential
from keras.layers import Dense
from keras.regularizers import l2
def build_model(lambda_parameter):
    model = Sequential()
    model.add(Dense(8, input_dim=8, activation='relu', kernel_
regularizer=l2(lambda_parameter)))
    model.add(Dense(8, activation='relu', kernel_regularizer=l2(lambda_
parameter)))
    model.add(Dense(1, activation='sigmoid'))
    model.compile(loss='binary_crossentropy', optimizer='sgd',
metrics=['accuracy'])
    return model
```

3. Perform **GridSearchCV()** on the model using the hyperparameters grid:

```
from keras.wrappers.scikit_learn import KerasClassifier
from sklearn.model_selection import GridSearchCV
# define a seed for random number generator so the result will be
reproducible
import numpy
seed = 1
numpy.random.seed(seed)
# create the Keras wrapper with scikit learn
model = KerasClassifier(build_fn=build_model, verbose=0)
# define all the possible values for each hyperparameter
lambda_parameter = [0.01, 0.5, 1]
epochs = [350, 400]
batch_size = [10]
```

```
# create the dictionary containing all possible values of hyperparameters
param_grid = dict(lambda_parameter=lambda_parameter, epochs=epochs, batch_
size=batch_size)
# perform 5-fold cross validation for to store the results
grid_seach = GridSearchCV(estimator=model, param_grid=param_grid, cv=5)
results = grid_seach.fit(X, y)
```

4. Print the results for the best cross-validation score:

```
print("Best cross validation score =", results.best_score_)
print("Parameters for Best cross validation scor e=", results.best_
params_)

# print the results for all evaluated hyperparameter combinations
accuracy_means = results.cv_results_['mean_test_score']
accuracy_stds = results.cv_results_['std_test_score']
parameters = results.cv_results_['params']
for p in range(len(parameters)):
    print("Accuracy %f (std %f) for params %r" % (accuracy_means[p],
accuracy_stds[p], parameters[p]))
```

Expected output:

```
Best cross validation score = 0.6979166676367944
Parameters for Best cross validation scor e= {'batch_size': 10, 'epochs': 400, 'lambda_parameter': 0.01}
Accuracy 0.669271 (std 0.044784) for params {'batch_size': 10, 'epochs': 350, 'lambda_parameter': 0.01}
Accuracy 0.671875 (std 0.062727) for params {'batch_size': 10, 'epochs': 350, 'lambda_parameter': 0.5}
Accuracy 0.651042 (std 0.052404) for params {'batch_size': 10, 'epochs': 350, 'lambda_parameter': 1}
Accuracy 0.697917 (std 0.040392) for params {'batch_size': 10, 'epochs': 400, 'lambda_parameter': 0.01}
Accuracy 0.674479 (std 0.042581) for params {'batch_size': 10, 'epochs': 400, 'lambda_parameter': 0.5}
Accuracy 0.652344 (std 0.014675) for params {'batch_size': 10, 'epochs': 400, 'lambda_parameter': 1}
```

Figure 5.23: Results for the best cross-validation scores

5. Repeat step 2 using **GridSearchCV()**, **lambda_parameter = [0.001, 0.01, 0.05, 0.1]**, and **epochs = [400]**, and repeat step 4. Print the results for the entire grid:

```
# define a seed for random number generator so the result will be
reproducible
numpy.random.seed(seed)
# create the Keras wrapper with scikit learn
model = KerasClassifier(build_fn=build_model, verbose=0)
# define all the possible values for each hyperparameter
lambda_parameter = [0.001, 0.01, 0.05, 0.1]
epochs = [400]
batch_size = [10]
# create the dictionary containing all possible values of hyperparameters
param_grid = dict(lambda_parameter=lambda_parameter, epochs=epochs, batch_
size=batch_size)
# search the grid, perform 5-fold cross validation for each possible
combination, store the results
grid_seach = GridSearchCV(estimator=model, param_grid=param_grid, cv=5)
results = grid_seach.fit(X, y)
```

Expected output:

```
Best cross validation score = 0.704427085390004
Parameters for Best cross validation score = {'batch_size': 10, 'epochs': 400, 'lambda_parameter': 0.05}
Accuracy 0.671875 (std 0.041515) for params {'batch_size': 10, 'epochs': 400, 'lambda_parameter': 0.001}
Accuracy 0.697917 (std 0.042438) for params {'batch_size': 10, 'epochs': 400, 'lambda_parameter': 0.01}
Accuracy 0.704427 (std 0.027547) for params {'batch_size': 10, 'epochs': 400, 'lambda_parameter': 0.05}
Accuracy 0.664063 (std 0.091266) for params {'batch_size': 10, 'epochs': 400, 'lambda_parameter': 0.1}
```

Figure 5.24: Results for the best cross-validation scores with different values of lambda_parameter and epochs

6. Repeat the previous step, using dropout regularization instead of L2 regularization, and using **rate = [0, 0.2, 0.4]** and **epochs = [350, 400]**:

```
# Create the function that returns the keras model
from keras.layers import Dropout
def build_model(rate):
    model = Sequential()
    model.add(Dense(8, activation='relu'))
    model.add(Dropout(rate))
    model.add(Dense(8, activation='relu'))
```

```
      model.add(Dropout(rate))
      model.add(Dense(1, activation='sigmoid'))
      model.compile(loss='binary_crossentropy', optimizer='sgd',
   metrics=['accuracy'])
      return model
```

7. Perform **GridSearchCV()** on the model and repeat step 4. Print the results for the entire grid:

```
# define a seed for random number generator so the result will be
reproducible
numpy.random.seed(seed)
# create the Keras wrapper with scikit learn
model = KerasClassifier(build_fn=build_model, verbose=0)
# define all the possible values for each hyperparameter
rate = [0, 0.2, 0.4]
epochs = [350, 400]
batch_size = [10]
# create the dictionary containing all possible values of hyperparameters
param_grid = dict(rate=rate, epochs=epochs, batch_size=batch_size)
# perform 5-fold cross validation for 10 randomly selected combinations,
store the results
grid_seach = GridSearchCV(estimator=model, param_grid=param_grid, cv=5)
results = grid_seach.fit(X, y)
```

Expected output:

```
Best cross validation score= 0.6901041681024557
Parameters for Best cross validation score= {'batch_size': 10, 'epochs': 400, 'rate': 0}
Accuracy 0.592448 (std 0.130434) for params {'batch_size': 10, 'epochs': 350, 'rate': 0}
Accuracy 0.666667 (std 0.053115) for params {'batch_size': 10, 'epochs': 350, 'rate': 0.2}
Accuracy 0.601563 (std 0.141879) for params {'batch_size': 10, 'epochs': 350, 'rate': 0.4}
Accuracy 0.690104 (std 0.040916) for params {'batch_size': 10, 'epochs': 400, 'rate': 0}
Accuracy 0.669271 (std 0.041091) for params {'batch_size': 10, 'epochs': 400, 'rate': 0.2}
Accuracy 0.653646 (std 0.052577) for params {'batch_size': 10, 'epochs': 400, 'rate': 0.4}
```

Figure 5.25: Results for the best cross-validation scores with different values for epochs, rate, and batch_size on L2 regularization

8. Repeat the previous step using **rate = [0.0, 0.05, 0.1]** and **epochs = [400]** and repeat step 4. Print the results for the entire grid:

```
# define a seed for random number generator so the result will be
reproducible
numpy.random.seed(seed)
# create the Keras wrapper with scikit learn
model = KerasClassifier(build_fn=build_model, verbose=0)
# define all the possible values for each hyperparameter
rate = [0.0, 0.05, 0.1]
epochs = [400]
batch_size = [10]
# create the dictionary containing all possible values of hyperparameters
param_grid = dict(rate=rate, epochs=epochs, batch_size=batch_size)
# perform 5-fold cross validation for 10 randomly selected combinations,
store the results
grid_seach = GridSearchCV(estimator=model, param_grid=param_grid, cv=5)
results = grid_seach.fit(X, y)
```

Expected output:

```
Best cross validation score= 0.6822916691501936
Parameters for Best cross validation score= {'batch_size': 10, 'epochs': 400, 'rate': 0.0}
Accuracy 0.682292 (std 0.056231) for params {'batch_size': 10, 'epochs': 400, 'rate': 0.0}
Accuracy 0.682292 (std 0.057025) for params {'batch_size': 10, 'epochs': 400, 'rate': 0.05}
Accuracy 0.673177 (std 0.059715) for params {'batch_size': 10, 'epochs': 400, 'rate': 0.1}
```

Figure 5.26: Results for the best cross-validation scores with different values for epochs and rate

Chapter 6: Model Evaluation

Activity 11: Computing Accuracy and Null Accuracy of Neural Network When We Change the Train/Test Split

Solution:

1. Import the required libraries. Load and explore the dataset:

```
#import the libraries
import numpy as np
import pandas as pd
#Load the Data
patient_data=pd.read_csv("Health_Data.csv")
##use the head function to get a glimpse data
patient_data.head()
```

The following figure shows the output of the preceding code:

	Patient_id	Age	Admission_type	PreExistingDisease	PreviousSurgery	Gender	Smoker	Homeless	DaysinHospital	Readmitted
0	1	33	Urgent	Y	0	M	1	0	1	0
1	2	34	Emergency	N	0	M	1	0	22	0
2	3	88	Trauma	Y	1	M	1	1	100	1
3	4	56	Elective	Y	0	M	1	0	2	0
4	5	45	Trauma	Y	0	M	1	0	34	0

Figure 6.30: A screenshot of the patient readmission dataset

2. Separate the independent and dependent variables. Since column 0, the **patient_ id** column, does not add any value, we discard that column. Columns 1 to 8 are independent variables, and the last column is the dependent variable.

The following figure shows the output of the preceding code:

```
mydata=pd.read_csv("Health_Data.csv")
X=mydata.iloc[:,1:9]
y=mydata.iloc[:,9]
X.head()
```

3. Create dummy variables for the categorical variables. Note that the input should all be numeric variables. Use the **get_dummies** function from pandas to create dummy variables:

```
##New Admission type
A_type=pd.get_dummies(X.iloc[:,1],drop_first=True,prefix='Atype')
##New Gender
New_gender=pd.get_dummies(X.iloc[:,4],drop_first=True,prefix='Gender')
##New Pre Existing Disease Variable
Pre_exdis=pd.get_dummies(X.iloc[:,2],drop_first=True,prefix='PreExistDis')
```

4. Drop the original categorical variables and replace them with the transformed numeric dummy variables:

```
## Drop the original categorical columns
X.drop(['Admission_
type','PreExistingDisease','Gender'],axis=1,inplace=True)
##Concat the new transformed data to X DataFrame
X=pd.concat([X,A_type,New_gender,Pre_exdis],axis=1)
```

5. Change the **test_size** and **random_state** from **0.30** to **0.25** and **110** to **500**, respectively:

```
from sklearn.model_selection import train_test_split
xtrain,xtest,ytrain,ytest= train_test_split(X, y, test_size=0.25, random_
state=500)
```

> **Note**
>
> If you use a different **random_state**, you may get a different train/test split, which may yield slightly different final results.

6. Scale the data using the **StandardScaler** function:

```
##Initialize StandardScaler
from sklearn.preprocessing import StandardScaler
sc=StandardScaler()
#Transform the training data
xtrain=sc.fit_transform(xtrain)
xtrain=pd.DataFrame(xtrain,columns=xtest.columns)
#Transform the testing data
xtest=sc.transform(xtest)
xtest=pd.DataFrame(xtest,columns=xtrain.columns)
```

> **Note**
>
> The `sc.fit_transform()` function transforms the data, and the data is also converted to a NumPy array. We may need the data later for analysis as a DataFrame object, so the `pd.DataFrame()` function reconverts data into a DataFrame.

7. Now convert the DataFrame again to NumPy using the **values** function:

```
#Convert DataFrame to NumPy array
x_train=xtrain.values
x_test=xtest.values
y_train=ytrain.values
y_test=ytest.values
```

> **Note**
>
> As a best practice, we should have training and testing data in both NumPy and DataFrames. We mostly use NumPy objects, but we may need DataFrame objects in some scenarios later in the chapter.

8. Import the libraries required to build a neural network architecture:

```
##Import the relevant Keras libraries
from keras.models import Sequential
from keras.layers import Dense
from keras.layers import Dropout
```

9. Initiate the **Sequential** class:

```
##Initiate the Model with Sequential Class
model=Sequential()
```

10. Add the first **Dense** layer and the **Dropout** layer. We have set a **Dropout rate** of 0.3:

```
## Add the 1st dense layer and Dropout Layer
model.add(Dense(units=6,activation='relu',kernel_
initializer='uniform',input_dim=11))
model.add(Dropout(rate=0.3))
```

11. Add the second **Dense** layer and the **Dropout** layer. We have used the **Dropout rate** as 0.3. Here, **Dropout** is used to avoid overfitting:

```
##Add the 2nd dense Layer and Dropout Layer
model.add(Dense(units=6,activation='relu',kernel_initializer='uniform'))
model.add(Dropout(rate=0.3))
```

12. Add an output **Dense** layer with a **sigmoid** activation function:

```
##Add Output Dense Layer
model.add(Dense(units=1,activation='sigmoid',kernel_
initializer='uniform'))
```

> **Note**
>
> Since the output is binary, we are using the **sigmoid** function. If the output is multi-class (that is, more than two classes), then the **softmax** function should be used.

13. Compile the network and fit the model. The metric used here is **accuracy**:

```
#Compile the Model
model.compile(optimizer='adam',loss='binary_
crossentropy',metrics=['accuracy'])
```

> **Note**
>
> The metric name, which in our case is **accuracy**, is defined in the preceding code.

14. Fit the model with **100** epochs and a batch size of **20**:

```
#Fit the Model
model.fit(x_train,y_train,epochs=100,batch_size=20)
```

15. Create two prediction variables, **y_pred_class** and **y_pred_prob**:

```
#y_pred_class is the predcition and y_pred_prob is probabilities of the
prediction
y_pred_class=model.predict(x_test)
y_pred_prob=model.predict_proba(x_test)
```

Two prediction variables are created here. One is the normal **predict** class, and the other is the probability of prediction. **y_predict_proba** will be used to adjust thresholds later in the chapter.

> **Note**
>
> **y_pred_class** contains the probabilities of prediction. It does not contain 0 or 1.

16. Set the threshold for class prediction. Any values that are above the threshold (0.5) will be 1, and values below 0.5 will be 0:

```
##Set threshold all values above threshold are 1 and #below 0
y_pred_class=y_pred_class>0.5
```

17. Calculate the accuracy by using the **accuracy_score** function of scikit-learn:

```
from sklearn.metrics import accuracy_score
accuracy_score(y_test,y_pred_class)
```

The following figure shows the output of the preceding code:

0.8555555555555555

Figure 6.31: The final calculated accuracy

The model returns an accuracy of 85.5%. But is it good enough? We can get the answer to this only by comparing it against the null accuracy.

18. Now, compute the null accuracy. The null accuracy can be calculated using the **value_count** function of the pandas library, which was used in *Exercise 16* of this chapter:

```
# Use the value_count function to calculate distinct class values
ytest.value_counts()
```

```
0    73
1    17
Name: Readmitted, dtype: int64
```

Figure 6.32: Value counts of distinct class values

> **Note**
>
> **ytest** is used here, not **y_test**. A pandas series is needed for the **value_count** method to work. Out of the total 108 values in **ytest**, 91 values are 0s and 17 values are 1s.

19. Calculate the null accuracy:

```
##use head function and divide it by lenght of ytest
ytest.value_counts().head(1)/len(ytest)
```

```
0    0.811111
Name: Readmitted, dtype: float64
```

Figure 6.33: Output showing the null accuracy

We can see that the accuracy and null accuracy will change as we change the train/test split. We will not cover any sampling techniques in this chapter as we have a very highly imbalanced dataset, and sampling techniques will not yield any fruitful results. Let's move onto Activity 12 and compute metrics derived from the confusion matrix.

Activity 12: Derive and Compute Metrics Based on the Confusion Matrix

Solution

1. Open a new Jupyter Notebook and run the whole code of *Exercise 17, Computing Accuracy and Null Accuracy with Healthcare Data*:

> **Note**
>
> The full code to execute step 1 is in the **Lesson06/Activity12.ipynb** file.

Lesson06/Activity12.ipynb

```
import numpy as np
import pandas as pd

#Load the Data
patient_data=pd.read_csv("Health_Data.csv")

//[...]

# Use the value_count function to calculate distinct class values
ytest.value_counts()

##use head function and divide it by lenght of ytest
print("Null Accuracy:",ytest.value_counts().head(1)/len(ytest))
```

https://bit.ly/2GuwRtp

2. Next, compute the confusion matrix using the **confusion_matrix** function from scikit-learn:

```
from sklearn.metrics import confusion_matrix
cm=confusion_matrix(y_test,y_pred_class)
print(cm)
```

The following figure shows the output of the preceding code:

```
array([[89,  2],
       [13,  4]], dtype=int64)
```

Figure 6.34: Computed confusion matrix

Always use **y_test** as the first parameter and **y_pred_class** as the second parameter so that you always get the correct results.

3. Calculate the true negative, false negative, false positive, and true positive:

```
##True Negative
TN=cm[0,0]
##False Negative
FN=cm[1,0]
##False Positives
FP=cm[0,1]
##True Positives
TP=cm[1,1]
```

> **Note**
>
> Using **y_test** and **y_pred_class** in that order is necessary because if they are used in reverse order, the matrix will still be computed without errors, but will be incorrect.

4. Calculate the sensitivity:

```
Sensitivity=TP/(TP+FN)
Sensitivity
```

The following figure shows the output of the preceding code:

0.23529411764705882

Figure 6.35: Output after calculating the sensitivity

5. Calculate the specificity:

```
##Calculating specificity
Specificity=TN/(TN+FP)
Specificity
```

The following figure shows the output of the preceding code:

0.978021978021978

Figure 6.36: Output after calculating the specificity

6. Calculate the precision:

```
##Precision
Precision= TP/(TP+FP)
Precision
```

The following figure shows the output of the preceding code:

0.6666666666666666

Figure 6.37: Output after calculating the precision

7. Calculate the FPR:

```
False_Positive_rate= FP/(FP+TN)
FalsePositive_rate
```

The following figure shows the output of the preceding code:

0.02197802197802198

Figure 6.38: Output after calculating the FPR

The following figure shows the output of the values:

Metrics	Value
Sensitivity	0.235 or 24% approximately
Specificity	0.978 or 98% approximately
Precision	0.666 or 66% approximately
False Positive Rate	.021 or 2% approximately

Figure 6.39: Metrics summary

Note

Sensitivity is inversely proportional to specificity.

As discussed earlier, our model should be more sensitive, but it looks more specific and less sensitive. So how do we solve this? The answer lies in the threshold probabilities. The sensitivity of the model can be increased by adjusting the threshold value for classifying the dependent variable as 1 or 0. Recall that originally, we set the value of **y_pred_class** to greater than 0.5. Let's change the threshold to 0.3 and re-run the code to check the results.

8. Go to step 16 and change the threshold from 0.5 to 0.3 and re-run the code:

```
y_pred_class=y_pred_class>0.3
```

9. Now create a confusion matrix and calculate the specificity and sensitivity:

```
from sklearn.metrics import confusion_matrix
cm=confusion_matrix(y_test,y_pred_class)
cm
```

The following figure shows the output of the preceding code:

```
array([[82,   9],
       [ 9,   8]], dtype=int64)
```

Figure 6.40: A confusion matrix with a threshold of 0.3

The following is the earlier confusion matrix with a threshold of 0.5:

```
array([[89,   2],
       [13,   4]], dtype=int64)
```

Figure 6.41: A confusion matrix with a threshold of 0.5

> **Note**
>
> Always remember that the original values of **y_test** should be passed as the first parameter, and **y_pred** as the second parameter.

10. Compute various components of the confusion matrix:

```
##True Negative
TN=cm[0,0]
##False Negative
FN=cm[1,0]
##False Positives
FP=cm[0,1]
##True Positives
TP=cm[1,1]
```

11. Calculate the new sensitivity:

```
## Calculating sensitivity
Sensitivity=TP/(TP+FN)
Sensitivity
```

The following figure shows the output of the preceding code:

```
0.47058823529411764
```

Figure 6.42: Output after calculating the recomputed sensitivity

12. Calculate the specificity:

```
Specificity=TN/(TN+FP)
Specificity
```

The following figure shows the output of the preceding code:

```
0.9010989010989011
```

Figure 6.43: Output after calculating the recomputed specificity

There is a clear increase in sensitivity and specificity after decreasing the threshold:

Threshold	Sensitivity	Specificity
0.5	24%	99%
0.3	47%	90%

Figure 6.44: Sensitivity and specificity comparison

So, clearly, decreasing the threshold value increases the sensitivity.

13. Visualize the data distribution. To understand why decreasing the threshold value increases the sensitivity, we need to see a histogram of our predicted probabilities. Recall that we created the **y_pred_prob** variable to predict the probabilities of the classifier:

```
import matplotlib.pyplot as plt
%matplotlib inline
#histogram of class distribution
plt.hist(y_pred_prob)
plt.title("Histogram of Predicted Probabilities")
```

```
plt.xlabel("Predicted Probabilities of patient readmission")
plt.ylabel("Frequency")
plt.show()
```

The following figure shows the output of the preceding code:

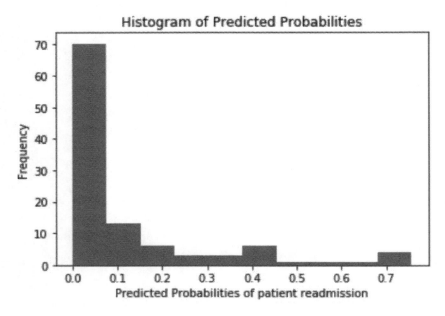

Figure 6.45: A histogram of the probabilities of patient readmission from the dataset

This histogram clearly shows that most of the probabilities for the predicted classifier lie in a range from 0.0 to 0.1, which is indeed very low. Unless we set the threshold very low, we cannot increase sensitivity of the model. Also, note that sensitivity is inversely proportional to specificity, so when one increases, the other decreases.

There is no universal value of threshold. It depends on the problem. The thing to do is to plot a histogram and then select the threshold. In our case, a very low threshold is needed, which we will try and compute in the following exercise. Let's do an exercise in which we further decrease the threshold and check the corresponding sensitivity and specificity.

Chapter 7: Computer Vision with Convolutional Neural Networks

Activity 13: Amending our Model with Multiple Layers and Use of SoftMax

Solution:

1. Import the libraries and classes:

```
#Import the Libraries

from keras.models import Sequential
from keras.layers import Conv2D
from keras.layers import MaxPool2D
from keras.layers import Flatten
from keras.layers import Dense
```

2. Now, initiate the model with a **Sequential** class:

```
#Initiate the classifier
classifier=Sequential()
```

3. Add the first layer of the CNN, followed by the additional layers:

```
classifier.add(Conv2D(32,3,3,input_shape=(64,64,3),activation='relu'))
classifier.add(Conv2D(32, (3, 3), activation = 'relu'))
classifier.add(Conv2D(32, (3, 3), activation = 'relu'))
```

   32, (3,3) means that there are 32 feature detectors of size 3x3. As a best practice, always start with 32 and then you can add 64 or 128 later.

4. Now, add the pooling layer with an image size of 2x2:

```
classifier.add(MaxPool2D(2,2))
```

5. The final step of building the CNN is flattening:

```
classifier.add(Flatten())
```

6. Add the first dense layer of the ANN. Here, **128** is the output of the number of nodes. As a best practice, 128 is good to get started. **activation** is **relu**. As a best practice, a power of two is preferred:

```
classifier.add(Dense(128,activation='relu'))
```

7. Add three more layers to the ANN:

```
classifier.add(Dense(128,activation='relu'))
classifier.add(Dense(128,activation='relu'))
classifier.add(Dense(128,activation='relu'))
```

8. Add the output layer of the ANN. Replace the sigmoid function with **softmax**:

```
classifier.add(Dense(1,activation='softmax'))
```

9. The next step is to compile the network:

```
#Compile The network

classifier.compile(optimizer='adam',loss='binary_
crossentropy',metrics=['accuracy'])
```

10. The following code will scale and transform the images, making them ready for processing:

```
from keras.preprocessing.image import ImageDataGenerator

train_datagen = ImageDataGenerator(rescale = 1./255,
                                   shear_range = 0.2,
                                   zoom_range = 0.2,
                                   horizontal_flip = True)

test_datagen = ImageDataGenerator(rescale = 1./255)
```

11. Create a training set from the training set folder. '**../dataset/training_set**' is the path of the folder where our data is placed:

```
training_set = train_datagen.flow_from_directory('../dataset/training_set',
target_size = (64, 64),
batch_size = 32,
class_mode = 'binary')
```

12. Create the test set:

```
test_set = test_datagen.flow_from_directory('../dataset/test_set',
target_size = (64, 64),
batch_size = 32,
class_mode = 'binary')
```

13. Finally, fit the data. **steps_per_epoch** is **10000**, as there are 10,000 images in the training set, **validation_steps** is **2500**, as the test set has 2,500 images:

```
classifier.fit_generator(training_set,
steps_per_epoch = 10000,
epochs = 2,
validation_data = test_set,
validation_steps = 2500)
```

The following figure shows the output of the preceding code:

```
10000/10000 [==============================] - 6705s 671ms/step - loss: 7.9712 - acc: 0.5000 - val_loss: 7.9688 - val_acc: 0.
5002
Epoch 2/2
10000/10000 [==============================] - 6169s 617ms/step - loss: 7.9712 - acc: 0.5000 - val_loss: 7.9702 - val_acc: 0.
5001
```

Figure 7.19: The accuracy of the model

Note that the accuracy has decreased to 50.01%, despite the increase in the CNN and ANN layers. Normally, the accuracy should increase while using multiple CNN and ANN layers. This must be because of the choice of the activation function, which we switched from sigmoid to softmax.

Activity 14: Classify a New Image

Solution:

1. Run one of the algorithms from the chapter.

2. Load the image and process it. '**../test/test_image_2.jpg**' is the path of the test image. Change the path in the code where you have saved the dataset:

```
new_image2 = image.load_img('../test/test_image_2.jpg', target_size = (64, 64))
```

3. Process the image:

```
new_image = image.img_to_array(new_image)
new_image = np.expand_dims(new_image, axis = 0)
```

4. Predict the new image:

```
result = classifier.predict(new_image)
```

5. The predict method will output the image as **1** or **0**. To map **1** and **0** to **Dog** or **Cat**, use the **class_indices** method with an if...else statement, as follows:

```
training_set.class_indices
if result[0][0] == 1:
    prediction = 'It is a Dog'
else:
    prediction = 'It is a Cat'

print(prediction)
```

It is a Cat

Figure 7.20: Image classification of a cat's image

test_image_2 is a cat's image, and was predicted to be a cat.

In this activity, we trained and, gave the model an image of a cat, and we found out that the algorithm is classifying those images correctly.

Chapter 8: Transfer Learning and Pre-trained Models

Activity 15: Use the VGG16 Network to Train a Deep Learning Network to Identify Images

Solution:

1. Import the libraries:

```
import numpy as np
from keras.applications.vgg16 import VGG16
from keras.preprocessing import image
from keras.applications.vgg16 import preprocess_input
```

2. Initiate the model. (Note that at this point, you can also view the architecture of the network, as follows.):

```
classifier = VGG16()
print(classifier.summary())
```

`classifier.summary ()` shows us the architecture of the network. The following points should be noted: It has a four-dimensional input shape (None, 224,224,3) and it has three convolutional layers.

The last four layers of the output are:

flatten (Flatten)	(None, 25088)	0
fc1 (Dense)	(None, 4096)	102764544
fc2 (Dense)	(None, 4096)	16781312
predictions (Dense)	(None, 1000)	4097000

```
=================================================================
Total params: 138,357,544
Trainable params: 138,357,544
Non-trainable params: 0
_____
None
```

Figure 8.29: The architecture of the network

3. Load the image. '**../Data/Prediction/test_image_1.jpg**' is the path of the image on our system. It will be different on your system:

```
new_image= image.load_img('../Data/Prediction/test_image_1.jpg', target_
size=(224, 224))
new_image
```

The following figure shows the output of the preceding code:

Figure 8.30: The sample cat image

The target size should be 224x 224 as VGG16 accepts only **(224,224)**.

4. Change the image in to an array by using the **img_to_array** function:

```
transformed_image= image.img_to_array(new_image)
transformed_image.shape
```

The following figure shows the output of the preceding code:

(224, 224, 3)

Figure 8.31: Shape of the image

5. To process this image further, it should be in a four-dimensional form for VGG16. So, we need to expand the dimension of the image as follows:

```
transformed_image=np.expand_dims(transformed_image,axis=0)
transformed_image.shape
```

The following figure shows the output of the preceding code:

(1, 224, 224, 3)

Figure 8.32: The new shape of the image after expanding to four dimensions

6. Preprocess the image:

```
transformed_image=preprocess_input(transformed_image)
transformed_image
```

The following figure shows the output of the preceding code:

```
array([[[[-102.939, -116.779, -121.68 ],
         [-102.939, -116.779, -121.68 ],
         [-102.939, -116.779, -121.68 ],
         ...,
         [-102.939, -114.779, -117.68 ],
         [-102.939, -114.779, -117.68 ],
         [-103.939, -116.779, -117.68 ]],

        [[-102.939, -116.779, -121.68 ],
         [-102.939, -116.779, -121.68 ],
         [-102.939, -116.779, -121.68 ],
         ...,
         [-103.939, -116.779, -117.68 ],
         [-103.939, -116.779, -117.68 ],
         [-103.939, -116.779, -117.68 ]],
```

Figure 8.33: Image preprocessing

7. Create the predictor variable:

```
y_pred= classifier.predict(transformed_image)
y_pred
```

The following figure shows the output of the preceding code:

```
array([[2.81155965e-09, 2.20523859e-07, 1.55958055e-08, 7.36266941e-08,
        5.88714784e-08, 4.52034413e-07, 5.20896615e-09, 7.53415520e-07,
        1.54636689e-06, 5.73676573e-08, 3.14125104e-09, 1.27633182e-09,
        1.64991093e-07, 1.30675195e-08, 7.48315909e-10, 6.14375262e-09,
        1.28625217e-08, 2.63904685e-08, 9.85927251e-09, 1.43010026e-09,
        1.54569069e-09, 2.27459168e-07, 5.58701139e-08, 1.67028162e-07,
        9.08437769e-08, 1.13857590e-09, 9.85258009e-09, 5.51692780e-09,
        4.85418861e-09, 1.93991994e-07, 7.10918380e-10, 2.34706343e-09,
        4.40968417e-09, 8.54253279e-10, 8.10707768e-09, 2.25196284e-09,
        1.13177991e-08, 3.08218673e-09, 1.77891295e-07, 3.37317196e-08,
        2.10853504e-08, 5.49144588e-08, 2.02370920e-08, 1.94341387e-09,
        2.82686869e-07, 2.08000692e-08, 8.02847282e-08, 1.44499754e-08,
        1.91879040e-10, 5.00411101e-10, 4.22271240e-09, 4.12553263e-08,
        5.78171040e-08, 1.05852660e-08, 2.50359534e-07, 2.45003728e-09,
        3.36756649e-08, 2.77800383e-09, 1.00973285e-09, 6.28951042e-08,
        4.18378193e-07, 4.93483654e-09, 2.23147474e-08, 1.26198749e-08,
```

Figure 8.34: Creating the predictor variable

8. Check the shape of the image. It should be of shape (**1,1000**). **1000** because, as mentioned previously, the ImageNet database has 1,000 categories of images. The predictor variable shows the probabilities of our image being one of those images:

    ```
    y_pred.shape
    ```

    The following figure shows the output of the preceding code:

    ```
    (1, 1000)
    ```

    Figure 8.35: Expected shape of the image

9. Out of the 1,000 labels that the VGG16 model has, the following code will select the top five probabilities of what our image label is:

    ```
    from keras.applications.vgg16 import decode_predictions
    decode_predictions(y_pred,top=5)
    ```

    The following figure shows the output of the preceding code:

    ```
    [[('n02124075', 'Egyptian_cat', 0.4049535),
      ('n02123045', 'tabby', 0.3942576),
      ('n02127052', 'lynx', 0.10080725),
      ('n02123159', 'tiger_cat', 0.05541087),
      ('n02123394', 'Persian_cat', 0.012944666)]]
    ```

    Figure 8.36: Top-five probabilities of our image

    The first column of the array is internal code number. The second is the label, and the third is the probability of the image being the label.

10. Transform the predictions in to a human-readable format. We extract the most probable label from the output as follows:

    ```
    label = decode_predictions(y_pred)
    # Most likely result is retrieved, for example highest probability
    decoded_label = label[0][0]
    # The classification is printed
    print('%s (%.2f%%)' % (decoded_label[1], decoded_label[2]*100 ))
    ```

    The following figure shows the output of the preceding code:

    ```
    Egyptian_cat (40.50%)
    ```

    Figure 8.37: The final image prediction

    This says, with a 40.50% probability, that the picture is of an Egyptian cat.

So, this completes activity 15. Unlike in *Chapter 7, Computer Vision with Convolutional Neural Networks*, we did not build a CNN from scratch. Instead, we used a pre-trained model. We just uploaded a picture that needs to be classified, and we can see that, with 40.50% accuracy, it is predicted to be an Egyptian cat. Now, in the next exercise, let's work with an image for which there is no matching image in the ImageNet database.

Activity 16: Image Classification with ResNet

Solution:

1. Import the libraries:

```
import numpy as np
from keras.applications.resnet50 import ResNet50
from keras.preprocessing import image
from keras.applications.resnet50 import preprocess_input
```

2. Initiate the model:

```
classifier=ResNet50()
print(classifier.summary())
```

classifier.summary () shows us the architecture of the network. The following points should be noted:

add_16 (Add)	(None, 7, 7, 2048)	0	bn5c_branch2c[0][0] activation_46[0][0]
activation_49 (Activation)	(None, 7, 7, 2048)	0	add_16[0][0]
avg_pool (GlobalAveragePooling2	(None, 2048)	0	activation_49[0][0]
fc1000 (Dense)	(None, 1000)	2049000	avg_pool[0][0]

```
Total params: 25,636,712
Trainable params: 25,583,592
Non-trainable params: 53,120
```

Figure 8.38: The last four layers of the output

> **Note**
>
> The last layer predictions (dense) has 1,000 values. This means that VGG16 has total of 1,000 labels and our image will be one of those 1,000 labels.

3. Load the image. '`../Data/Prediction/test_image_2.jpg`' is the path of the image on our system. It will be different on your system:

```
new_image= image.load_img('../Data/Prediction/test_image_2.jpg', target_
size=(224, 224))
new_image
```

The following is the output of the preceding code:

Figure 8.39: A sample image of an elephant

The target size should be 224x224, as ResNet50 accepts only **(224,224)**.

4. Change the image to an array by using the **img_to_array** function:

```
transformed_image= image.img_to_array(new_image)
transformed_image.shape
```

5. To process this image further, it has to be in a four-dimensional form for ResNet50. So, we need to expand the dimensions of the image as follows:

```
transformed_image=np.expand_dims(transformed_image,axis=0)
transformed_image.shape
```

6. Pre-process the image:

```
transformed_image=preprocess_input(transformed_image)
transformed_image
```

7. Create the predictor variable:

```
y_pred= classifier.predict(transformed_image)
y_pred
```

8. Check the shape of the image. It should be of the **(1,1000)** shape.

```
y_pred.shape
```

The following is the output of the preceding code:

$$(1, 1000)$$

Figure 8.40: The expected shape of the image

9. Select the top five probabilities of what our image is:

```
from keras.applications.resnet50 import decode_predictions
decode_predictions(y_pred,top=5)
```

The following is the output of the preceding code:

```
[[('n02504458', 'African_elephant', 0.6968602),
  ('n01871265', 'tusker', 0.26584822),
  ('n02504013', 'Indian_elephant', 0.03676174),
  ('n02410509', 'bison', 0.00026724974),
  ('n02412080', 'ram', 4.000693e-05)]]
```

Figure 8.41: The top five probabilities of our image

The first column of the array is the internal code number, the second is the label, and the third is the probability of the image matching the label.

10. Transform the predictions in to a human-readable format. We extract the most probable label from the output as follows:

```
label = decode_predictions(y_pred)
# Most likely result is retrived, for example highest probability
decoded_label = label[0][0]
# The classification is printed
print('%s (%.2f%%)' % (decoded_label[1], decoded_label[2]*100 ))
```

The following is the output of the preceding code:

African_elephant (69.69%)

Figure 8.42: The final predicted image using ResNet50

So, the network says, with close to 70% accuracy, that the image is that of an elephant. This time, we used a ResNet50 pre-trained model to classify the image of an elephant.

Chapter 9: Sequential Modeling with Recurrent Neural Networks

Activity 17: Predict the Trend of Microsoft's Stock Price Using an LSTM with 50 Units (Neurons)

Solution

1. Import the required libraries:

```
import numpy as np
import matplotlib.pyplot as plt
import pandas as pd
```

2. Import the dataset:

```
dataset_training = pd.read_csv('MSFT_train.csv')
dataset_training.head()
```

The following figure shows the output of the preceding code:

	Date	Open	High	Low	Close	Adj Close	Volume
0	2013-12-31	37.400002	37.580002	37.220001	37.410000	33.032299	17503500
1	2014-01-02	37.349998	37.400002	37.099998	37.160000	32.811550	30632200
2	2014-01-03	37.200001	37.220001	36.599998	36.910000	32.590809	31134800
3	2014-01-06	36.849998	36.889999	36.110001	36.130001	31.902086	43603700
4	2014-01-07	36.330002	36.490002	36.209999	36.410000	32.149307	35802800

Figure 9.23: The first five rows of the dataset

3. We are going to make the prediction using the **Open** stock price, so we will extract this column first:

```
training_data = dataset_training.iloc[:, 1:2].values
training_data
```

The following figure shows the output of the preceding code:

```
array([[ 37.400002],
       [ 37.349998],
       [ 37.200001],
       ...,
       [ 95.139999],
       [ 99.300003],
       [102.089996]])
```

Figure 9.24: The extracted column (the open stock price) from the dataset

4. Then, perform feature scaling by normalizing the data:

```
from sklearn.preprocessing import MinMaxScaler
sc = MinMaxScaler(feature_range = (0, 1))
training_data_scaled = sc.fit_transform(training_data)

training_data_scaled
```

The following figure shows the output of the preceding code:

```
array([[0.03308963],
       [0.03246992],
       [0.03061099],
       ...,
       [0.74866775],
       [0.80022313],
       [0.83479982]])
```

Figure 9.25: Normalizing the data

5. Create the data to get 60 timestamps from the current instance:

```
X_train = []
y_train = []
for i in range(60, 1258):
    X_train.append(training_data_scaled[i-60:i, 0])
    y_train.append(training_data_scaled[i, 0])
X_train, y_train = np.array(X_train), np.array(y_train)
```

6. Reshape the data as follows:

```
X_train = np.reshape(X_train, (X_train.shape[0], X_train.shape[1], 1))
```

7. Import the following libraries to build the RNN:

```
from keras.models import Sequential
from keras.layers import Dense
from keras.layers import LSTM
from keras.layers import Dropout
```

8. Initiate the sequential model as follows:

```
model = Sequential()
```

9. Build the ANN architecture using the LSTM:

```
model.add(LSTM(units = 50, return_sequences = True, input_shape = (X_
train.shape[1], 1)))

# Adding a second LSTM layer and some Dropout regularisation
model.add(LSTM(units = 50, return_sequences = True))

# Adding a third LSTM layer and some Dropout regularisation
model.add(LSTM(units = 50, return_sequences = True))
# Adding a fourth LSTM layer and some Dropout regularisation
model.add(LSTM(units = 50))

# Adding the output layer
model.add(Dense(units = 1))
```

10. Compile the network as follows:

```
# Compiling the RNN
model.compile(optimizer = 'adam', loss = 'mean_squared_error')

# Fitting the RNN to the Training set
model.fit(X_train, y_train, epochs = 100, batch_size = 32)
```

11. Load and process the test data (which is treated as the actual data here):

```
dataset_testing = pd.read_csv('MSFT_test.csv')
actual_stock_price = dataset_testing.iloc[:, 1:2].values
actual_stock_price
```

12. Concatenate the data, as we will need 60 previous instances to get the stock price of each day; therefore, we will need both the training and testing data:

```
total_data = pd.concat((dataset_training['Open'], dataset_
testing['Open']), axis = 0)
```

13. Reshape and scale in the input:

```
inputs = total_data[len(total_data) - len(dataset_testing) - 60:].values
inputs = inputs.reshape(-1,1)
inputs = sc.transform(inputs)
X_test = []
for i in range(60, 81):
    X_test.append(inputs[i-60:i, 0])
X_test = np.array(X_test)
X_test = np.reshape(X_test, (X_test.shape[0], X_test.shape[1], 1))
predicted_stock_price = model.predict(X_test)
predicted_stock_price = sc.inverse_transform(predicted_stock_price)
```

14. Visualize the results, as follows:

```
# Visualizing the results
plt.plot(actual_stock_price, color = 'green', label = 'Real Microsoft
Stock Price',ls='--')
plt.plot(predicted_stock_price, color = 'red', label = 'Predicted
Microsoft Stock Price',ls='-')
plt.title('Predicted Stock Price')
plt.xlabel('Time in days')
plt.ylabel('Real Stock Price')
plt.legend()
plt.show()
```

Please note that your results may differ slightly from the actual stock price of Microsoft.

Expected output:

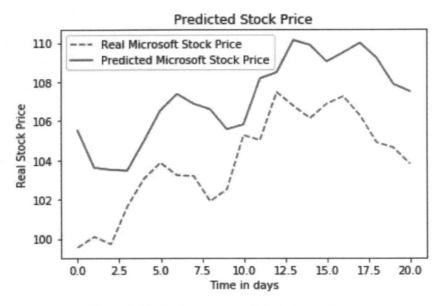

Figure 9.26: Real versus predicted stock prices

As you can see in the preceding plot, the trends of the predicted and real prices are pretty much the same; the line has the same peaks and troughs. This is possible because of LSTM's ability to remember sequenced data. A traditional feedforward neural network would not have been able to forecast this result. This is the true power of LSTM and RNNs.

Activity 18: Predicting Microsoft's stock price with added regularization

Solution:

1. Import the required libraries:

```
import numpy as np
import matplotlib.pyplot as plt
import pandas as pd
```

2. Import the dataset:

```
dataset_training = pd.read_csv('MSFT_train.csv')
dataset_training.head()
```

3. We are going to make the prediction on the open stock price, so we will extract the **Open** stock price column as follows:

```
training_data = dataset_training.iloc[:, 1:2].values
training_data
```

The following figure shows the output of the preceding code:

```
array([[ 37.400002],
       [ 37.349998],
       [ 37.200001],
       ...,
       [ 95.139999],
       [ 99.300003],
       [102.089996]])
```

Figure 9.27: Extracted data from the open stock price column

4. Perform feature scaling by normalizing the data:

```
from sklearn.preprocessing import MinMaxScaler
sc = MinMaxScaler(feature_range = (0, 1))
training_data_scaled = sc.fit_transform(training_data)

training_data_scaled
```

The following figure shows the output of the preceding code:

```
array([[0.03308963],
       [0.03246992],
       [0.03061099],
       ...,
       [0.74866775],
       [0.80022313],
       [0.83479982]])
```

Figure 9.28: Normalizing the data for feature scaling

5. Create the data to get 60 timestamps from the current instance:

```
X_train = []
y_train = []
for i in range(60, 1258):
    X_train.append(training_data_scaled[i-60:i, 0])
    y_train.append(training_data_scaled[i, 0])
X_train, y_train = np.array(X_train), np.array(y_train)
```

6. Reshape the data as follows:

```
X_train = np.reshape(X_train, (X_train.shape[0], X_train.shape[1], 1))
```

7. Import the following libraries to build the RNN:

```
from keras.models import Sequential
from keras.layers import Dense
from keras.layers import LSTM
from keras.layers import Dropout
```

8. Initiate the sequential model, as follows:

```
model = Sequential()
```

9. Build the ANN architecture with dropout regularization:

```
model.add(LSTM(units = 50, return_sequences = True, input_shape = (X_
train.shape[1], 1)))
model.add(Dropout(0.2))

# Adding a second LSTM layer and some Dropout regularisation
model.add(LSTM(units = 50, return_sequences = True))
model.add(Dropout(0.2))

# Adding a third LSTM layer and some Dropout regularisation
model.add(LSTM(units = 50, return_sequences = True))
model.add(Dropout(0.2))

# Adding a fourth LSTM layer and some Dropout regularisation
model.add(LSTM(units = 50))
model.add(Dropout(0.2))

# Adding the output layer
model.add(Dense(units = 1))
```

10. Compile the network as follows:

```
# Compiling the RNN
model.compile(optimizer = 'adam', loss = 'mean_squared_error')

# Fitting the RNN to the Training set
model.fit(X_train, y_train, epochs = 100, batch_size = 32)
```

11. Load and process the test data, which is treated as the actual data here:

```
dataset_testing = pd.read_csv('MSFT_test.csv')
actual_stock_price = dataset_testing.iloc[:, 1:2].values
actual_stock_price
```

12. Concatenate the data, as we will need 60 previous instances to get the stock price of each day; therefore, we will need both the training and testing data:

```
total_data = pd.concat((dataset_training['Open'], dataset_
testing['Open']), axis = 0)
```

13. Reshape and scale the data in the input:

```
inputs = total_data[len(total_data) - len(dataset_testing) - 60:].values
inputs = inputs.reshape(-1,1)
inputs = sc.transform(inputs)
X_test = []
for i in range(60, 81):
    X_test.append(inputs[i-60:i, 0])
X_test = np.array(X_test)
X_test = np.reshape(X_test, (X_test.shape[0], X_test.shape[1], 1))
predicted_stock_price = model.predict(X_test)
predicted_stock_price = sc.inverse_transform(predicted_stock_price)
```

14. Visualize the results:

```
# Visualising the results
plt.plot(actual_stock_price, color = 'green', label = 'Real Microsoft
Stock Price',ls='--')
plt.plot(predicted_stock_price, color = 'red', label = 'Predicted
Microsoft Stock Price',ls='-')
plt.title('Predicted Stock Price')
plt.xlabel('Time in days')
plt.ylabel('Real Stock Price')
plt.legend()
plt.show()
```

Please note that your results may differ slightly to the actual stock price.

Expected output:

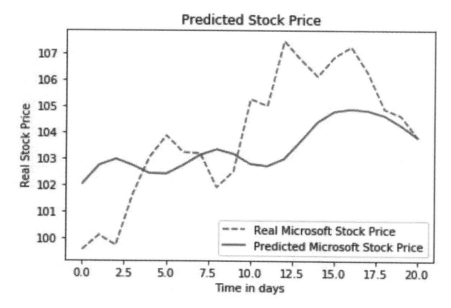

Figure 9.29: Real versus predicted stock prices

In the following figure, the first plot with regularization represents Activity 17 and the other represents Activity 18. You can see that adding dropout regularization is giving us a worse trend. So, in our case it is better to not use regularization:

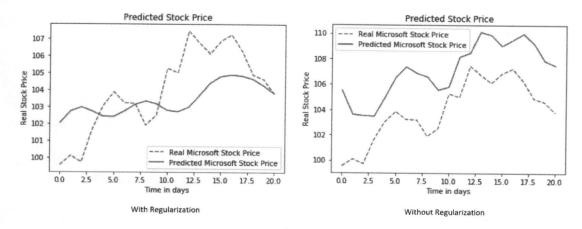

Figure 9.30: Comparing the results of Activity 17 and Activity 18

Activity 19: Predicting the Trend of Microsoft's Stock Price Using LSTM with 100 Units

Solution:

1. Import the required libraries:

    ```
    import numpy as np
    import matplotlib.pyplot as plt
    import pandas as pd
    ```

2. Import the dataset:

    ```
    dataset_training = pd.read_csv('MSFT_train.csv')
    dataset_training.head()
    ```

3. We are going to make the prediction using the **Open** stock price, so we will extract the **Open** stock price column:

    ```
    training_data = dataset_training.iloc[:, 1:2].values
    training_data
    ```

4. Perform feature scaling by normalizing the data:

    ```
    from sklearn.preprocessing import MinMaxScaler
    sc = MinMaxScaler(feature_range = (0, 1))
    training_data_scaled = sc.fit_transform(training_data)
    training_data_scaled
    ```

5. Create the data to get 60 timestamps from the current instance:

    ```
    X_train = []
    y_train = []
    for i in range(60, 1258):
        X_train.append(training_data_scaled[i-60:i, 0])
        y_train.append(training_data_scaled[i, 0])
    X_train, y_train = np.array(X_train), np.array(y_train)
    ```

6. Reshape the data as follows:

    ```
    X_train = np.reshape(X_train, (X_train.shape[0], X_train.shape[1], 1))
    ```

382 | Appendix

7. Import the following libraries to build the RNN:

```
from keras.models import Sequential
from keras.layers import Dense
from keras.layers import LSTM
from keras.layers import Dropout
```

8. Initiate the sequential model as follows:

```
model = Sequential()
```

9. Build the ANN architecture as follows:

```
model.add(LSTM(units = 100, return_sequences = True, input_shape = (X_
train.shape[1], 1)))

# Adding a second LSTM layer and some Dropout regularisation
model.add(LSTM(units = 100, return_sequences = True))

# Adding a third LSTM layer and some Dropout regularisation
model.add(LSTM(units = 100, return_sequences = True))

# Adding a fourth LSTM layer and some Dropout regularisation
model.add(LSTM(units = 100))

# Adding the output layer
model.add(Dense(units = 1))
```

10. Compile the network as follows:

```
# Compiling the RNN
model.compile(optimizer = 'adam', loss = 'mean_squared_error')

# Fitting the RNN to the Training set
model.fit(X_train, y_train, epochs = 100, batch_size = 32)
```

11. Load and process the test data, which is treated as the actual data here:

```
dataset_testing = pd.read_csv('MSFT_test.csv')
actual_stock_price = dataset_testing.iloc[:, 1:2].values
actual_stock_price
```

12. Concatenate the data, as we will need 60 previous instances to get the stock price of each day; therefore, we will need both the training and testing data:

```
total_data = pd.concat((dataset_training['Open'], dataset_
testing['Open']), axis = 0)
```

13. Reshape and scale the data in the input:

```
inputs = total_data[len(total_data) - len(dataset_testing) - 60:].values
inputs = inputs.reshape(-1,1)
inputs = sc.transform(inputs)
X_test = []
for i in range(60, 81):
    X_test.append(inputs[i-60:i, 0])
X_test = np.array(X_test)
X_test = np.reshape(X_test, (X_test.shape[0], X_test.shape[1], 1))
predicted_stock_price = model.predict(X_test)
predicted_stock_price = sc.inverse_transform(predicted_stock_price)
```

14. Visualize the results as follows:

```
plt.plot(actual_stock_price, color = 'green', label = 'Actual Microsoft
Stock Price',ls='--')
plt.plot(predicted_stock_price, color = 'red', label = 'Predicted
Microsoft Stock Price',ls='-')
plt.title('Predicted Stock Price')
plt.xlabel('Time in days')
plt.ylabel('Real Stock Price')
plt.legend()
plt.show()
```

Please note that your results may differ slightly from the actual stock price.

Expected output:

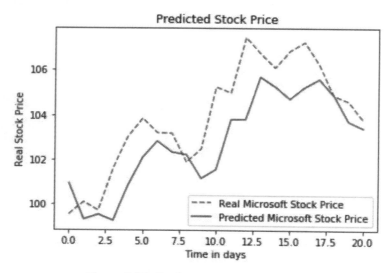

Figure 9.31: Real versus predicted stock prices

So, if we compare the results of the LSTM with 50 units (from Activity 17) and the LSTM with 100 units in this activity, we get trends with 100 units. Also, note that when we run the LSTM with 100 units, it takes more computational time than the LSTM with 50 units. A trade-off needs to be considered in such cases:

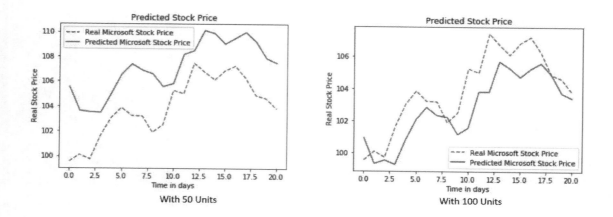

Figure 9.32: Comparing the real versus predicted stock price with 50 and 100 units

Index

About

All major keywords used in this book are captured alphabetically in this section. Each one is accompanied by the page number of where they appear.

A

absolute: 42, 86, 147-148, 170
abstracts:68
accuracies:183
accuracy: 2, 35, 38-42, 45, 50, 52, 72, 74, 97, 105-107, 126-128, 137-138, 143-144, 150, 174-175, 177-184, 188, 194-195, 197-202, 205, 219-227, 229, 242, 247, 250, 284
accurate: 35-36, 48, 112, 114, 128-129, 181, 217, 220, 256, 282
accurately: 28, 34
activate:51
activation: 25, 28, 68-71, 73-74, 78-79, 81-85, 91-92, 94-96, 98, 106-107, 120-121, 125, 127, 130, 132, 135-139, 150, 154-157, 162, 164, 166, 169-171, 174, 195, 199, 208-209, 215, 218-219, 221-225, 227, 230, 250, 269-271
active: 26, 158
activities: 7, 23, 54, 90, 108, 112, 120, 137, 144, 150, 174, 179, 188, 218, 239, 271
activity: 40, 44-45, 73-74, 93-96, 105, 107, 114, 125, 127-128, 137-140, 144, 150-151, 154, 157-158, 161, 169, 173-175, 181, 199-201, 221, 229, 234, 238, 242, 255, 277, 282-284

actual: 53, 179, 183, 185-186, 212, 267, 271, 274-278, 280, 282-283
actually: 185, 203
adaptable:50
adding: 29, 44, 93, 102-103, 146, 148, 156-158, 164-169, 174, 213, 215, 218, 221, 227, 230, 238, 250, 274, 279, 282
addition: 53-54, 56-57, 62-63, 74, 81, 108, 124, 169, 270
additional:221
additions: 52, 54
address: 35, 144, 168, 175
algebra: 11, 28, 62, 68, 74
algorithm: 2, 27, 33-34, 48-49, 87-89, 146, 148, 152-153, 178-179, 185, 199, 212, 217, 221, 227-230, 242, 252, 255, 265, 278
algorithms: 11-12, 25-26, 28-29, 33-34, 45, 48, 50-51, 184, 208, 227, 229-230, 265
analyzing:4
append: 133-134, 136, 273, 275, 279-280
applied: 3, 17, 28, 31, 34, 43, 50, 54, 56, 59, 65, 69-71, 74, 79, 96, 119, 141, 145, 148-149, 158, 161, 169, 284
applies: 15, 37, 216
applying: 29, 68, 85, 147, 169, 216, 242, 255, 284
arrays: 53, 57, 60, 65, 96, 122

arrive:185
artificial: 12, 48, 208, 235, 264
attribute:53
attributes: 7, 12, 73, 139, 157
auc-roc: 175, 284
available: 5, 28, 51, 78, 83, 86, 90-92, 96, 98, 105-106, 112, 115-116, 123, 126-127, 130, 144, 150, 158, 168-169, 172, 174, 179, 261
average: 38, 41, 70, 83, 86-87, 89, 195, 213
averaging: 85, 115, 117 A

B

backend:215
background:237
balance: 13, 34, 91
balanced:35
banking: 4, 7
bank-names:7
baseline: 40-42, 44, 160
binary: 2, 5, 10-11, 13-14, 16, 22-23, 26, 32, 35, 38, 41, 72, 83-84, 86, 91-92, 94-98, 105-106, 127, 137, 145, 150, 154-156, 162, 164, 166, 174, 195, 219-221, 223-224, 226, 250-251
boolean:62
booleans:197
boundary: 94-96, 100-102
bounding:70
bounds: 12, 14

C

calculate: 35-36, 38, 40-41, 72, 194, 197-198, 200-205
callback: 160-161, 164-167
choice: 83, 89, 95, 128, 130, 151, 160, 172
circles: 94, 182, 270
cleaning:12
clustering: 26-28, 48
clusters:27
clutch:234
colname:19
compile: 72-73, 92, 96-98, 121, 126, 132, 135, 155-156, 162, 164, 166, 171, 195, 199-200, 219, 223, 225, 250, 274, 280
complexity: 146, 159
computing: 51, 78, 85-87, 96, 181, 188, 199-201, 238
concat: 18-19, 192, 275, 280
connection:6
correlated:27
counted:81
counts: 14, 17, 41, 179-180, 198, 202
cyclical:264
database: 6, 238, 241-243, 246

D

debugging:29
dependency:269
dependent: 5, 33, 70, 116, 181, 191, 199, 220, 260, 271
depending: 6, 16, 68, 73, 81, 85, 92, 113, 117, 122, 126, 129, 157, 160, 168
depends: 115, 185, 237
depiction:69
derivative: 78, 83, 86-87, 89
detection: 168, 185, 205, 207
detector: 210-211
detectors: 212, 215, 219
detects:160
dimension: 4, 31, 65, 70, 91-93, 105, 215, 240, 244, 253
dimensions: 27, 37, 53, 58-65, 68-69, 81, 234, 277, 282-283
diverse:216
download: 7, 54, 90, 106, 120, 150, 218, 239, 271, 277, 282
downloaded: 188, 218, 227, 229, 239, 242, 248
dramatic:146
drawback: 115, 118
drawbacks: 49, 78, 113, 115, 144
duration:13

E

encode: 11-12, 20, 23-24
encoded: 3, 11, 23
encoding: 11-12, 20, 23
entropy: 164, 166
epochs: 72-73, 89-90, 92, 95-96, 98, 106-107, 120, 122, 126-127, 130, 133-135, 137-138, 140, 150, 155-158, 160-162, 164-167, 170-171, 174, 196, 199, 216, 220, 224, 226, 251, 274, 280
explicitly:34

F

factors:271
feature: 7, 9-10, 12-14, 18-24, 30, 33-34, 37, 39-40, 42, 44, 50-51, 72-73, 90, 120, 125, 131, 154, 161, 207-208, 210-215, 219, 233, 235-236, 256, 272-273, 279
fields:230
figsize:162
figure: 2-5, 8-11, 13-19, 21-22, 24-25, 27, 30-39, 41, 43-44, 48-69, 79-84, 87-88, 91, 93, 96, 98, 100-104, 106, 113-114, 116-119, 121, 126, 129-131, 133, 135-136, 145-148, 152, 155-156, 159, 162-163, 165, 167, 170, 173, 180, 182-184, 186-194, 196-198, 203-205, 209-217, 220, 224, 226, 228, 235-236, 240-255, 260-270, 272-273, 275-276, 281
filename:6
filter: 199, 210-211
finally: 7-8, 10, 13, 19, 23, 25, 40, 45, 78, 94, 108, 112, 149, 205, 220, 224, 226-227, 252, 259, 283
floats:5
formats:12
fscore: 38-39, 41
function: 2, 6-10, 14-20, 24, 35, 38, 41, 55, 61,

65, 70-73, 79, 81-88,
91-92, 94-96, 106-108,
120-123, 125-127, 130,
132, 135-137, 139, 145,
147-149, 155, 159, 162,
164, 166, 170-171, 174,
179-180, 189-195,
197-203, 208-209, 215,
218, 221-222, 224, 240,
244, 253, 269, 271

G

github: 7, 54, 90, 106, 120,
127, 137, 150, 157, 174,
179, 188, 218, 227, 229,
239, 248, 271, 277, 282
google: 239, 256,
261-263, 265, 284
gradient: 72, 78, 87-89,
104, 108, 256, 259-260,
266-269, 271, 284
gradients: 51, 71, 89,
108, 168, 268
gradually:108

H

height: 4, 27
high-level: 28, 208
histogram:201
historical:35
horizontal: 217, 219,
223, 226, 250
horzintal:221
hospital: 185, 188
hypotheses:23
hypothesis: 23-25

I

in-depth: 112, 284
indexes:84
indexing:191
inherent:20
inline: 12, 14, 72, 94, 162
instagram:208
installed: 7, 54
instance: 45, 69, 73,
265, 268, 273, 279
instances: 5, 36, 179-180,
245, 260, 265-267,
273, 275, 280
intercepts:79
interface: 120, 122,
126-127, 172
interfaces:120
internal: 189, 200-201,
242, 246, 254
internet: 25, 94, 208
interpret: 3, 51
intervals:269
iteration: 43, 72, 89, 92,
95, 104, 115, 117-118, 122,
127, 148, 151-153, 157, 162
iterations: 37, 43,
90, 104-105
iterative: 23, 36, 50, 104
iterator: 126-127
iterators: 123-124

K

kernel: 69, 149, 195
kernels:34
k-means: 27-28, 48
knowing: 130, 144, 234
knowledge: 48, 65, 234

L

labeling:33
limits: 70, 151
linear: 11, 28, 33-34, 37,
42, 45, 47-48, 52, 62,
68-69, 71, 74, 81, 100
listed:53
little: 19, 146, 159, 238

M

matplotlib: 12, 14, 72, 94,
105, 162, 202, 271, 278
median:139
members: 26, 51
metadata: 189-191
moderate:278
multiclass:195
multiple: 20, 49, 69,
74, 78, 80, 95, 108,
111, 187, 209, 212, 217,
221-222, 226-227, 266
multiplied: 62-65,
69, 79, 86, 147
multiplies:271
multiply: 64-66, 268, 271
mydata:191

N

network: 26, 28-31, 33-34,
45, 48-49, 51, 62, 71,
78-81, 84-86, 89-90,
92-96, 98, 100, 102-104,
106-108, 112, 114, 118,
127, 130, 137-139,
146-150, 152-154, 156,
158-159, 168, 170, 181,
194-195, 199-200, 207,
209, 212, 219, 223, 225,
234-235, 237-239,

242-243, 246-247, 250, 252, 255-256, 260, 263-264, 266-269, 271, 274, 277, 280, 282-283

networking:208

networks: 12, 25, 28-29, 48-49, 51-52, 68, 70-71, 78, 80-81, 84, 87, 95-96, 105, 108, 114, 125, 127-128, 130, 138-140, 144, 146, 148-149, 153, 158, 168, 170, 207-209, 230, 234, 238-239, 247, 250-251, 256, 259-261, 263-264, 269, 284

neural: 12, 25-26, 28-31, 33-34, 45, 48, 51-52, 62, 68, 70-71, 78-81, 84, 86-87, 89-90, 93-96, 98, 100, 102-103, 105-108, 114, 125, 127-128, 130, 137-140, 144, 146, 148-149, 152-153, 158-159, 168, 170, 181, 194, 199-200, 207-209, 212, 230, 234-235, 238, 247, 250-251, 256, 259-261, 263-264, 267-268

neurons: 25, 33-34, 48, 208, 271, 276-278, 281-283

nfscore: 38, 41

nonlinear:79

non-linear: 2, 95

non-spam:185

nonzero:71

non-zero:42

normalized:94

notebook: 7, 14, 24, 54-55, 59, 64-65, 90, 120, 150, 179, 201, 218, 239, 271

notebooks: 7, 179

nrecall: 38, 41

numerical: 3, 5, 9, 11-16, 20-23, 25, 33, 45, 121, 190

O

object: 168, 190, 209, 238, 242, 248

objective: 2, 4, 178, 188, 269

objectives: 1, 47, 77, 111, 115, 143, 177, 207, 233, 259

objects: 5, 30, 50, 193-194, 208, 234

optimizers: 25, 28, 78, 90, 135-136, 138, 140, 143-144, 169, 173-175

optimum: 44, 203-204

outcomes: 48, 179, 181, 184

P

pandas: 5-8, 10, 12-13, 24, 36, 40, 45, 73, 179-180, 189, 192, 198, 200, 202, 271, 278

parameter: 10, 37, 41-45, 144, 147-148, 153, 171, 173-174, 193, 202

parameters: 27, 51, 72, 78-79, 81, 84-89, 104, 108, 120, 128, 130-131, 141, 145, 148, 170-171, 173

params:120

percentage: 86, 188

pipelines:27

plotted:96

plotting: 14, 94, 96, 160, 162

plugged:29

population:27

precision: 35-36, 38, 41, 45, 175, 177-178, 185-186, 200-201, 205, 284

prediction: 33, 39, 68, 84, 178-179, 185-186, 196, 200, 205, 228-229, 239, 242, 244, 246, 248-249, 251, 253, 255, 263, 272, 278, 284

predictive: 23, 30, 40, 51

predictor: 197, 241-242, 245-246, 254-255

predictors:91

proximity:27

pydata:6

pyplot: 72, 94, 105, 162, 202, 271, 278

pyramid: 243-244, 247

Q

queries: 5-6

R

recurrent: 70, 256, 259-261, 263, 269

redundancy: 18, 20

redundant:18

resampling: 108, 112-113, 141

robotics:208

robust: 29, 36, 40, 112, 114-115, 128-129, 153, 183, 221, 261

row-vector:61

running:179

S

sampling: 35, 124,
172, 183, 199
scalar: 53-54, 57, 64, 71
scikit: 120, 122, 126,
133, 172-173
screenshot: 55, 66,
241, 245, 261
select: 6, 81, 112, 116,
122, 128, 159, 183, 213,
241, 246, 254, 271
sequential: 69-71, 73,
77, 79, 91, 94-96, 98,
120-121, 125, 132, 135,
154-156, 162, 164,
166, 169, 171, 194, 199,
218-219, 221-222,
224-225, 249, 256,
259-261, 264-265,
274, 279, 284
series: 41, 52, 179,
198, 256, 284
sigmoid: 71, 73, 79, 81-85,
92, 95-96, 98, 155-156,
162, 164, 166, 169,
195, 199, 219, 221-224,
227, 250, 270-271
similarity:209
skewed: 15, 35, 179
skiprows:6
sklearn: 37-38, 41, 73, 90,
94, 98, 120, 122-126, 131,
133, 139, 150, 154, 157,
161, 172-173, 183, 193,
197, 202, 205, 272, 279
slicing:217
systems:234

T

tables:4
tabular: 10, 25
tangent:81
target: 7, 9-10, 12, 22-23,
25-27, 31-32, 34-37,
40-41, 44-45, 68,
72-74, 88, 220, 223,
226, 228, 239-240,
244, 250-251, 253
targeted:24
technique: 26-27, 42-43,
77-78, 108, 112, 115,
117, 141, 144, 149,
168-169, 178, 199, 205,
230, 252, 256, 261
techniques: 12, 20,
25-28, 40, 42, 96, 105,
112, 143-144, 146, 153,
158, 168, 175, 178, 181,
183, 207, 256, 284
templates: 90, 120,
150, 218, 239, 271
tensor: 53, 55-56,
58-60, 65-69
tensorflow: 28, 215
tensors: 52-55, 58-59,
62, 65, 67, 74
testing: 37, 44, 183,
193-194, 218,
274-275, 280
test-set:226
test-train:193
themselves:268
threshold: 71, 177,
196-197, 200-205
thresholds: 196,
202-203, 264
trainable:249
training: 3, 12, 25, 27-28,
31-32, 34-38, 40, 42-45,
50-51, 68, 72-74, 78,
81, 86, 89-92, 95-99,
101-108, 112-119, 122,
124, 127-129, 137-138,
144-146, 148, 150-168,
170, 174, 178, 183,
193-194, 208, 216, 218,
220-221, 223-224,
226, 228, 237, 248,
250-251, 267-268,
272-275, 277-280, 284
train-test:118
traits:237
transfer: 233-234, 256
transform: 24, 124, 193,
210, 219, 221, 223, 226,
272, 275-276, 279-280
transforms:193
transpose: 58-59,
61, 64, 66
transposed: 58, 61
treated: 112, 217, 274, 280
tree-based: 12, 42
tree-like:33
trends: 103, 106,
150-151, 157-158,
162, 256, 276, 284
tutorials:25
tweaking: 238, 252,
256, 278
two-class: 86, 96, 105
two-layer: 80-81, 84

U

uniform: 195, 215
unlabeled: 27, 32, 51
unseen: 43, 97-98,
113, 128-129
unusable:70
update: 72, 87-89, 108, 148
updating: 87, 104, 153, 237

uploading:208
upper-left:187
utilizing: 2, 20, 25, 27, 45, 73

V

validating:227
validation: 35, 43-44, 72-73, 99, 105, 118, 124, 157, 160-162, 164, 166, 169, 216, 220, 224, 226, 251
valuable:104
values: 5, 8, 11, 13-18, 20, 22, 32, 35, 38-42, 45, 51, 56-57, 70-71, 87-90, 92, 94-96, 105-106, 116, 120, 125, 127, 131, 136-138, 140, 144, 147-148, 150, 153-154, 157-158, 160-161, 169-174, 179-180, 188, 190, 194, 196-203, 205, 239, 243, 263, 267-268, 271-272, 274-275, 277-278, 280, 282-283
valves:271
variable: 7-10, 19-20, 22-23, 25-27, 32, 35, 40, 73, 181, 189, 191-193, 199, 201, 203, 241-242, 245-246, 254-255
variables: 3, 7, 9, 12, 26, 33, 40-41, 179, 189, 191-192, 196, 199-200
variance: 78, 99, 102-103, 116-119, 129, 145-146, 153, 157
variation: 12, 43, 114, 117
variations: 12, 112-113, 123, 141, 144, 147

various: 4-5, 7, 25, 27-28, 32, 51-52, 54, 58, 72-74, 78, 144, 169, 188, 208, 266, 284
vector: 28, 34, 53, 55-56, 58, 61, 84
vectors: 52-55, 58, 62, 74, 84, 208
vendors:239
verbose: 92, 95, 97, 99, 122, 126, 133-134, 136, 155-156, 162, 164, 166, 172-173
verified:21
verify: 7-10, 21, 37, 61
verifying:241
version: 71, 89
versions: 124, 168, 217
vertical:151
visualize: 201, 276-277, 280, 283-284
visualized: 27, 72
volumes:208

W

weight: 27, 43, 68, 147-148, 150-151, 153, 158, 168, 174, 237, 268, 271
weighted: 79, 89, 208
weighting:20
weights: 12, 42, 50-51, 68-71, 79, 84-85, 87-89, 138, 146-149, 153, 168, 264, 267-268
window:70
workflow: 112, 119-120, 125, 169
working: 3, 5, 25-26, 29, 51-52, 81, 96, 183, 215, 218, 220, 223, 227, 229-230,

239, 242, 248, 260
workspace: 227, 229
wrapper: 108, 111, 119-120, 122, 126, 133, 141, 169, 172, 174, 284
wrappers: 111-112, 120, 122, 126, 133, 157, 169, 172-173
writing: 97, 141, 160, 169
written: 28, 87, 187, 271
wsofin:90

X

xception:238
xlabel: 162, 202, 276, 280
x-rays:52
xtrain: 193-194

Y

ylabel: 162, 202, 276, 280
youtube:208
ytrain: 193-194

Z

zeroes:147